John Bunyan's

The Holy War:

A Reawakening

Duane W. Priset

God bless you always.

EMETH PRESS
www.emethpress.com

*Sincerly
Duane*

John Bunyan's The Holy War: A Reawakening

Library of Congress Cataloging-in-Publication Data

Names: Bunyan, John, 1628-1688, author. | Priset, Duane Walter, editor.
Title: John Bunyan's The holy war : a reawakening / Duane W. Priset.
Description: [Dardenne Prairie] : Emeth Press, [2022] | Includes
   bibliographical references. | Summary: "This is a re-presentation of
   John Bunyan's allegory, The Holy War. It offers the reader
   thought-provoking discussion questions that will prompt careful
   consideration of the meaning of the gospel of Jesus Christ in current
   personal, cultural, and ecclesiastical conflicts. Priset's brief and
   fascinating biography of Bunyan in historical context sets the stage for
   the reappearance of Bunyan's brilliantly characterized figures such as
   Diabolus, Lord Willbewill, Mrs. Piety, Mr. Sloth, Captain Credence,
   Prince Emanuel, and many others in the spiritual struggle for good over
   evil, the eternal Kingdom of God over the forces of hell"-- Provided by
   publisher.
Identifiers: LCCN 2022023635 | ISBN 9781609471811 (paperback ; acid-free
   paper)
Subjects: LCSH: Spiritual warfare--Fiction. | LCGFT: Christian fiction. |
   Allegories. | Novels.
Classification: LCC PR3329 .H1 2022 | DDC 828/.407--dc23/eng/20220523
LC record available at https://lccn.loc.gov/2022023635

Stained Glass of John Bunyan
Seated at his Desk on the front cover
By permission of the Trustees of Bunyan's Meeting,
Bedford, England

Dedication

I dedicate this rendering of John Bunyan's classic *The Holy War* to my parents John and Edith Priset, who brought me up in God's love and faithful service, and to my wife Beth's parents, Donald and Betty Ashbery, who were great blessings, supports and encouragers, as well.

Endorsements

Archbishop Elias Chacour

It is with a special feeling of gratitude that I received Duane Priset's manuscript of *John Bunyan's The Holy War: A Reawakening* written with so much eloquence. Here follows what I would write about Dr. Priset's work.

Many thousands of people from all venues have come to visit our institution during the past thirty years. Few of them have kept in touch, and among these is the Reverend Duane Priset. Soon he conquered our attention. We have learnt from him far more than whatever we might have taken from him. The Sermon on the Mount and especially the Beatitudes are our common calling to get up to move, to do something positive to establish Justice, and to spread Peace. I think that Rev. Priset interpreted the Sermon on the Mount and other passages from the Bible with the conviction of one who lives what he teaches. Peace is important for him, but Justice is a fundamental requirement to establish Peace.

Duane Priset attracts people and enriches them to become his friends; this is what he is doing for us at Mar Elias Educational Institutions. Surely, it's not any money which impresses us; it's his openness and his appreciation for human beings being created in the image and in the likeness of God. His comments on Bunyan's book on the holy war is an inspiration and a motivation to take courage. Peace is possible. It needs witnesses. The holy war ultimately is not with human weapons. This is a war against the evil and the bad spirits roaming around to divert people and to make them blind.

Against the fact all people, regardless of race, religion, or any other factor, and respecting that they have been created in the image and likeness of God, this book is an inspiration and invitation to get our hands dirty, to make Justice, and to pursue Peace.

Abuna [Father] Elias Chacour
Mar Elias Educational Institutions, Ibillin, Israel
Archbishop em. of Galilee

Wendy J. Deichmann, Ph.D.

In a well-timed re-presentation of John Bunyan's allegory, *The Holy War,* Duane Priset offers the reader thought-provoking discussion questions and powerful prayer suggestions that will prompt careful consideration of the meaning of the gospel of Jesus Christ in current personal, cultural, and ecclesiastical conflicts. Priset's brief and fascinating biography of Bunyan in historical context sets the stage for the reappearance of Bunyan's brilliantly characterized figures such as Diabolus, Lord Willbewill, Mrs. Piety, Mr. Sloth, Captain Credence, Prince Emanuel, and many others in the spiritual struggle for good over evil, the eternal Kingdom of God over the forces of hell.

Wendy J. Deichmann, Ph.D.
Professor of History and Theology
Director of the Center for Evangelical United Brethren Heritage
United Theological Seminary, Dayton, Ohio

John Dilworth

I so enjoyed reading Duane Priset's prior book, *John Bunyan's, The Pilgrim's Progress: A Reimagining: Parts 1 & 2.* My appreciation for the quality of his research and thoroughness of his research and writing even further heightened as I read *John Bunyan's The Holy War: A Reawakening.* The hundreds of footnotes Duane added anchor Bunyan's allegory to the Scriptures. The biographical summary of Bunyan's life experiences gives critical context to the metaphors used to develop the story. The appendix reflections connect several key aspects of *The Holy War* to current times and inspire deeper thought. I find that a story written well over three hundred years ago is as fresh as the today's news on the topic of good and evil is fascinating. The scriptural references work together with the story to highlight the brokenness of humankind and that brokenness intensifies our great need for God's salvation. Reading the book, I was reawakened to the infinite, subtle, deceptive, and manipulative ways that evil constantly seeks to lure us and to the amazing extravagance of the grace of God when a lost soul comes back to Him! *John Bunyan's The Holy War: A Reawakening* will generate rich discussion during small group studies using the extensive list of questions included in the appendix. This is a book to read, to study and to keep!

John Dilworth, Discipleship Ministry Team Chairperson,
The Church of the Lakes, Canton, Ohio, and
Writer for the *Daily Guideposts*

Abby Manzella, LMSW

I met Duane Priset as he was starting on his journey through grief, in losing his wife, Beth. I met him along his way as a source of support and guidance. Moreover, many others with whom Duane shared his workings on Bunyan's stories became important characters who had offered him support in some way that promoted strength and healing, as well.

Exploring the many feelings that arise during one's grief journey are found to be comparable to that of the characters in John Bunyan's famous books *The Pilgrim's Progress* and *The Holy War*. Christian's journey in *The Pilgrim's Progress* tells of a man in search of the Celestial City. Along the way, he faces many challenges that attempt to deter him, but also individuals who provide physical and emotional strength to finally get him to his destination. Similarly, in the book The Holy War, there is a story about a physical war that represents the human soul fighting the ongoing battle between good and evil. In the town of Mansoul, which was created by Shaddai (God) and close to perfection, Diabolus (Satan) tries to penetrate the gates and take rule. The townspeople engage in a battle between both rulers, that damage the town both physically and spiritually. Ultimately, the town of Mansoul was saved, but evil elements remain.

Duane's rewritings of the stories reflect faith being challenged, emotions being heavy, and fighting to walk in God's grace. These allegories represent the ever-present challenge of staying near to God while enduring challenges and obstacles in life. In order to withstand the attacks, we must depend on God's strength and use every piece of his armor.

In Ephesians 6:12-15, Paul says: "For our struggle is not against flesh and blood, but against the rulers, against the authorities, against the powers of this dark world and against the spiritual forces of evil in the heavenly realms. Therefore put on the full armor of God, so that when the day of evil comes, you may be able to stand your ground, and after you have done everything, to stand. Stand firm then, with the belt of truth buckled around your waist, with the breastplate of righteousness in place, and with your feet fitted with the readiness that comes from the gospel of peace" (NIV).

Abby Manzella, LMSW
Wellness Counselor

Reverend Dr. Daniel V. Runyon, Ph.D.

Duane Priset's refreshing probe into John Bunyan's neglected *The Holy War* is best understood in light of a few historical realities lost on modern readers. First, we must realize that in place of academic credentials or ordination papers, dissenting preachers in Bunyan's time wrote spiritual autobiographies to establish their own credibility, and they demonstrated their authority via thoroughly biblical preaching. *In Grace Abounding to the Chief of Sinners* Bunyan penned the finest spiritual autobiography of his time, and his preaching demonstrated spiritual authority to match or transcend the work of ordained clergy.

Bunyan then raised the bar by authoring the finest of allegories, first with *The Pilgrim's Progress*, a journey allegory portraying a fictionalized saga of one individual's struggle and conquest over sin, and then with *The Holy War*, a battle allegory portraying the Church in a battle-to-the-death struggle against systemic evil in a fallen universe. Both allegories are theologically astute as well as autobiographical, informed by Bunyan's personal experience, first as a pilgrim, then as a leader in the salvation history narrative of the Church.

The imagery of spiritual warfare via the word "battle" turns up 117 times as Priset references heroic conflicts ranging from Abram to Armageddon. Such battles run the gamut from emotional angst to out-and-out physical struggles that end in death. In *The Holy War* depicted by Bunyan, the "battle" ranges far wider than mere skirmishes with the devil. If every day of obedience to the upward call of God through Christ Jesus empowered by the Holy Spirit "seems like a battle" (see the "Prayer Starter" on page 104) that's because every day is a battle – every inch of every day. Remember, they also serve who only stand and wait.

Priset's goal is to awaken modern warriors in God's Kingdom to strap on the same tools of holy warfare offered by Bunyan to the Church of his time that still today can result in victory for individuals in this life-long battle, and therefore ultimate success in the full scope of salvation history for the corporate Body of Christ—the Church—until such time as the saga of human history closes with the strenuous victory of the returning Son of the living God.

Reverend Dr. Daniel V. Runyon, Ph.D.
Professor of English and Communication (retired), Spring Arbor University Preaching Chaplain, Vista Grande Villa Retirement Com-munity

Reverend Dr. Tom Schwanda, Ph.D.

John Bunyan's *The Holy War* is a classic retelling of the biblical story that reminds readers that the journey through life is filled with challenges and temptations. We can be grateful for Duane Priset's meticulously researched yet readable edition that brings Bunyan's message to life for us today. Detailed annotations provide helpful background to assist in understanding and applying this powerful allegory. This book seeks to reawaken any who read it to the reality that we never need to face life's obstacles alone since God is always willing to guide and protect us. May this fine book be well-received and applied to every person's life!

Reverend Dr. Tom Schwanda, Ph.D., Associate Professor, Emeritus
Christian Formation and Ministry, Wheaton College
Author of *The Emergence of Evangelical Spirituality:*
The Age of Edwards, Newton, and Whitefield

Bishop Mark J. Webb

Providing a glimpse into the life of John Bunyan and through a rendition of his work, *The Holy War*, Duane Priset invites us into a journey of spiritual reawakening towards the life God invites us to know and experience. With guided prayer moments and questions for thought and discussion, students of Bunyan's writings will find a fresh approach to a classic work.

Bishop Mark J. Webb
Upper New York Area
The United Methodist Church

Reverend Dr. Janet Wooton

'I once observed a tinker's anvil put on view in Bunyan Meeting House and Museum in Bedford, England . . . large . . . and undoubtably heavy! I can only imagine the tinker lugging it around,' so writes Duane Priset. The anvil belonged to John Bunyan, a tinker, skilled at his craft, a practical man and writer of life-changing allegorical works. Priset offers a guide to Bunyan's *The Holy War*, that is contextual, spiritual, and practical. At the centre is an annotated text of what he calls this 'mesmerizing and thoughtful classic'. Each section is introduced with a well-chosen quotation from the Geneva Bible, which helps the reader to relate the allegory to his or her own discipleship. The wider context is set by reference to Bunyan's military service, but also in the writer's own family experience of war, and by reference to world conflicts, including the situation in the Middle East. The book offers spiritual guidance through prayer suggestions, and topics for group discussions. And in practical terms, the reader is challenged to 'get your hands dirty', to do good. At the end there are three appendices from experts in relevant fields of study, and an extensive annotated list of resources. This is an encounter with John Bunyan and *The Holy War* from which the attentive reader will gain a fascinating insight into the battles between good and evil in the world, and in each human life.

Reverend Dr. Janet Wootton
The John Bunyan Museum and Library
Bedford, England

Table of Contents

Martin Luther's Hymn

John Bunyan's *The Holy War*: A Reawakening

For a Wrap-up

Appendices

Questions for Individuals and Groups / 235

For Reflective Moments and Discussion

Annotated Bibliography

Helpful Resources / 249

Foreword

Reverend Dr. D. Gregory Van Dussen
Northeastern Seminary

In this new volume, Duane Priset provides a lavishly annotated, yet accessible version of *The Holy War*, with reflections on its enduring significance as an allegory for the Christian journey. The world through which God's people must travel, and the dynamics of each pilgrim's life, contain every kind of challenge, obstacle, and distraction, as we make our way toward the destiny for which we were created. Dr. Priset's presentation of *The Holy War* continues his work on Bunyan's better known *Pilgrim's Progress* and its companion, *Christiana's Journey*, showing in a rich variety of personifications the sinister influences and manipulations which together form the gauntlet which humanity must navigate.

The author provides resources that place Bunyan's work in Biblical, theological, biographical, and historical contexts taking into account the insights of commentators over the centuries. He explains or translates arcane vocabulary and applies its story to our own life and times. In this he shows both the instincts of a careful historian and the spiritual concern of a dedicated pastor, shown in his "prayer for us all … that we grow through the years to be a faithful people of God and a more constructive and kindlier presence to others around us" (16). He also offers a "prayer starter" to begin each section and highlight its particular importance.

While the characters and incidents in Bunyan's work serve as warnings, the story is ultimately one of hope, based upon the grace and power of God himself. For example, while "the powers with which we do battle are those which would seek to despoil our lives, in whatever way, at whatever time, and however long it takes," Bunyan envisions death as "only a passage out of a prison into a palace, out of a sea of troubles into a haven of rest, out of a crowd of enemies to an innumerable company of true, loving, and faithful friends" (10, 27).

The struggles involved in the journey are part of the larger drama of salvation; "the great Biblical drama of sin, the fall, the struggle with evil, God's undaunted love, so great salvation [a familiar term in the writings of John and Charles Wesley, signifying not only conversion but grace-driven transformation], and the outcome of redemption from Genesis to Revelation" (40). For "Shaddai and his Son," completely aware of the tempter and temptations we face, counter with "their divine plan that something profoundly better and more redemptive would unfold" (63).

That plan involves the restoration of God's original connection with his creatures. "The crucial question was whether the Mansoulians would be brought back into relationship with the King." (67) That relationship would overcome the powers of sin and death and transform us into the likeness of Christ (II Corinthians 3:18; I John 3:2, NIV). While, when left to us, we are too often trivialized caricatures, easily deceived and led astray to participate in the character and schemes of "Diabolus," grace restores us to God's vision, inviting and leading us to actually "participate in the divine nature and escape the corruption in the world caused by evil desires" (II Peter 1:4, NIV).

Dr. Priset seeks to provide not only a complete context for the work itself, but also encourages us to fully participate with our own thoughts and experiences as we ponder this journey. To accomplish this, he provides the perspectives of three people, whose vocational lives equip them to read Bunyan's work in diverse and distinctive ways. The reflections of a psychological counselor, a trial attorney, and a retired military chaplain exemplify the rich interaction of this book with its readers.

Each one highlights elements in *The Holy War* that speak out of their respective areas of observation and expertise. In one of these, drawing upon his theological and military experiences, Dr. Paul Womack sees limitations in Bunyan's perspective – that of perseverance under persecution – and suggests other ways to see and respond to life's struggles, 231-233.

As in his earlier work on Bunyan, our author has done a great service by empowering many more people to read and benefit from this significant work. I invite you to dive in and fully appreciate the world he opens to our understanding and growth.

D. Gregory Van Dussen
Northeastern Seminary

Acknowledgments

To Brian Stahler who, over fifty years ago, as my High School English teacher, encouraged me to read John Bunyan's *The Pilgrim's Progress*, guided my earliest attempts in creative writing, and set into motion an interest that carries on into Bunyan's other writings.

To Abby Manzella, LMSW, Wellness Counselor, for psychological insights she perceived as an underlayment to Bunyan's story and for suggesting the insertion of various music titles to lead the reader into reflective moments along the way.

To Lynda Ashbery Dodd, prosecuting attorney, for helpful insights culled in reflection upon the arrest and trial scenes in Bunyan's life story and allegory.

To the Reverend Dr. J. Paul Womack (Colonel), Vietnam, Desert Storm, and Operation Iraqi Freedom veteran and military chaplain, for expressing his heart on war and peace-making.

To the Reverend Darryl Barrow, pastor, and Heather Pitzrick Salonis, secretary, at Emmanuel United Methodist Church, Lockport, New York, for feedback on the story content and prayer components.

To the Reverend Dr. Janet Wootton; and Joint Curators Jennifer Ayley and Helen O'Hara at Bunyan Meeting and Museum, Bedford, England, for their gracious response and support.

To Joyce Foley, retired elementary teacher, and Kevin Foley, retired college professor; Janice McKinney, church musician and retired public-school music teacher; Dr. Thomas Skraitz, chiropractor; Carol Erickson, my sister, and her daughter Kristy, all for various informational checks and suggestions.

Also, to Kevin Foley, previously head of wood technology at Rochester Institute of Technology, who reviewed and made suggestions on the chapter "The Master Craftsperson."

To Meredith Sears Priset, MLS, my daughter-in-law, Student Engagement and Acquisitions Librarian at Walsh University, North Canton, Ohio; and Janis M. Gibbs, JD, Ph.D., Associate Professor of History, Hope College, Holland, Michigan for substantial proofreading, grammatical suggestions, and content clarifications.

To my granddaughter Kaitlyn, a Clarence, New York, high school senior, for her pen and ink drawings featured throughout the book. And to my grandson Zachary who, as a third grader, did a read-aloud with me through Bunyan's *Holy War* and, as a fourth grader, did a read-through my rewrite, which, at times, brought his asking clarifying questions, thus helping to refine word choices and develop enriching footnotes.

To the Reverend Fung Kiu (Alice) Priset, M.Div., my daughter-in-law and pastor of the Marilla and Williston United Methodist Churches, for her technical support, troubleshooting, song title suggestions and clerical help; and to her husband Jonathan, my son, for helpful assistance, as well.

Also to George Streit's adult Sunday school class and Pastor Alice Priset's JOY group, respectively involving people from the Marilla and Williston, New York, United Methodist Churches for meaningful study, reflection and discussion experiences engaging Bunyan's classic writings.

Why a Reawakening?

The American writer Washington Irving in *The Sketch Book* relates the story of Rip Van Winkle said to have fallen asleep for twenty years and, upon awakening, brought to discover so much of himself and his world had changed.

The King of England no longer controlled the Colonies. The United States of America was a nation under the leadership of a president. Then, too, there was a whirlwind of changes that befell his perception of family and friends! Quite bluntly, Rip Van Winkle had to catch up from the past in order to discover where he belonged in the present. Comprehending past and present were both important for spiriting him on into the next years of his life!

Later, Irving writes of another repose. At Westminster Abbey, London, he is drawn into the library of its chapter house. After dealing with a door "double-locked, and opened with some difficulty, as if seldom used," Irving entered a treasure trove of old books. At first, he looked upon the scene as a "harem," but then quickly shifted the metaphor to that of an "infirmary." There were so many volumes he presumed had been opened no more than once every two hundred years or so. Oh, there were times and places wherein such writings "flourished." But now, "more worn by time than use," they were left collecting dust on shelves. Possibly once a year the dean might brisk past these tomes suffering "the tint of age," which brought Irving to a pondering: What if Westminster school would just turn its students loose to happen upon the insight, enjoyment, and refreshment couched in such literary treasures?

> They are caskets which enclose within a small compass the wealth of the language – its family jewels, which are thus transmitted in a portable form to posterity. The setting may occasionally be antiquated and require now and then to be renewed . . . but the brilliancy and intrinsic value of the gems continue unaltered.[1]

---

[1] Washington Irving, "The Mutability of Literature," *The Legend of Sleepy Hollow and Other Stories from The Sketch Book*, with an Introduction by Wayne Franklin (New York: Signet Classics by Penguin Group, 1961, 2006), 131, 132, 133, 139; all in all, 130-140.

In still another setting, Washington Irving found his interest peaked in the library of the British Museum wherein he came upon a strange cast of people. At first, Irving thought they were Magi! No, they were bookworms! Or sages! Working away in a room marked by a hushed stillness, a silence broken only "by the racing of pens over sheets of paper," they were folks busy at "long tables" surrounded by "great cases of venerable books."

On watching these "studious personages poring intently over dusty volumes, rummaging among moldy manuscripts," his curiosity grew. Then, interrupting his thoughts one or another of the researchers would send a "familiar" back into the stacks for additional resources. However, when Irving's time in the library came abruptly to an end – confronted with the way-out-of-there because he did not have "a card of admission" – Irving realized that these "bookworms" (maybe even "poachers" he had mistaken for Magi) were authors "in the very act of manufacturing books."

Nonetheless, this American author and visitor to Europe had a helpful way of describing how such an engagement could air-lift the worth and wisdom of the past to bring a sense of renewal to the present.

> Nature has wisely, though whimsically, provided for the conveyance of seeds from clime to clime, in the maws of certain birds, so that animals, which, in themselves, are little better than carrion, and apparently the lawless plunderers of the orchard and the cornfield, are, in fact, Nature's carriers to disperse and perpetuate her blessings. In like manner, the beauties and fine thoughts of ancient and obsolete authors are caught up by these flights of predatory writers and cast for again to flourish and bear fruit in a remote and distant tract of time. Many of their works, also, undergo a kind of metempsychosis[2] and spring up under new forms. What was formerly a ponderous history revives in the shape of a romance, an old legend changes into a modern play, and a sober philosophical treatise furnishes the body for a whole series of bouncing and sparkling essays. Thus it is in the clearing of our American woodlands; where we burn down a forest of stately pines, a progeny of dwarf oaks start up in their place, and we never see the prostrate trunk of a tree moldering into soil, but it gives birth to a whole tribe of fungi.[3]

---

[2] In some belief systems, metempsychosis, which at times converges on the occult, is, in death, the supposed transmigration of the soul of a human being or animal into a new body of the same or a different species. The idea goes as far back as Pythagoras. Interestingly, Irving is using this word to depict a literary process.

[3] Washington Irving, "The Art of Bookmaking," *The Legend of Sleepy Hollow and Other Stories from The Sketch Book*, with an Introduction by Wayne Franklin (New York: Signet Classics by Penguin Group, 1961, 2006), 80, 81, 82, 85; all in all, 79-85.

Consequently, it is with this in mind, I hope my handling of John Bunyan's *The Holy War* might serve more than the re-manufacturing of an old book, an updated commentary, a poaching, or even a trivial pursuit, but an inspiration for one to get digging back into vintage Bunyan itself and find a good word – indeed, many good words – for the present.

Reawakening is a powerful image. There are times when, metaphorically speaking, we may have fallen asleep in some phase of life and, upon awakening, must catch back up with the changes, or even reexamine those matters from which we may have drifted off, laid aside or failed to comprehend. What then is good, we have the chance to discover a renewed manifestation of life which reaches us on through the next passing of the years!

The way in which C. S. Lewis introduces the love poetry of the Medieval world may help us appreciate what is going on in Bunyan's literary craft of allegory.

> Humanity does not pass through phases as a train passes through stations: being alive, it has the privilege of always moving yet never leaving anything behind. Whatever we have been, in some sort we are still. Neither the form nor the sentiment of this old poetry [and to this, I would add Bunyan's works] has passed away without leaving indelible traces on our minds. We shall understand our present, and perhaps even our future, the better if we can succeed, by an effort of the historical imagination, in reconstructing that long-lost state of mind.[4]

In a similar frame of thought, I have seized the chance for us to go back and reclaim something of which many of us may have lost sight. In a somewhat interdisciplinary approach, I have examined John Bunyan's *The Holy War* through several past and present-day lenses. Starting with thousands of scriptural texts that provided an underlayment for Bunyan's allegory,[5] I moved on to a Vietnam War veteran who also served as a military chaplain during Desert Storm and Operation Iraqi Freedom. I have gone, as well, to a prosecuting attorney and to a wellness counselor for professional insights they respectively might view at places throughout

---

[4] C. S. Lewis, *The Allegory of Love: A Study in Medieval Tradition* (New York: Oxford University Press, 1936; Paperback, 1958), 1.

[5] According to Mark S. Burrows, "The original Greek word, *allegorein*, 'to interpret allegorically', derives from *allos*, 'other', and *agoreuein*, 'to proclaim in the assembly [*agora*]'. To allegorize was to publicize a meaning other than the obvious or literal one, revealing a meaning supposedly hidden *in* the text and *from* the reader. It was also a way of retrieving from obscure narratives a meaning with universal significance" Mark S. Burrows, "Allegory," in *The New Westminster Dictionary of Christian Spirituality*, by Philip Sheldrake, ed. (Louisville, Kentucky: Westminster John Knox Press, 2005), 100.

the text. Then, with the realization that Martin Luther's *Commentary on Galatians* played a significant role in John Bunyan's spiritual awakening and development, I have taken what I shall call soundings from Luther's Commentary, where a number of remarkable parallels and significant contributions come to light.

In all these turns of attention, I am intrigued how I – indeed, any of us – often lose sight of the insights and encouragements a three-hundred-year-old allegory, a five-hundred-year-old Bible commentary, other testimonies past and present, and the Scriptures themselves may reawaken and resource our lives today.

Early on in my endeavors, Matt Redman's song "10,000 Reasons (Bless the Lord)" had been pressing upon my heart and mind. Maybe it was because I loved the song during times that we used it in Praise Team for worship at church. Then, Redman's repetition of the words "my soul" comes so close to an echo of Bunyan's word "Mansoul." In due course, I went on to realize the sketch of theology threading its way through Redman's song. For instance, the lines sounding out Shaddai's creation and God's new creation are expressed in Matt Redman's "a new day's dawning." Then, there is Bunyan's sense of Shaddai and Redman's sense of God "rich in love," "slow to anger," of a great name and of a kind heart.

From this, it is a short step to point to a sampling of additional song titles (many available as music videos, too) wherever a Text and Song Interactional footnote appears throughout the book. One may refer to the entire song list on the first discussion question page toward the end of the book.

By connecting with my rendition of John Bunyan's notable story for insight, inspiration, and enjoyment, one may also engage in any of the notes placed at various points for additional depths of insight, too.

Enjoy a revitalization of your own thoughts and aspirations via this re-expression of Bunyan's life story and his compelling allegory, *The Holy War*.

"10,000 Reasons (Bless the Lord)"

By Jonas Myrin and Matt Redman
(Psalm 103:1-5)

Bless the Lord, O my soul,
O my soul, worship His holy Name.
Sing like never before, O my soul.
I'll worship Your holy Name.

The sun comes up, it's a new day dawning;
It's time to sing Your song again.
Whatever may pass and whatever lies before me,
Let me be singing when the evening comes.

Bless the Lord, O my soul,
O my soul, worship His holy Name.
Sing like never before, O my soul.
I'll worship Your holy Name.

You're rich in love and You're slow to anger,
Your Name is great and Your heart is kind;
For all Your goodness I will keep on singing,
Ten thousand reasons for my heart to find.

Bless the Lord, O my soul,
O my soul, worship His holy Name.
Sing like never before, O my soul.
I'll worship Your holy Name.

And on that day when my strength is failing,
The end draws near and my time has come;
Still my soul sings Your praise unending,
Ten thousand years and then forever more.

Bless the Lord, O my soul,
O my soul, worship His holy Name.
Sing like never before, O my soul.
I'll worship Your holy Name.

Bless the Lord, O my soul,
O my soul, worship His holy Name.
Sing like never before, O my soul.
I'll worship Your holy Name.

Whatsoever Is of Good Report

The boy had just turned sixteen. It was an age at which he could get away from home and join the military. At home, so many things had been happening. His mother had just died. Within a month his sister, his childhood playmate, had died. Then, a stepmom came into the family mix. All these significant life transitions came about inside of three months. At any rate, when lads back then turned sixteen, they were included in "levies" set by Parliament among those pressed into military service.[6]

The boy was John Bunyan. This was the 1600s and, in England, Scotland and Ireland, it was the time of the Civil Wars when the King's forces were fighting against the Parliamentary forces. It is not clear how much fighting Bunyan experienced, for this phase of the war in which he was engaged was nearing its end. Yet, military images hung within his heart and mind throughout the years and eventually contributed to what became one of his most enduring writings, *The Holy War*.[7]

Across the years, the boy came to comprehend that what fell out of sorts in people's lives – indeed, his own life – did not happen by chance. Rather so many problems had a spiritual basis. These spiritual challenges would gnaw away within an individual for years with great effects. Bunyan articulated this through the various unhealthy and unholy characters populating his story – take, for example, Hard-Heart, Strife, Bragman,

---

[6] John Brown, *John Bunyan: His Life, Times and Work* (London: Wm. Isbister Limited, 1885), 49.

[7] Alexander Whyte points out: "The *Pilgrim's Progress* sets forth the spiritual life under the scriptural figure of a long and an uphill journey. The *Holy War*, on the other hand, is a military history; it is full of soldiers and battles, defeats and victories. And its devout author had much more scriptural suggestion and support in the composition of the *Holy War* than he had even in the composition of the *Pilgrim's Progress*. For Holy Scripture is full of wars and rumours of wars; the wars of the Lord; the wars of Joshua and the Judges; the wars of David, with his and many other magnificent battle-songs; till the best-known name of the God of Israel in the Old Testament is the Lord of Hosts; and then in the New Testament we have Jesus Christ described as the Captain of our salvation. Paul's powerful use of armour and of armed men is familiar to every student of his epistles; and then the whole Bible is crowned with a book all sounding with the battle-cries, the shouts, and the songs of soldiers, till it ends with that city of peace where they hang the trumpet in the hall and study war no more. Military metaphors had taken a powerful hold of our author's imagination even in the *Pilgrim's Progress*, as his portraits of Greatheart and Valiant-for-truth and other soldiers sufficiently show, while the conflict with Apollyon and the destruction of Doubting Castle are so many sure preludes of the coming *Holy War*. Bunyan's early experiences in the great Civil War had taught him many memorable things about military art; memorable and suggestive things that he afterwards put to the most splendid use in the siege, the capture, and the subjugation of Mansoul" Alexander Whyte, *Bunyan Characters – Third Series* [Public Domain] (Astounding-Stories.com, 2015), 5.

Pitiless, Fooling, Despair, and many, many more. Bunyan also amplified the sense of this with such hyphenated name characters like Scorn-Truth, High-mind, Love-no-Good, and others present in this rogues' gallery. All were held under the serpentine influence of lord Diabolus (Satan)!

So as not to leave anyone hanging in a negativity, Bunyan went on to populate his story with wholesome characters as Think-Well, Desires-awake, True-heart and many others pleading, praying, and pressing for the good. Above all, they were those who had a heart toward God whom Bunyan called Shaddai[8] and His Son, Emmanuel (Jesus). Nonetheless, there were times, as in life, when the seemingly good individuals drift off track and need God's gracious and redemptive work in their lives. Which if we are honest, we all need every day! Thus, we have set the stage for Bunyan's distinguished allegorical war story.

One of the early Bible story battles happened when Abram, in Genesis 14, went to rescue his nephew Lot who had been captured in a conflict when four kings pitted themselves against five kings. During the conflict Sodom and Gomorra were pillaged and Lot was taken captive.[9] The last battle the Bible mentions is the Battle of Armageddon. The word appears only in Revelation 16.[10] It depicts the ultimate struggle between good and evil, with the power of God on the one side against the demonic forces of evil on the other side.

In Exodus 17, there is the account of a battle Israel fought on the way to the Promised Land. It was retaliation for an unprovoked surprise attack by an enemy. Still, Matthew Henry, a contemporary of John Bunyan, remarks about the story. "[The children of Israel] had been quarreling with Moses, and now God sends the Amalekites to quarrel with them." There is an interesting touch of body language throughout the story. If Moses could keep his arms extended to raise his staff, which was a sign of his reaching to God in trust, Israel would be on the winning side. When Moses grew tired and lowered his staff, success would turn toward the Amalekites. Then, Aaron and Hur slipped in close to Moses seated on a rock and

---

[8] El Shaddai, one of the most common Hebrew words used in Christian worship for God, means "Almighty God." Without the word El preceding it, Shaddai means "the Almighty." The word primarily appears among the patriarchs (especially Job). In the New Testament, the word which is translated into Greek as "pantokratōr" appears once in 2 Corinthians and eight times in Revelation. In Revelation, it is associated closely with the songs of heaven. Moreover, some understand Shaddai to mean "the mountain god" while others view Shaddai to mean the "thunderer" or "overpowerer." R. C. Sproul points out: "Scripture often borrows words from the Semitic language-speaking peoples of its day and invests them with brand-new, divinely-inspired meanings."

[9] Genesis 14:1-17

[10] Revelation 16:16

by standing each side of him propped his arms up. And thus, Israel won the battle.[11]

But who were these Amalekites?

A group of people in somewhat of a shirttail relationship to Israel, the Amalekites were descendants of Jacob's brother Esau. As a nomadic desert tribe to the east of Egypt, the Amalekites bore quite a vested interest in the caravan routes linking Arabia with Egypt. Do not mess with anyone's commerce! Even though they were Israel's so-called distant relatives, we find Israel and Amalek never kept on friendly terms. Even worse, Israel regarded the Amalekites as merciless killers. For instance, Deuteronomy 25:17-19 referred to a time they preyed upon the travel-weary Hebrews lagging at the rear in the wilderness wanderings, ruthlessly cutting the children of Israel down.

When all was said and done, from the time of Moses during the Exodus until the years of King David who brought them into check – roughly four hundred years – the Amalekites were in perpetual conflict with the Israelites.

Years later, though, Obadiah had an interesting remark about some of their relatives, the Edomites, who lived in Petra – a city one hundred and two miles square with some parts of it carved out of rock – in the Jordanian desert. As descendants of Esau, too, they displayed such arrogance to gloat over Israel's misfortunes and believed nothing could bring themselves, the unassailable Edomites, down! Obadiah decreed:

> 3 You live in the safety of the rocks.
>
> You make your home high up in the mountains.
>
> But your proud heart has tricked you.
>
> So you say to yourself,
>
> 'No one can bring me down to the ground.'
>
> 4 You have built your home as high as an eagle does.
>
> You have made your nest among the stars.
>
> But I will bring you down from there,
>
> Announces the Lord.[12]

You do not have to be on a military battlefield, though, for life to be painfully hard. Evil-Eye, Mistrust, False-Peace, Let-Good-Slip, and oth-

---

[11] Exodus 17:8-16

[12] Obadiah 1:3-4, New International Reader's Version, 1995, 1996, 1998, 2014 by Biblica, Inc.®

ers (still more of Bunyan's character names) raise additional problems and reflect broken relationships which can ache on for years. Nevertheless, there are those like Aaron and Hur in Exodus 17 from whom we draw help and encouragement. Gifts such people in our lives exemplify come to the greatest focus in the redemptive strength, love, and power of the Lord Jesus Christ.

As John Bunyan grew to manhood, he went through quite a wild and reckless time of life. You might say he sowed his wild oats, struggled to find God's peace but, once connecting with God's love, became one of the most gifted, unable-to-be-ignored, and humble communicators of God's grace.

There is a passage in the Apostle Paul's letter to the Philippians that might nicely stream out as a banner regarding the good with which I believe Bunyan tried to live. I draw this from the Geneva Bible of 1599 which, with the King James Bible of 1611, Bunyan would have had access.

> Whatsoever things are true, whatsoever things are honest, whatsoever things are just, whatsoever things are pure, whatsoever things are worthy of love, whatsoever things are of good report, if there be any virtue, or if there be any praise, think on these things.[13]

John Bunyan published *The Holy War* six years before he died and four years after he had published Christian's journey, which was part of *The Pilgrim's Progress* – the book by which we know him best. In addition to Bunyan's journey literature, *The Holy War* brought another dimension to the drama of life. In his account of goodness battling against evil, *The Holy War* depicted the long and arduous campaign – indeed, the whole saga of salvation – directed against Diabolus (Satan)[14] and his evil entourage who in the beginning ambushed God's people of Mansoul in an Eden-like setting.[15]

Notwithstanding this, some of the heroes Bunyan would have us draw upon are Charity, Piety, Humble, Gracious, Patience, True-heart, Conviction, Promise, and others (all highlighting spiritual qualities) that the Bible held high for the wholesome living of our lives. Consequently, the importance of these spiritual counterforces![16]

---

[13] Philippians 4:8, Geneva Bible

[14] Biblical images of Satan: "Abaddon, Beelzebub, Belial, devil, god of this age, king of Tyre, Lucifer, prince of the power of the air, ruler of this world" (Walter Martin, Jill Martin Rische and Kurt Van Gorden, *The Kingdom of the Occult* [Nashville, Tennessee: Thomas Nelson, 2008], 5, 729).

[15] Genesis 3:1-6

[16] Ephesians 6:13-18

As the Apostle Paul says in Ephesians, the powers with which we do battle in life are not flesh and blood.[17] In effect, the powers with which we do battle are those which would seek to despoil our lives in whatever way, at whatever time, and however long it takes.[18]

Engaging in these life battles, though, we are not alone. Even if at times we think that help is far away, we still are not left alone.

John Bunyan brings forth several commanding officers leading God's forces to rescue the people from the power of the Evil one. All these captains are God's well-equipped, undaunted, and indefatigable forces.

Shaddai's commanding general is Boanerges – a name the Gospel lays upon James and John, sons of thunder[19] – and under him, there are Captain Conviction, Captain Judgment, Captain Execution, and their troops – thus, providing an Old Testament prophetic flavor to the allegory. In due course, though, Shaddai sends another force. This time it is Emmanuel with Captain Credence, Captain Good-Hope, Captain Charity, Captain Innocent, Captain Patience, and their soldiers. Consequently, a New Testament Gospel flavor!

As earlier I had pointed out, one of John Bunyan's mentors was Martin Luther who lived more than a hundred years before Bunyan. The mentoring came through Luther's commentary on Paul's letter to the Galatians, which Bunyan happened upon. Therein, Martin Luther gave Bunyan a most valuable understanding of God's grace which provided him profound help while going through his spiritual wilderness.

To circle back upon the episode regarding Moses, Aaron, Hur, and Joshua: Think now. Who is holding your arms up? Whose arms are you holding up?

Eugene Peterson in his distinctive paraphrase of the Scriptures called *The Message* has a poignant way of stating our Christian calling:

> Summing it all up, friends, I'd say you'll do best by filling your minds
> and meditating on things true, noble, reputable, authentic, compelling, gra-

---

[17] Ephesians 6:12

[18] During World War II, Clive Staples Lewis imagines Satan's evil notables playing a game for keeps – howsoever long it takes – bringing people prey to temptation; as in *The Screwtape Letters*, we see it expressed through Screwtape's counseling Wormwood: "You should be guarding him [the one Satan had been trying to take down] like the apple of your eye. If he dies now, you lose him. If he survives the war, there is always hope. The Enemy [Shaddai God] has guarded him from you through the first great wave of temptations. But, if only he can be kept alive, you have time itself for your ally. The long, dull, monotonous years of middle-aged prosperity or middle-aged adversity are excellent campaigning weather. You see, it is so hard for these creatures to *persevere*" (C. S. Lewis, *The Screwtape Letters*, section 28, pp. 154-155).

[19] Mark 3:17

cious – the best, not the worst; the beautiful, not the ugly; things to praise, not things to curse. Put into practice what you learned from me, what you heard and saw and realized. Do that, and God, who makes everything work together, will work you into his most excellent harmonies.[20]

You Have Heard It Said

The grave misunderstandings and conflicts that plague people take a substantial toll not only upon those who are engaging in them, but also upon others around them. Sometimes, as the misunderstandings and conflicts arise, their effect seems to know no boundaries. They disrupt families, churches, local communities, and larger clusters of people anywhere. Often, the sources which bring disputes into place ache for a long time, blocking almost anything constructive and healing.

The time before a conflict breaks out is what I would call an incubation period. It does not matter how long or short the period may be. As it keeps on gnawing away, the collateral damages become myriad.

In the Sermon on the Mount, Jesus provides serious reminders about both individual and social dynamics. In one regard, Jesus draws us to the root of attitudes which can develop into something worse when he says, "you have heard it said, but I say unto you" and so on.[21]

Another ancient writing, *The Shepherd of Hermas*, which had nearly come to acceptance for inclusion in the New Testament canon, envisions two spirits – a good one and a bad one – pulling separate ways within a person. The choices made bring about the crucial results.

> There are two angels with a [person], one of righteousness and one of wickedness . . . The angel of righteousness is delicate and bashful and gentle and tranquil. When then this one enters into thy heart, forthwith he speaketh with thee of righteousness, of purity, of holiness, and of contentment, of every righteous deed and of every glorious virtue. When all these enter into thy heart, know the angel of righteousness . . . [and know] the angel of wickedness also. First of all, he is quick tempered and bitter and senseless, and his works are evil, overthrowing the servants of God . . . Recognizing his works, stand aloof from him, and trust him in nothing for his works are evil and inexpedient for the servants of God. Here then thou hast the workings of both . . . it is good to follow the angel of righteousness, and to bid farewell to the angel of wickedness.[22]

---

20 Philippians 4:8-9, *The Message*, 1993, 2002, 2018 by Eugene H. Peterson
21 Matthew 5:21-48
[22] *The Shepherd of Hermas*, trans. J. B. Lightfoot (London: Macmillan, 1891; reprint, CrossReach Publications, 2017), Mandate 6, pp. 37-38.

As a child back in the early days of television I remember a cartoon character engaged in a decisive moment depicted with a good angel and a bad angel floating above his or her head and trying to pull one way or the other. Whether the cartoonist realized it or not, this was a play upon an ancient insight found in *The Shepherd of Hermas*.

In John Bunyan's 17th century classic, *The Holy War*, we come across an array – no, an expanse – of good and bad characters maneuvering throughout people's lives and accordingly working upon human hearts and minds, hopes, behaviors, and relationships. The setting for all this is the corporation of Mansoul[23] on the famous continent of Universe, a very large and spacious country, a place well-watered and richly adorned and as originally intended, an exceptionally fine place to live!

Delving into Bunyan's story, a professional counselor or psychologist might find quite an array of interest areas at various depths for examination. A prosecuting attorney and a defense attorney would have a heyday sifting through various characterizations Bunyan stages in this tangle of life, too. In one way or another, the storyteller pricks our interests while laying out quite a potpourri of dynamics across a patchwork quilt of human life.

There is a quotation I first intended to save until the end as a wrap for this whole retelling of *The Holy War*. After further reflection, I felt it made more sense to share it right as we start. It thus becomes a lens through which we may view each stage of the story. The quotation comes from the concluding pages of a significant history on war and peace by Roland Bainton, a twentieth-century Yale professor and church historian. Though the quotation articulates what a pacifist might remark, it relates to what-

---

[23] According to Suzanne Noffke in Philip Sheldrake's *Dictionary of Christian Spirituality*: "The human individual's inherent capacity for selfhood, self-awareness and subjectivity, the principle of human knowing and responsible freedom, has in Christian tradition and much of philosophical history been called 'soul' "(592). In William D. Mounce's *Expository Dictionary of Old & New Testament Words*: The Hebrew נֶפֶשׁ / *nepeš* often translated "soul" carries a range of meanings. It means "breath," but also "soul, life, entire being." Not only referring to human beings, the "breath" of life is something all creatures share (Genesis 1:30). In Greek, the word is ψυχή / *psychē*. In a biblical sense, the Greek, much as the Hebrew, shares a spectrum of meanings. In the Biblical creation story, when humanity comes to life it is because of God's breathing into them life (Genesis 2:7). Noffke continues to clarify that body and soul are not separate entities from each other as in dualistic Greek Platonic thought. "Whatever may be the form of human immortality it must somehow ultimately encompass both the spiritual and the physical aspects of one's individual being; it cannot be simply a matter of 'saving one's soul'. And while one lives in time, an integrated spirituality cannot address the soul without addressing bodiliness as essential to humanness and holiness" (594). Thus, we come to interact with Bunyan's "Mansoul."

ever view – just war, crusade, or pacifism – pertains to one's engaging in conflict:

> If in withstanding the beast he [the warrior] descend to the methods of the beast, he will himself become the beast, and though the field be won the cause will be lost.[24]

John Bunyan's beast throughout *The Holy War* is the dragon Diabolus. The designation for almighty God is Shaddai and his Son, Jesus, is Emmanuel. The people inhabiting life are Mansoulian. In the Bible, however, the more common word for Diabolus is Satan.

Combing through an array of ancient biblical and extrabiblical sources – e.g., Job, Daniel, Zechariah, 1 Enoch, 3 Enoch, Jubilees, Testament of Job, Qumran writings – Daniel G. Reid remarks:

> In broad strokes, Satan was understood to be a personal spiritual being of the highest order, originally created by God for good purposes, but now engaged as the leader of a cosmic rebellion. While he exercises his power on earth, he does not seem to have been barred from appearing in the courts of heaven to bring accusation against God's people. He rules over a destructive force of fallen angels or spirits and actively and strategically works evil against God's people, whether as individuals, leaders, sect, or nation. Israel, or at least the righteous remnant within Israel, is protected by God or his archangelic agent, typically Michael, the Prince of Israel. And both individual and corporate Israel are enjoined to resist Satan's falsehoods, his malevolent schemes and his dangerous assaults. In due course Satan will be defeated by God.[25]

John Bunyan's story as well as his life is respectfully sensitive to such a spirit in daily life and practice. *The Holy War* is what goes on within each one of us. At its core, Diabolus's design is to damage life. Shaddai's design has ever and always been to graciously redeem and bless life.

If, in what I have laid out as each episode of *The Holy War*, there is a reawakening to that reality, I pray for us to be sensitive to God's leading us to reexamine what insights may have escaped us, been laid aside by us, or obscured through the years.

As we engage in this venture, we, soon, shall review John Bunyan's fascinating life. Then, we shall trace our way through Bunyan's mesmerizing and thoughtful classic.

---

[24] Roland H. Bainton, *Christian Attitudes Toward War and Peace* (Nashville: Abingdon Press, 1960), p. 249.

[25] D. G. Reid, "Satan, Devil," in *Dictionary of Paul and His Letters*, ed. Gerald F. Hawthorne, Ralph P. Martin, and Daniel G. Reid, (Downers Grove, Illinois: InterVarsity Press, 1993), 863.

"Where Have All the Flowers Gone"

I have never been a soldier and probably would miss what experienced soldiers might be able to draw from Bunyan's tale. However, my father, a World War II veteran, served under Major General George Churchill Kenney in the 5th Army Airforce Service Command in the South Pacific[26] My father-in-law served in Battery A, 209th Coast Artillery under Major General Alexander McCarrell Patch who, after his experience in the South Pacific, commanded the 7th Army from the Mediterranean into Southern France as backup for General George S. Patton at Normandy.[27]

All through the years afterwards, besides watching my father carry the flag and march with his buddies in the local Memorial Day and Fourth of July parades, I do not remember Dad ever telling me about his war time experiences. So, also, my father-in-law hardly spoke of the war. I believe this is nothing unusual. I once asked a World War II army sergeant if the movie *The Saving of Private Ryan* were accurate? "Yes, except for one thing," he said and then he went on to explain, "We did not curse and swear like that." All in all, I have sensed that old soldiers do not speak much about what they went through and yet war remains profoundly imprinted upon their lives.

Aside from research my sister has done, intimating our father's facing some of the most challenging conditions in war,[28] while battling through New Guinea, Bismarck Archipelago (among the bloodiest), Southern Philippines and Luzon, there was something in which my dad gave me a sliver of insight.

During my college years, I learned to play the guitar so that I, as a student chaplain, could lead the singing at our Intervarsity Christian Fellowship meetings. One of the songs I learned and grew to love was a classic protest song, "Where Have All the Flowers Gone." I, as a teen during the Vietnam War era, would have been drafted except for a lottery system the government was using at the time, with my birthday having drawn such a number that placed me off the active list.

My cousin, Lance Corporal[29] John Fredrick Priset, a Marine, who bore the same name as my father and our grandfather, except our grandfather's

---

[26] Major General Kenney fought in WW1 and WW2 and commanded forces in the South Pacific

[27] Major General Patch fought in WW1 and WW2 and commanded forces in Pacific and Europe

[28] Monsoons, rain-saturated downpours, streams turned into raging rivers, enemy forces tunneled into mountains and led to fight until death, as well as dealing with malaria and other tropical diseases

[29] In the United States Marine Corp, a Lance Corporal is the third enlisted and highest

middle name spelled Frederick, was not so fortunate and, at the age twenty, became a Vietnam War casualty whose name appears among the 58,320 inscribed in the Vietnam Memorial Wall in Washington, DC.

I would sometimes ask my father if he had a song, he wanted me to play and sing. Although a man of very few words, invariably he would say he wanted me to sing the one about the "young girls." I knew exactly what he wanted. It was the 1955 song by Pete Seager (expanded in 1960 by Joe Hickerson), popularized by the Kingston Trio, and Peter, Paul, and Mary, and others, to which Winter Olympics figure skater Katarina Witt performed at Lillehammer in 1994.

Where have all the flowers gone? Long time passing.

Where have all the flowers gone? Long time ago.

Where have all the flowers gone?

Young girls have picked them everyone.

Oh, when will we ever learn?

When will we ever learn?[30]

I would start playing the guitar and singing, "Where have all the flowers gone? . . . Long time passing. When will [they] ever learn?" The song would pick up on "young girls" in place of "flowers" for the next verse. It then transitioned from "young girls" to "young men" and on to "soldiers." Then, "Where have all the soldiers gone . . . Gone to graveyards everyone." On my reaching the end, however, the going was from graveyards back to flowers again. A cycle of life song, but rhetorically speaking, circling on to what?

It was at this point this quiet-mannered man, my father, who hadn't much to say about anything and yet lived a continually gracious and giving life, was making a heart sensitive statement as an old soldier could never have forgotten.

---

in rank in order of seniority a Marine can hold without being a non-commissioned officer (Wikipedia).

[30] According to *Wikipedia*, founded by Jimmy Wales and Larry Sanger in 2001, Pete Seager drew his tune from an Irish lumberjack song, its lyrical inspiration was a traditional Cossack folk song, "Koloda-Duda."

I realize conflict and war – the failure of diplomacy, as some would claim[31] – brings a great wreckage and deeply-wounded spirits. So much so dearly lost![32]

I also realize, as renowned mid-twentieth century journalist Dorothy Thompson once put it: "It is doubtful whether the sight and experience of monstrous suffering breed compassion . . . All the publicizing of the Dachau and Belsen horrors [has] not made mankind more tender of humanity."[33]

Oh, for a legacy of humble goodness and kindness as articulated in Bunyan's vision of the flower garden in Christiana's part of *The Pilgrim's Progress*, published two years after *The Holy War* and four years before Bunyan died!

> [The Interpreter] led [Christiana, Mercy, and the boys] into his Garden, where was a great variety of flowers: And he said, do you see all these? So, Christiana said, Yes. Then said he again, Behold the flowers are divers in stature, in quality, and colour, and smell, and virtue; and some are better than some: Also, where the gardener has set them, there they stand, and quarrel not one with another.[34]

As I think of my father and my father-in-law and the wholesome, giving, constructive and productive lives they lived, my remembrance of them is a segue into this greater and profoundly more well-known story I am about to relate.

Thus, my prayer is for us to go on and grow to be a faithful people of God and a more constructive and kindlier presence to others around us.

---

[31] Tony Benn in a speech on 28 February 1991

[32] As a lead into a moving portrayal of what some soldiers experienced during the Vietnam War, refer to Scott P. Munson's *A Gift from Saint George* cited in the Annotated Bibliography.

[33] Peter Kurth, *American Cassandra: The Life of Dorothy Thompson* (Boston, Toronto, London: Little, Brown and Company, 1990), 378

[34] John Bunyan, *The Pilgrim's Progress*, with an introduction by David Hawkes (New York: Barnes and Noble Books, 2005), 224.

John Bunyan, Tinker

During the English Civil Wars,[1] a boy, at the impressionable age of sixteen, served for a brief period in the Parliamentary Army of Sir Oliver Cromwell. The boy's biographer, John Brown, wraps up this soldiering phase of Bunyan's life story with a meaningful glimpse of such a time.

> It must have been a curious school of experience to be among these fighting, preaching, praying majors and captains, who could one day storm and take Grafton or Hillesdon House, and the next preach to edification in Newport church. Eagerly taking in this new world, all so vivid to him, he marches, it may be, with Captain Bladwell to Aylesbury and the Surrey Downs, or stands with the men in Lathbury Field to hear Captain Hobson preach, or gives military salute in Newport garrison to Sir Samuel Luke, or along with Major Ennis fights amidst the rain of death on Leicester walls.[2]

The lad of whom I write was John Bunyan, especially known as author of *The Pilgrim's Progress* and *The Holy War*. He was born November 28, 1628 in a small cottage about halfway between Elstow and Bedford, England. His home was at the foot of a gentle slope on a nine-acre plot through which passed two streams, one running so close to their cottage

---

[1] From August 22, 1642 to September 3, 1651, three English Civil Wars overall involving England, Scotland and Ireland raged between the Royalist (Cavalier) supporters of King Charles I and his successor Charles II and the Parliamentary (Roundhead) forces regarding issues of government and religious freedom. The word Cavaliers was a derogatory term for Royalists in courtly dress. The Parliamentary forces were called Roundheads for their short, cropped hair. All in all, 34,000 Parliamentarian soldiers and 50,000 Royalist soldiers died throughout the conflict. At least 100,000 men and women died from war-related diseases, leaving the death toll nearly 200,000. The first of this series of the three Civil Wars – the one in which Bunyan would have been involved – ran from 1642 to 1646. The Battle of Edgehill, the first in this first set of assaults, took place in open country between Banbury and Warwick, on October 23, 1642, in Warwickshire. Although the results of the battle were a stalemate, the forces loyal to the English Parliament, commanded by Robert Devereux, 3rd earl of Essex, fatally delayed Charles I's march on London.

[2] John Brown, *John Bunyan: His Life, Times and Work* (London: Wm. Isbister Limited, 1885), 52.

that heavy rains often turned the field near the house into a virtual Slough of Despond.[3]

Bunyan's elementary education at best was meager, as children in poor families often had to leave such learning aside to go help in their parents' work. Thus, John's schooling was cut short when he moved from the school bench to his father Thomas's forge. As his biographer John Brown notes, "the education he received was mainly that given in the great school of human life."[4]

In June 1644, the boy's mother died. He was just fifteen years old. Within a month, his sister Margaret, his childhood playmate, died. Both mother and sister were buried in Elstow churchyard. If the timing of such life passages were not difficult enough, John's father married soon afterwards. In three months, the Bunyan family had gone through a cascade of three significant life changes.

By November 1644, as John Bunyan turned sixteen, he was eligible – in reality, levied, pressed, or drafted – for military service. However, his time in the Army could not have been long because the Battle of Naseby which practically ended the first of England's Civil Wars was in June 1645.[5] Still, there has been debate regarding which side of the war Bunyan served. Macaulay posits Bunyan served in the Parliamentary Army whereas Froude puts forward the idea that Bunyan was a Royalist.[6]

Emerging from Bunyan's classic writings, it has been suggested that Greatheart in *The Pilgrim's Progress* of Christiana's journey and Captain Boanerges and Captain Credence in *The Holy War* are portraits of military saints in the army of Sir Thomas Fairfax, Commander in Chief of the Parliamentary Army. On the other hand, Froude claims support for the Royalist theory in that Bunyan's own father belonged to the Anglican church and John Gifford, the Bedford pastor who played a significant role in Bunyan's spiritual development (the person believed to be Evangelist in *The Pilgrim's Progress* of Christian's journey) was a Royalist soldier. What may distract from the theory, though, is that Bunyan and Gifford never met until years after the war. Besides, though Bedfordshire had a few identifiable Royalist supporters, the county primarily was a hotbed of Parliamentary enthusiasm.

---

[3] As imagined in the beginning of *The Pilgrim's Progress*

[4] Brown, *John Bunyan: His Life, Times and Work*, 41

[5] Other resources posit Bunyan's military service extended into 1647 or 1648. However, in 1905 an anvil, stamped with Bunyan's name and the date, 1647, was drawn from some garbage in St. Neots, near Bedford, England (John Bunyan, *The Holy War Made by King Shaddai* [Made in the USA: Monee, IL: n.p., n.d.], p. 4.

[6] Brown, *John Bunyan: His Life, Times and Work*, 42

During his military service in the Parliamentary forces, Bunyan probably marched under the leadership of Sir Samuel Luke, a Presbyterian of Coplewood, whose character was lauded by many, including Oliver Cromwell. Drawing upon a few phrases crafted seriatim from an extensive depiction that John Brown provides:

> Sir Samuel Luke was one of shrewd observation, godly life, considerable breadth, humor, humanness, keen insight, and strong common sense. His personal valor was as unquestioned as his military skill. There was also a strong possibility that Luke's father enjoyed the assistance of a confidential servant named Edward, who, interestingly, was John Bunyan's uncle married to Bunyan's mother's sister, Rose, as well. Such a small world! Moreover, Sir Samuel Luke drew enjoyment from the finer things of life – including good wine, red deer pie, pheasant, buttons, loops – as well as the practical equipages pertaining to his work – including spades, mattocks, drums – all listed within his personal and military correspondence. Such incidentals being far off from fitting the stereotypical caricature of a narrow, parsimonious, and ascetic Puritan![7]

After a short stint of military service, Bunyan returned to Elstow and resumed work as a tinker. The years following Army life were marked by matters vividly described in *Grace Abounding to the Chief of Sinners* as those of quite the ungodly person. Quite bluntly, Bunyan was a notorious sinner, curser, swearer, liar, and blasphemer. However, there was a time he was struck by the disdain of a woman, who had an extremely ill-mannered reputation herself, scolding him for his wicked, blasphemous, and vulgar tongue.

In 1648, John Bunyan married. Plagued with poverty, Bunyan's wife, possibly being an orphan, could bring only two books, cherished by her beloved, godly father, as a dowry to their marital home. Unfortunately, almost every detail a biographer would love to have – his wife's name, where she came from, any particulars regarding the wedding, where it took place, and a few married life stories – is lost to the historical record. If the oldest child – a blind girl Mary – were given her mother's name, it is possible Bunyan's wife's name was Mary.

One of the wedding dowry books was *The Plain Man's Pathway to Heaven*, published in 1601, by Arthur Dent, a minister of Shoebury in Essex. Although John Brown considered Dent's book long, wearisome, heavy, and theologically narrow, it was popular enough to go through twenty-four editions by 1637. The story woven throughout the book was of a day in May when four characters had time on their hands and the at-

---

[7] Brown, *John Bunyan: His Life, Times and Work*, 45, 46

tractive setting of an arbor, with comfortable seating under an [oak]-tree, to talk of heavenly things. The four conversationists were a divine, a plain honest man, an ignorant man, and a caviller.[8] With an intensely English style of expression, the book held several racy sayings which may have filtered into Bunyan's imagination.

One of Dent's proverbs was that "he that never doubted never believed" – an interesting contrast to the ungodly regiments of doubters drawn into Diabolus's army to attack Mansoul in *The Holy War*! At the close of Dent's book, the ignorant man grew so concerned about his own moral state that the caviller, sounding a bit like the evil manipulator Carnal-Security picking on Godly-Fear in *The Holy War*, said he had a speedy remedy for such anxious troubles. One just had to go away and get lost in any pleasant and merry books.

Of a much more substantial nature than Dent's book was *The Practice of Piety*, by Lewis Bayly of Evesham, who afterwards became the Anglican bishop of Bangor, which was the other book Bunyan's bride brought into the marriage. First published in 1612, *The Practice of Piety* had gone through more than fifty printings by 1673 and had been translated into several languages. Notwithstanding its distinctly ecclesiastical tone, *The Practice of Piety*, with its many Bible references, was a favorite writing among the Puritans. For instance, Joseph Alleine, educated at Lincoln College, Oxford, and tutor and chaplain of Corpus Christi College, as well as one of the most beloved and respected of Nonconformists, found great consolation in Bayly's book while dying; and James Frazer of Brea, one of the Scottish Confessors, spoke of his conversion by reading it.

Significantly, Bishop Bayly had a thought-provoking thesis in that he endeavored to draw "out of the chaos of endless controversies the old practice of true piety which flourished before the controversies were hatched."[9]

Certainly sounds like a challenge every generation faces!

Bayly, also, advocated a person's reading the Bible through each year, first by means of a chapter each morning, then one at noon, and one in the evening, leaving six chapters left over for completion on the last day of the year. The Apocrypha could be read for one's pleasure but accepted only

---

[8] Those engaged in talk were: Theologus, a divine; Philagathus, a plain honest man; Assunetus, an ignorant man; and Antilegan, a Caviller. To clarify the difference in meaning between a caviller and a cavalier: a *caviller* was a disgruntled disputant who quibbled; one who raised annoying petty objections. A *cavalier*, historically, referred to a supporter of King Charles I in the English Civil War. Moreover, the word *cavalier*, used as an adjective, referred to one showing a lack of proper concern or saying or doing something offhand.

[9] Brown, *John Bunyan: His Life, Times and Work*, 57

as according with the Canonical scriptures.[10] As Spring Arbor University professor, Dr. Daniel V. Runyon summarizes Bayly's counsel:

> [The Bible reading is] in order to find 1) good advice resulting in good works or holy living; 2) threats of judgement motivating an appropriately Godly fear; 3) blessings and promises that will lead to all the Christian virtues; 4) reminders of God's gracious deliverance and special blessings; 5) suggestions to apply what is learned, not as mere historical discourse, but as personal letters from God in heaven; 6) admonitions for reverence for God's Word "as if God himself stood by and spake these words unto thee" (Piety 210-12).[11]

Between 1649 and 1652, John Bunyan attended Elstow Church where Christopher Hall served as the vicar. Hall entered the ministry when William Laud, a strict Anglican, was Archbishop of Canterbury, which gives one a sense that the worship was well-prescribed, strict, and liturgical. However, Bunyan's struggle to find peace with God required something other than this. With a tortured conscience, he engaged in a share of enjoyments, eventually becoming convinced of his sinfulness each time, and repeatedly walking away from what he thought stood between him and God. For instance, after enjoying a game of Cat[12] played at the market cross, he was struck with thoughts of God's displeasure for such frivolity, so he abandoned what some might regard just an innocent diversion. He enjoyed ringing the bells for church, but eventually felt ashamed of the enjoyment he was finding, and so, stepped away from the job. Nevertheless, he kept lurking in the doorway, watching his replacement pull the rope and wishing he were doing it still, until he felt he had to step away from the door, fearing the bell might come crashing down upon him. Sometime later, he heard of a church bell crashing down and killing a bell ringer in another place. Quite interestingly, many years later, when penning *The Pilgrim's Progress*, Bunyan described the bells of heaven ringing

---

[10] Corrective: 3 chapters daily, plus another 7 or 8 monthly, would keep spirit with Bayly's plan for a 12 months' read.

[11] Daniel V. Runyon, "John Bunyan's Master Story: The Holy War as Battle Allegory in Religious and Biblical Context" (Published version of Ph.D. dissertation, Lampeter, Wales: Edwin Mellen Press, 2007), 88.

[12] Tip cat or One-a-Cat was a 17th century outdoor game also taken to Colonial America – possibly the forerunner of baseball or cricket. Basically, it involved a 3 ft. long stick, and a 4-inch (1-inch to 2-inch thick) piece of wood called a cat. The cat was placed on the ground, struck at one end in a way to propel it upward (tipping the cat), and then slammed as far as possible with the stick. Then, the batter would run around the bases and try to get back to home base before a fielder could throw it there. However, if the batter missed the cat three times or the fielder caught the cat, the batter was out. For more details: http://www.1771.org/cd_tipcat.htm

so loudly and clearly celebrating people entering the Celestial City. At another stage of life, Bunyan turned to dancing with the village girls, and then to Bible reading (especially the historical books), but nothing seemed to ultimately help him.

To help get a grasp of Bunyan's supersensitive conscience, his 19th century biographer John Brown had a kindly and sensitive analysis of this part of John Bunyan's turbulent faith journey.

> The intensity of these struggles was, of course, largely due to the intensity of the spiritual nature in which they took place. As the storm sweeps most wildly and makes its dolefullest moaning through the tops of the tallest trees, the greatness of the man contributed to the greatness of his sufferings. They were intensified also by his ignorance and lack of spiritual guidance. Many of the shapes with which he wrestled in deepest anguish were the phantoms of his own heated imagination, the result of his own misinterpretation of the book of God. The battle which he was fighting was, of course, no phantom; it is the one battle of the ages for all who in a world of sin are seeking for the life of God; yet it might have been shortened and simplified by enlightened friendly aid. But it was Bunyan's misfortune to be surrounded by men who, either from want of sympathy or lack of light, could help him very little till his fiercest battle was fought out and ended.[13]

One day, while in Bedford, Bunyan overheard some women having a discussion on their Christian faith. Finding himself eavesdropping on what these godly women were saying, Bunyan's heart warmed with their thoughts. They were active participants in a Free Church founded in Bedford two or three years previously. Though Bunyan could be quite the talker himself, he was struck by how much he was out of depth listening to these women.

At still another time, Bunyan came across a tattered copy of Martin Luther's *Commentary on Paul's Epistle to the Galatians*. Upon reading page after page, he felt his heart drawn forward with insights which became guidance he cherished for the rest of his life. A sample from the beginning of Luther's text illustrates a tone that Bunyan found there.

> The greeting of the Apostle is refreshing. Grace remits sin, and peace quiets the conscience. Sin and conscience torment us, but Christ has overcome these fiends now and forever. Only Christians possess this victorious knowledge given from above. These two terms, grace and peace, constitute Christianity. Grace involves the remission of sins, peace, and a happy conscience. Sin is not canceled by lawful living, for no person is able to live up to the Law. The Law reveals guilt, fills the conscience with terror,

---

[13] Brown, *John Bunyan: His Life, Times and Work*, 60

and drives men to despair. Much less is sin taken away by man-invented endeavors. The fact is, the more a person seeks credit for himself by his own efforts, the deeper he goes into debt. Nothing can take away sin except the grace of God.[14]

How fitting were the words for one so haunted by sin, guilt, a yearning for forgiveness and peace! In time, Luther's insights would do much to shape Bunyan's understanding of the faith and ministry.[15] Moreover, Luther, an earlier pilgrim sufferer,[16] was the very guide for John Bunyan's troubled heart.[17] Then, in time, by means of the direction of the four Bedford Christian women, Bunyan came under the influence of John Gifford, their pastor.

During the Civil Wars, John Gifford, a Kentish man, and Royalist, was a major in the King's army. In June 1648, at the Battle of Rochester, where some of the fiercest fighting took place, Gifford was taken prisoner and among a few singled out to die upon the gallows. Tipped off by his sister, who happened to be visiting him in his cell, that the guards had fallen asleep, Gifford escaped, holed up in ditches, and made his way to London to seek a hiding place in the homes of friends. Within a passage of time, as his notoriety faded, he traveled to Bedford and apparently engaged as a

---

[14] Martin Luther, *Commentary on Galatians*, trans. by Theodore Graebner (Digireads. com Publishing, 2019), content on Galatians 1:3; p. 11.

[15] "In spiritual matters a person is by nature full of darkness, error, ignorance, malice, and perverseness in will and in mind. In view of this, Paul declares that Christ began and not we. 'He loved me, and gave Himself for me. He found in me no right mind and no good will. But the good Lord had mercy upon me. Out of pure kindness He loved me, loved me so that He gave Himself for me, that I should be free from the Law, from sin, devil, and death'" Martin Luther, *Commentary on Galatians*, trans. by Theodore Graebner (Digireads.com Publishing, 2019), Galatians 2:20; p. 55.

[16] Daniel V. Runyon, citing Richard Greaves, says the "quest for religious peace was a momentous psychological experience" for both Luther and Bunyan, but for different reasons. While Luther suffered an identity crisis, Bunyan had a "distinctly psychopathic temperament" characterized by "doubts, fears, and insistent ideas, and [...] verbal automatisms, both motor and sensory" Daniel V. Runyon, "John Bunyan's Master Story: The Holy War as Battle Allegory in Religious and Biblical Context" (Published version of Ph.D. dissertation, Lampeter, Wales: Edwin Mellen Press, 2007), 44.

[17] "The sins of the whole world, past, present, and future, fastened themselves upon Christ and condemned Him. But because Christ is God, He had an everlasting and unconquerable righteousness. These two, the sin of the world and the righteousness, met in a death struggle. Furiously the sin of the world assailed the righteousness of God. Righteousness is immortal and invincible. On the other hand, sin is a mighty tyrant who subdues all men. This tyrant pounces on Christ. But Christ's righteousness is unconquerable. The result is inevitable. Sin is defeated and righteousness triumphs and reigns forever" Martin Luther, *Commentary on Galatians*, trans. by Theodore Graebner (Digireads.com Publishing, 2019), Galatians 3:13; pp. 80-81.

physicke.[18] Even so, Gifford was quite a vile man, a gambler, and of a wild reputation. But then, he came to a saving faith in the Lord Jesus Christ and, though the people were reluctant at first to trust his conversion, he offered himself to serve as their pastor. Eventually accepted by a cadre of people, "apostolic in number as well as in simplicity of spirit,"[19] Gifford became pastor of Bedford Church.

John Bunyan was drawn to John Gifford's ministry by 1653, although he may have heard him preach a bit before that. Basically, it was another stage in an interesting path Bunyan was to pursue in his pilgrim's progress toward a vital faith. Moreover, this, at this stage, was what some theologians might identify as God's prevenient grace leading a confused and rough-and-tumble person through the years to a gradual and profound spiritual awakening.

Essentially, Gifford entered Bunyan's life at just the right place at just the right time to guide his faith journey. Interestingly, Bunyan's attachment to Gifford's ministry also brought the Elstow people curious to see what it was that brought their notorious "town-sinner"[20] Bunyan into such a change of life.

The Bunyan family's move from Elstow to Bedford most likely happened in 1655. This was about the time, Bunyan, in his late 20s, became gravely ill and fearful of his own death. If not enough of an ordeal, his wife died, leaving behind a blind daughter and three other children at a time Bunyan was still battling with his own inner conflicts. And then, in the same year, Pastor John Gifford died.

All in all, Gifford served as a pastor in Bedford not quite five years, and yet, his impact upon people's lives – especially Bunyan's – was powerful. In the short duration of time, Gifford's influence upon Bunyan's spiritual development directly was no more than two years. And yet, Bunyan, under Gifford's evangelical influence, had come to a faith community with which he would be associated for the next thirty-five years.

Among the Bedford Church records there was a most interesting purpose statement to which the Bedford Free Church people were committed:

> To propagate the Gospell and help it forward, both by purse and presence, always keeping a door open and a table furnished, and free for all such

---

[18] Physicke (middle English from old French *fisique* 'medicine,' from Latin *physica*, from Greek *phusike*) "an archaic variant of physic, the art or practice of healing disease; the practice or profession of medicine; a medicinal agent or preparation; natural science" Roderick W. McConchie, *Lexicography and Physicke: The Record of Sixteenth-Century English Medical Terminology* (Oxford University Press UK, 1997.

[19] Brown, *John Bunyan: His Life, Times and Work*, 85

[20] Brown, *John Bunyan: His Life, Times and Work*, 96

ministers and Christians who shewed their zeale for and love to the Gospell of Christ . . . non-conforming men, such as in those days did beare the name of Puritans.[21]

In the early 1650s, Oliver Cromwell called a short-lived Little Parliament into being and by the mid-1650s, there was a movement to remove the Stuart family line from the kingship and bring Cromwell and his family into place. Interestingly, although it was an effort promoted by many government officials, it met with a significant measure of discontent from others and was no less strongly rejected by Cromwell himself.

In the wake of the first of the English Civil Wars, spiritual and political crosscurrents, and subsequent reconstruction of the government, at the least it could be said that England needed significant reconciliation and house-cleaning.

By 1657, John Bunyan's congregation urged him to speak a word of exhortation at their gatherings. Bunyan humbly agreed and thus began his engagement with preaching. It was two years after he had joined the Bedford church that he spoke that first word. Although modest in his own self-estimate, people observed that Bunyan displayed significant ability, depth, and spirit. It all commenced with his Christian friends having him accompany them out into the countryside to teach and add an inspirational word. From the get-go it was obvious his was no ordinary ministry. As he commenced making more extended speeches, soon hundreds throughout the area came to listen to the tinker preacher.

By the end of the 1650s, John Bunyan made his debut as an author with *Some Gospel Truths Opened.* The book was volley against an influx of Quaker work in the Bedford area. In the writing, Bunyan was countering a mystical inner light theology he viewed as disparaging God's written word and Christ's bodily resurrection. John Burton, the current pastor at the Bedford church, wrote a preface for Bunyan's book emphasizing its author as –

Not [being] chosen out of an earthly but out of the heavenly university, the Church of Christ . . . He hath through grace taken these three heavenly degrees, to wit, union with Christ, the anointing of the Spirit, and experiences of the temptations of Satan, which do more fit a man for that mighty work of preaching the Gospel than all university learning and degrees that can be had.[22]

---

[21] Note the pairing of words, "non-conforming" and "Puritan" - Brown, *John Bunyan: His Life, Times and Work*, 81

[22] Brown, *John Bunyan: His Life, Times and Work*, 113

Bunyan's biographer of later years, John Brown, would remind the readers that although Bunyan's first written works were the controversial, his best works that drew upon people's hearts were not the controversial. The ones that touched people's hearts more significantly came later. Quite poignantly the best played out the main and central verities that many Christians held dear. Interestingly, an array of Bunyanesque insights pertaining to Bunyan's preaching style provide helpful insights:

> A word cast in by the by hath done more execution in a Sermon than all that was spoken besides." Sometimes, when he thought he had done no good he did most, and at other times, when he thought he should catch men, he has fished for nothing. Occasionally he has been about to take up some smart and searching portion of the Word, when up starts the Tempter and asks him if he really is going to preach a Truth which so plainly condemns himself; but he thanks God, who helped him to put down these horrid suggestions, and to bow himself with all his might to condemn Sin and Transgression wherever found even upon his own conscience . . .

> When tempted to vanity over his success, "the Lord of his precious mercy hath so carried it towards me that for the most part I have had but small joy to give way to such a thing. For it hath been my every day's portion to be let into the evil of my own heart, and still made to see such a multitude of corruptions and infirmities therein that it hath caused hanging down of the head under all my Gifts and Attainments. I have felt this thorn in the Flesh the very God of mercy to me." He saw that, if he had gifts, but wanted saving grace, he was but as a tinkling cymbal. "This consideration was as a maul on the head of Pride and desire of vain glory. What, thought I, shall I be proud because I am a sounding brass? Is it so much to be a Fiddle?" Love will never die, but gifts will cease and vanish; gifts are not our own, but the Church's, and to be accounted for in stewardship. Gifts, indeed, are desirable, but yet great grace and small gifts are better than great gifts and no grace.[23]

Before *The Pilgrim's Progress* and *The Holy War* came about, Bunyan produced several books on diverse topics, but all containing interesting twists and turns of phrase that snare the imagination. In his *Signs from Hell*, a work on Jesus' parable of the rich man and Lazarus, published in 1658 when he was at the age of thirty, he spun out the thought, "Some men despise the Lazaruses of our Lord Jesus Christ because they are not gentlemen because they cannot with Pontius Pilate speak Hebrew, Greek, and Latin."[24] In another place, he said, "Death can do thee no harm. It is only a

---

[23] Brown, *John Bunyan: His Life, Times and Work*, 116-117
[24] Brown, *John Bunyan: His Life, Times and Work*, 118

passage out of a prison into a palace, out of a sea of troubles into a haven of rest, out of a crowd of enemies to an innumerable company of true, loving, and faithful friends."[25] Then, in 1659, he published *The Doctrine of the Law and Grace Unfolded* emphasizing Christ's person and work as the one Priest and Mediator for a sinful world, where he also gave a glimpse of his own "struggles of doubt up to the daylight of faith."[26]

By 1660, so much in Bunyan's world was in flux: e.g., the death of Oliver Cromwell who was capable of keeping in check the diverging forces throughout the land; the inability of Richard Cromwell to succeed his father in leadership; the surging power of the Army; the on-again, off-again, and on-again Parliament, excluding a number of members because of their Presbyterian affiliations; the death of Reverend Burton, the beloved Bedford pastor; the forced removal of the Bedford congregation from their building; and a movement throughout the country that brought Charles II back from the Hague and restored the kingship to him. For the meantime, Bunyan was engaged in a number of preaching moments despite a mounting drive against him.

Some easily noted Bunyan a tinker, either because of belittlement or fascination, and there were those who questioned the legitimacy of his calling by the Bedford church. But it was not an evenly measured appraisal. Whether or not those criticizing him or affirming him were credentialed churchmen or political leaders, they could not dismiss Bunyan from their thoughts. Bunyan's supporters and detractors alike included those who held university credentials and those who did not. Some charged him with gross immoralities – all untrue. Others called him a wizard, a Jesuit, or a highwayman – not so. Yet, Bunyan could not help but draw comfort from the treasured words of Jesus about how people persecuted the faithful prophets in times past.[27] In the face of both praise and condemnation, Bunyan demonstrated a deep sense of humility through his life.[28]

As King Charles II entered London on May 29, 1660, he quickly turned his attention to deal with those involved in his father King Charles I's execution. After dealing with the regicides, the question of what to do with the Church came next. At this moment, the great body of the Convention Parliament, though Royalist in sympathy, were Presbyterian in opinion. At first, it seemed the King would be taking a more consensual stand upon religious life, providing that various church people were not disturbing the

---

[25] Brown, *John Bunyan: His Life, Times and Work*, 119

[26] Brown, *John Bunyan: His Life, Times and Work*, 125

[27] Matthew 5:11-12

[28] Brown, *John Bunyan: His Life, Times and Work*, 125-126

peace. That seemed to have been his spirit while still in the Netherlands. Once back home, however, Charles II, affected by the swells of opinion, and greatly influenced by Edward Hyde (afterwards Lord Clarendon) narrowed his view of the church-state situation. At first, the way things were working favored the Presbyterians. Meanwhile, the old Anglican clergy who had been deprived of their livings under Cromwell were coming forward in droves, claiming that they should be reinstated to their livings. By September 13, 1660, an Act was passed to confirm and reinstate these ministers.

On October 17, 1660, during the Parliamentary recess of September 13 - November 6, 1660, Robert Sanderson, age seventy-three, was elected Bishop of Lincoln. It was a diocese that did not have a bishop since Thomas Winniffe had been elected in 1642 to hold the position for a few months until the Episcopacy was overthrown by the Long Parliament.[29] Winniffe died in 1658 at the age of seventy-eight, thus leaving Lincoln open for the consecration of a new bishop. When Bishop Sanderson entered Bedford a few weeks later, the appearance took on more of the guise of an approaching victorious general, with a handsome volley and musket salute, than the processional of spiritual leader.

In October 1660, the royal justices in Bedford ordered that the *Book of Common Prayer*, which had been mandated by Archbishop Laud and eliminated by Cromwell, be used in all worship.[30]

---

[29] In November 1640, King Charles I summoned the Long Parliament. The word "Long" would distinguish it from "Short" which convened previously April–May 1640. The existence of the Long Parliament carried into April 1653 when its remaining members were forced out by Cromwell's army, or into March 1660, when its members, finally restored, passed an act for its dissolution. Legally, the ejection of 1653 and the act of 1660 were both invalid in that they did not have royal assent. An act of the Convention Parliament which convened April–December 1660 dissolved the Long Parliament. Yet, the Convention Parliament was not lawful, too, in that the king did not call it, but later legislation reinforced its act (Editors of the Encyclopedia Britannica, "Long Parliament," 23 Jun. 2019, https://www.britannica.com/topic/Long-Parliament. Accessed 22 May 2021).

[30] Runyon reaches back into some earlier history: "Queen Elizabeth's first public act when Parliament met in 1559 was to pass the two pillars that would define the Church of England for four centuries: the Act of Supremacy which titled the queen as "Supreme Governor of the Church of England," and the Act of Uniformity which established the *Book of Common Prayer* as the only recognized order of public worship. A minister using any other form of service could lose a year's income and be imprisoned for six months at the first offence. For a second offence he could be deprived of his benefice, and for a third face life imprisonment. Nonconformist preachers not licensed in the Church of England felt pressured by the Act of Uniformity, the same pressure Bunyan experienced in 1660 with the restoration of the monarchy" Daniel V. Runyon, "John Bunyan's Master Story: The Holy War as Battle Allegory in Religious and Biblical Context" (Published version of Ph.D. dissertation, Lampeter, Wales: Edwin Mellen Press, 2007), 21.

A little more than a month later, on November 12, 1660, Bunyan held a service at Lower Samsell, a small hamlet about thirteen miles from Bedford in the finely wooded and undulating terrain of a property almost surrounded by Elm trees. Though Bunyan often preached beneath a Hawthorne tree there, he was to lead the service on that day in the farmhouse. As with many residences in remote areas, the house was surrounded by a moat and serviced by a drawbridge which could be raised at night. At the time Bunyan arrived, there was a bit of whispering going on and Bunyan was asked to refrain from preaching that day because a local magistrate, Francis Wingate, was ready with a warrant for his arrest. Yet, Bunyan said: "No, by no means; I will not stir, neither will I have the meeting dismissed for this. Come, be of good cheer, let us not be daunted. Our cause is good, and we need not be ashamed of it; to preach God's word is so good a work that we shall be well rewarded even if we suffer for it."[31] It would take many years before the public would comprehend how far-sighted and prophetic a statement such as this would be.

As the time of the meeting came about for the few gathered there, Bunyan started with a prayer. Upon opening his Bible, he got set to preach as the constable arrived and ordered him to stop and go with him. Meanwhile, Bunyan turned to go, but then turned back to tell his people not to be discouraged. As Bunyan was talking, the constable grew more impatient. To top it all, Wingate was not at home and the constable had to place the preacher in a hold until the morrow. However, a neighboring farmer and friend of Bunyan offered to house him overnight and bring him to the magistrate the next day. Consequently, the constable would not have to detain the prisoner overnight.

On the next day, Bunyan's examination happened in Magistrate Wingate's home. When Wingate asked the constable how he found Bunyan's gathering the day before, it seemed he was hoping to come upon some dirt that the people gathered for this religious meeting were armed and dangerous. To the contrary, the constable attested to their orderly behavior. No new law had been enacted that would have called for the hearing. No similar arrests had happened in other places. The Act of Uniformity, which would have had a bearing on this, did not become law for another year and a half.[32] One might posit that Wingate, probably through a grudge,

---

[31] Brown, *John Bunyan: His Life, Times and Work,* 138

[32] The Act of Uniformity was one of four pieces of legislation, known as the Clarendon Code, named after Edward Hyde, the Earl of Clarendon, who was the Lord Chancellor for the reinstated King Charles II. First, there was the Corporation Act of 1661 requiring all municipal officials to take Anglican Communion. Second, there was the Act of Uniformity of 1662, mainly targeting Nonconformist ministers, making the *Book of Common Prayer*

was acting with unnecessary zeal, for which, as the years would unfold, he would go down in history as the one most responsible for Bunyan's arrest and imprisonment.[33] However, such is the perspective from the vantage of the future looking back.

When the magistrate could not gather any sense of foul play having happened nor even intended – all that could be ascertained was that those gathered to hear Bunyan were harmless, peaceable folk – he turned to Bunyan and asked him why he was not minding his own business. He was a tinker, right? In response, Bunyan said his intention was to bring people "to forsake their sins and close with Christ."[34] At this point, Wingate stormed he would break the neck of these kinds of meetings and Bunyan calmly responded it might be so.

Once the magistrate sentenced Bunyan to be held in jail until the Sessions, Bunyan kindly dismissed his supportive friends. On the way to the jail, though, some other friends met him and the constable and said they wanted to approach the magistrate to see if anything further might be done to clear up the matter. On returning from their mission, the friends told Bunyan if he would just say certain things, he would be cleared. Bunyan turned to his friends and said, if they were words he could express with a clear conscience, he would do it. However, if not, he'd proceed to jail. Thus, they turned around and headed back to Wingate's house. All the way there, Bunyan was praying God would give him light and strength to keep his composure and do nothing "that might either dishonor Him or wrong my own soul or be a grief or discouragement to any that were inclining after the Lord Jesus Christ."[35]

At the Wingate's Harlington House, who should come into the room holding up a candle – it was the darkening of a November day – but William Foster, a Bedford lawyer, Wingate's brother-in-law. "What, John

---

mandatory for use in all church services. Third, there was the Conventicle Act of 1664, greatly affecting the people, which forbade conventicles, namely unauthorized gatherings for worship of no more than five people, not of the same household. Fourth, there was the Five Mile Act of 1665, targeting Nonconformist ministers forbidding them to come within five miles of an incorporated town or their place of former residence and forbidding them to teach – thus, respectively severing a too easily known pool of encouragement and support for the unauthorized pastor.

[33] According to a notable church historian, "The magistrate is as much subject to the Christian ethic as the minister, though in a much more difficult position because the magistrate in executing a malefactor must be completely devoid of any personal rancor, resentment, or revenge" (Roland H. Bainton, *Christian Attitudes Toward War and Peace* [Nashville: Abingdon Press, 1960], 139).

[34] Brown, *John Bunyan: His Life, Times and Work,* 142

[35] Brown, *John Bunyan: His Life, Times and Work,* 144

Bunyan!" he cried, pretending affection. A syrupy sweet, conniving flatterer, Foster tried to convince Bunyan a genuine minister needed to be sent by a bishop and Parliament. A so-called call from God and a fire in the soul were no authorization for ministry! Knowing there were no grounds for discussion, Bunyan was ready to say he was at peace with God. Instead, he held his peace and felt blessed as he was going "away to prison with God's comfort in my poor soul."[36]

Jailed and facing the January Quarter Session which would come to Bedford in seven or eight weeks, his simple prayer was whether he might accomplish a greater good by being set at liberty or remaining in prison, and that God's will might be done awakening the saints throughout the country.

There were five magistrates tending to Bunyan's trial. None of them would favor Bunyan's case. The five were John Kelynge, Henry Chester, George Blundell, William Beecher, and Thomas Snagg. Sir John Kelynge of Southhill, a blustering, unfeelingly harsh, and insulting personality, was the chairperson. A feisty individual with a nasty reputation, Kelynge once fined the members of a jury a hundred marks each for acquitting some poor people who came to church with Bibles but no Books of Common Prayer. He also served as Counsel for the Crown during the Regicide trial of those responsible for the execution of King Charles I. At still another time, Kelynge landed in trouble with the House of Commons for making contemptuous allusions to the Magna Carta. And still another time, he was brought before the House of Lords for insolence. Some believe Bunyan had Kelynge in mind as he created the sketch for Judge Hategood in *The Pilgrim's Progress.*

Among the magistrates handling the case there also was Sir Henry Chester of Liddington, who was Francis Wingate's uncle. It was Chester who, at another time, sought to turn Sir Matthew Hale's heart against Elizabeth Bunyan as she pled for her husband to have a fair trial. There also was Sir George Blundell of Cardington whose Bedford estate had been decimated in 1655 and was begrudging enough to present no friendly presence with such a case. Then, there was Sir William Beecher of Howbury who was knighted the same day that Bunyan was arrested. Finally, there was Thomas Snagg of Millbrook, who, for a time, had been disinherited by his father, but eventually rose to become high sheriff of the county. Basically, John Bunyan would be appearing before justices gathered in this time who would do him no justice.

---

[36] Brown, *John Bunyan: His Life, Times and Work*, 145

At the trial, John Bunyan faced charges of "devilishly and perniciously abstaining from coming to an established church to hear divine services and for being a common upholder of unlawful meetings and conventicles to the great disturbance and distraction of the good subjects of the kingdom, contrary to the laws of our sovereign lord the King."[37]

When Bunyan said he did go to the church of God, Kelynge railed at him, saying that he, Bunyan, knew what they were asking! The point was whether Bunyan was attending the parish church, to which Bunyan replied, "No."

Then, the interrogation turned to the practice of prayer. Bunyan said he did not need a book to pray. When one of the magistrates deemed this was an outrage, Kelynge, as if a matter of fact, remarked the Prayer Book stood in no danger, its having been around since the Apostolic times!

Apparently, no historian prior to Kelynge came up with such a statement!

Eventually, one of the magistrates asked Bunyan if Beelzebub were his god and if he were possessed by a spirit of delusion. Then, Kelynge proceeded to teach Bunyan some scripture, but the magistrate was quickly out of his depth.

Finally, Kelynge declared he would send Bunyan back to jail for three months. If that did not accomplish anything, he would banish him from the realm. And if that did not work, he would stretch him by the neck.[38]

In response, Bunyan replied that if he were released today, he would resume proclaiming the Gospel tomorrow. Thus commenced a jail time that would pass into six years and then, beyond, into twelve years.

Just before Bunyan had completed three months of jail time, Mr. Cobb, the clerk of the peace, came in a semi-official capacity hoping to make Bunyan willing to quit preaching. While Cobb tried both threats and friendly persuasion, his visit proceeded rather cordially. When asked why he couldn't submit to the teaching of an authorized parish priest, Bunyan responded that he was willing to teach and be taught. Cobb, seeking to worry or perhaps warn Bunyan of further consequences, threatened him with the thought that he could be sent in exile to some faraway land, like Spain or Constantinople. In response, Bunyan said that he was a law-abid-

---

[37] Brown, *John Bunyan: His Life, Times and Work*, 152

[38] In *Grace Abounding*, Bunyan writes: "I saw what was coming, and had especially two Considerations warm upon my heart; the first was, How to be able to endure, should my imprisonment be long and tedious; the second was, How to be able to encounter death, should that be here my portion" John Bunyan, *Grace Abounding*, edited with Introduction and Notes by John Stachniewski with Anita Pacheo (New York: Oxford University Prewss, 1998), p. 88.

ing Christian citizen, respectful of the King's government, and was only hoping for the opportunity to express his loyalty to the prince by word and by deed. By the end of the visit, Bunyan thanked Cobb for his meek and civil conversation, and, at Cobb's parting, Bunyan humbly remarked, "O! that we might meet in heaven!"

Three weeks later, April 23, 1661, it was King Charles II's coronation day. At the time, various prisoners were given clemency and released in honor of the event. There were many who benefitted from that special act. However, Jesus did not benefit before Pontius Pilate, nor did John Bunyan before any English tribunal. For such a release, the King depended upon the word of the local authorities. Also, it did not help that a newsworthy item at the time was a riot in London by a group of religious fanatics led by Thomas Venner, a Fifth Monarchist, to overturn the government.

By August 1661, the Midsummer Assize would come to Bedford. Elizabeth Bunyan made her way to it to plead for her husband. Initially, she approached Sir Matthew Hale, notably a kindly Christian man, whose first response was he would do what good he could. Upon the next day, as a judicial carriage passed through St. Paul's Square, in Bedford, Elizabeth directed a petition into the carriage through the window and Judge Twisden grabbed it and angrily snapped that her efforts were of no use. Undaunted, Elizabeth approached Judge Hale again. Sir Henry Chester happened to be nearby, and stressed Bunyan was duly convicted. Consequently, Sir Matthew Hale, at this point, displayed no further interest. Meanwhile, Edmund Wylde, high sheriff, kindly approached Elizabeth in her crestfallen condition with the suggestion she approach the judges in chamber before they left town.

Imposing herself again into such a menacing setting, Elizabeth made her way through the crowd of notables to Sir Matthew Hale to plead for mercy and understanding. At this point, Twisden and Chester, hanging nearby, accosted her. Persisting with Hale, though, she told of going to London to Lord Barkwood, who directed her back to the assize. As Hale seemed to be ignoring her, Sir Henry Chester deflected her plea with a caustic remark that her husband was a pest like no one else in the country. Notwithstanding, Elizabeth kept pleading for her husband's well-being. All he wanted was the chance to live peacefully and follow his calling! Gaining a greater sense of the woman's desperate situation ignited Sir Matthew Hale's interest once again. And yet, Twisden, true to form, butted in with a caustic word. But Sir Matthew queried: "Just what is his calling?" To which a chorus of voices replied, "A tinker, my lord!" And once again, this beautifully undaunted woman raised her passionate response:

"Yes, and because he is a tinker and a poor man, therefore, he is despised and cannot have justice!"[39]

The twelve years Bunyan spent in the jail for county offences was in the county gaol at the corner of High Street and Silver Street, in Bedford. He was thirty-two years old and had the prime of life ahead of him at the time he was incarcerated. At times, the jail was crowded with more than sixty prisoners. The two books comprising Bunyan's "library" while there especially were the Bible and Foxe's *Book of Martyrs*. Years later, around 1785, John Howard, the renowned prison reformer, visited Bunyan's gaol and described it.

> [It consisted] mainly of a ground floor and first floor. The ground floor was appropriated to felons, and had two dayrooms, besides sleeping rooms. There were also two dungeons underground, one in total darkness, and reached by a descent of eleven steps. The first floor, which was for debtors, consisted of four sleeping rooms and one common day room, which was also used for a chapel, all the rooms being eight-and-a-half feet high. There was a small courtyard which was common to all the prisoners.[40]

The first year or so, notably between the Autumn Assize in 1661 and the Spring Assize in 1662, depending upon the openness of the jailer, Bunyan was given a few liberties not evident at other times. However, contradicting some people's suspicions that Bunyan could get away to his church meetings, there was no reference that such happened between October 28, 1661 and October 9, 1668, in the Bedford Church records. Between 1669 and 1672, his presence was noted occasionally.

No doubt Bunyan's time in jail had a significant impact on his wife and four children. He would describe it as "a man who at the bidding of conscience was pulling down his house upon the heads of those he loved best."[41] Sometimes, there would be a point where Elizabeth and the children would benefit from the compassion of their Christian community. Still, at times, Bunyan discovered his temporal affairs had become a wreck.

Even so, while in Bedfordshire jail, John Bunyan was not idle. In those days, prisoners had to provide for their own maintenance. He learned in prison how to make long Tagg'd Laces to the extent of producing many hundred gross.[42] He also served as spiritual counselor to the inmates, many

---

[39] Brown, *John Bunyan: His Life, Times and Work*, 158

[40] John Howard, *State of the Prisons in England and Wales*, 3rd edition, 1785, p. 283; in *John Bunyan: His Life, Times and Work*, by John Brown, 162-163.

[41] Brown, *John Bunyan: His Life, Times and Work*, 168

[42] Regarding "long Tagg'd Lace" – According to Sophie Ploeg, artist, writer and tutor, lace furnishings for clothing, introduced in the 16th century, became popular by its end and

of whom were from his own church fellowship, and he would preach and pray with fellow prisoners in the Day Room. Some of these sermons led into books Bunyan authored which, with the help of good friends, were directed to Francis Smith, publisher at the Elephant and Castle, near Temple Bar, London.[43] Although a supportive person of great sincerity and contentment, Smith, too, suffered his own house searched, his windows broken, and, at times, jailing at the hands of the King's Messengers.[44]

After having been behind bars for six years, 1660 to 1666, Bunyan was jailed for another six years, 1666 to 1672, stretching his jail time into the twelve years. Over this second span of time, England went through several desperate situations. For instance, the plague which had desolated London also raged through Bedford goal. This, too, was the time of the great London Fire. In addition, the power of Lord Clarendon, arch instigator of acts against the Nonconformists, was beginning to crumble.

During this second period, Bunyan published only two books: *Confession of Faith* and *A Defense of the Doctrine of Justification by Faith*. John Brown posed various reasons for his meager output.

> Was it because he was not able to get any of his writings licensed and Francis Smith was now too carefully watched to be able to publish them unlicensed? Was it that the claims of his family's maintenance made great demands upon his time now that the long continuance of persecution had made friends fewer? Or was it that he was becoming more broken-spirited and for a time at least had lost something of his old elasticity of mind?[45]

---

fashionable from the early 17th century onwards. Early cut-out lace, called Reticella, was crafted stitch by stitch with a needle and thread, and led to complex patterns of squares, circles, and rose, but over time the patterns became more free and less geometric. In the 17th century the craft of lace making was mainly a female domain. Nine-year-old girls could be fully trained. However, spinning the linen in damp and dark places to guard against thread breaking, the lace maker was working in some of the worst conditions – some going blind by the age of thirty. Furthermore, in an April 6, 2021 text message, Sophie Ploeg thought Bunyan's "long Tagg'd Lace" was in his making the shoelaces and not the elaborate decorative types of lace [https://www.sophieploeg.com/blog/historyofearlylace/].

[43] In 1661, Bunyan had published *Profitable Meditations*, a supposed conversation between Satan and a tempted soul; in 1662, *Praying in the Spirit* against relying on forms in *The Book of Common Prayer*; in 1663, *Christian Behaviour* with a precursor to the scene in Christiana's journey featuring the unity of flowers in a garden; between 1663 and 1665, two poetry renditions, *Serious Meditations on Four Last Things*, and *Ebal and Gerizim*; in 1665, *Holy City*; *The Resurrection of the Dead*; and *Prison Meditations*; and in 1666, *Grace Abounding to the Chief of Sinners*, a spiritual autobiography on the par with Augustine's *Confessions* and the heart-utterances of Martin Luther.

[44] Brown, *John Bunyan: His Life, Times and Work*, 182

[45] Brown, *John Bunyan: His Life, Times and Work*, 185

Prior to 1672, when the Conventicle Act was suspended by King Charles's Declaration of Indulgence and the penal laws in ecclesiastical matters against the Nonconformists were suspended, there was an intensification of persecution. The Conventicle Act had expired on March 2, 1668 and was reenacted on April 11, 1670. Roughly between May 1670 and April 1671, under the Cavaliers in Parliament, the Nonconformists fared the worst. People were fined, excommunicated, or imprisoned for such matters as not paying church dues, not coming to church in more than a month, and not having their children baptized.

There was a legal action taken against a Henry Thurrowgood of Northill for burying his mother in a garden. Apparently not engaging the services of an authorized priest! There was another legal action against Thomas Hawkins and Mary Herbert of Dunstable for celebrating their marriage in a "phanatique" manner at a Quaker Meeting.

By the early 1670s, some locals worked as hirelings for the authorities who investigated religious misdeeds. In some cases, they hid in trees to catch people gathering for unauthorized religious services, and then drew an allotment from the fines collected for hunting down these peaceable citizens.

Yet, by the next year, the severity was greatly lightened. Bunyan was accorded such liberty that the Bedford Church, by November 24, 1671, was considering naming Bunyan as their pastor. A process of discernment continued through December until January 21, 1672, when the church formally extended to Bunyan the call. All in all, it had been twelve years since the congregation had left the church of St. John's and met for years as homeless wanderers in one another's houses, fields, and woods.

On March 15, 1672, John Bunyan was officially licensed as teacher of the congregation. Seven weeks after Bunyan's election, the King's Declaration opened the possibilities of times and places for legal religious gatherings.

Meanwhile, Josias Ruffhead of Bunyan's congregation purchased from Justice Crompton of Elstow an orchard in Mill Lane, where stood a barn that at once became officially certified as a place of meeting. In the wake of all these happenings, there were twenty-five preachers and thirty buildings throughout the area for which Bunyan applied for licenses.

Although Bunyan was probably released from the jail in May 1672, his general pardon was dated September 13, 1672. From 1672 to 1675, "Bishop Bunyan," as he came to be called, partly in jest and in earnest, was extremely busy far and wide as pastor of a large flock. Yet, Bunyan's release and legal exoneration did not come without some people's chatter.

In one regard, Edward Fowler, vicar of Northill, later Bishop of Gloucester, to whom Bunyan had directed a criticism regarding *The Design of Christianity*,[46] a book Fowler had written, was outraged that such a "Pestilent Schismatick" was released – a jab Bunyan chose to ignore. In another matter, Bunyan, who did not have strong feelings about the sacraments, nevertheless entered the debate about them in 1673, with his *Differences in Judgment about Water Baptism no bar to Communion*. His view that differences in opinions about the sacraments were minor came close to the views of another area pastor, William Dell, who affirmed that character rather than ritual should be the foundation of fellowship."[47]

By the mid-1670s, Bunyan seemed rather busy authoring books. In 1674, his *Peaceable Principles and True* came as response to critics for his previously published *Confession of Faith* where he touched on baptism and communion again.

There arose a scandal in that Bunyan escorted a young woman to a meeting – reluctantly, by the way, knowing her father, previously one of his devoted congregants, would discountenance it – then, shortly afterwards, her father died. A sprouting up of rumors! Despite this, Bunyan and the young woman were eventually vindicated. Still, it impelled Bunyan to add something to his *Grace Abounding* stressing his innocence and chastity.

In 1675, Bunyan published four books. There was: *Light for them that sit in Darkness*; and there was: *Instruction for the Ignorant*, a question-and-answer writing to provide elementary truths on the nature of God, sin, faith in Christ, prayer, and self-denial. Then, too, there were *Saved by Grace* and *The Strait Gate*, which contained a fascinating zinger: "Some professors do with religion just as people do with their best apparel – hang it against the wall all the week and put it on Sundays."[48]

By the winter and early spring 1675-1676, John Bunyan was jailed again. At this time, it was for six months in the small Bedford Town Gaol located on a bridge over the River Ouse. Drawings of this building in its picturesque setting have captured people's imagination. It was during this

---

[46] Bunyan's argument with Fowler: "It is not enough for the old nature to go forth in holiday clothes, there must be a new creation in righteousness and true holiness. In Bunyan's judgment Fowler makes too light of Christ's great sacrifice in its character as an expiation for human guilt, making it to appear that Christ merely holds the point of the sword of justice, not that he received it into his own soul, that he suspended the curse from us, not that He Himself was made a curse for us, and in this way he steppeth over Christ's sacrifice as a spider straddleth over a wasp. A pale shadowy gospel . . ." Brown, *John Bunyan: His Life, Times and Work*, 186.

[47] Brown, *John Bunyan: His Life, Times and Work*, 236

[48] Brown, *John Bunyan: His Life, Times and Work*, 307

time, though, Bunyan in the guise of dreaming a dream began writing his great pilgrim allegory which catapulted him into distinction!

A lovely piece of the ambience comes while imagining Bunyan doing a read-aloud with his six or seven fellow inmates – basically the capacity of this small jail. His biographer John Brown points out that Bunyan penned the part of *The Pilgrim's Progress* up to Christian and Hopeful's arrival at the Delectable Mountains during this half year of imprisonment. Moreover, at the next part of the book, there appears another reference to a dream, then, we move into Bunyan's continuation of the storytelling following his release from jail.

‹ In 1676, Archbishop Sheldon ordered a religious census to be taken, which numbered the Nonconformists living in Bedfordshire as nearly two thousand over the age of sixteen years old – thus, some 3,000 to 4,000 of all ages. In Bedford itself, this measured out to around one in every ten individuals to account for the number of Nonconformists there. From such calculations, Bunyan was responsible for the spiritual care of a considerable number of people.

The Pilgrim's Progress went through three editions in its very first year it was published. Once it hit the market, the story, as we best know it, was fine-tuned, and augmented two additional times during that initial year. Incidentally, Mr. Worldly Wiseman entered the story with the second edition, and By-Ends appeared by the third edition. It was a best seller right from the start. All sorts of people bought the book up in a flash!

After its many interested readers started to pick up on John Bunyan's pilgrim story, there were the story cobblers who attempted to fill in the blanks created by the absence of Christian's wife with their own renditions.

Meanwhile, in 1678 and 1679, Bunyan authored two other books: *Come and Welcome to Jesus Christ* in 1678 and *A Treatise of the Fear of God* in 1679, with insights on noble fear and ignoble fear.[49] By 1680, though, he drew a sharp contrast to the pilgrim story with *The Life and Death of Mr. Badman*, which, as well, took on a dialogical form like Dent's *Plain Man's Pathway to Heaven*,[50] the book Bunyan's first wife brought into their marriage. Drawing from J. A. Froude's description, in his *English Men in Letters*, John Bunyan's *Mr. Badman* story provided:

> A picture of vulgar English life in a provincial town, such as Bedford was when Bunyan lived there. The drawing is so good, the details so minute, the conception so unexaggerated, that we are disposed to believe that

---

[49] Brown, *John Bunyan: His Life, Times and Work*, 310-312
[50] Brown, *John Bunyan: His Life, Times and Work*, 316-317

we must have a real history before us. But such a supposition is only a compliment to the skill of the composer . . . Bunyan conceals nothing, assumes nothing, and exaggerates nothing. He makes his bad man sharp and shrewd. He allows sharpness and shrewdness to bring him the rewards which such qualities in fact command. Badman is successful; he is powerful; he enjoys all the pleasures which money can buy; his bad wife helps him to ruin, but otherwise he is not unhappy, and he dies in peace. Bunyan has made him a brute because such men do become brutes.[51]

In 1681, the people outside of the established church entered another grave period, when King Charles II twice dissolved Parliament and for the next four years ruled without it. In a Declaration from Whitehall, he excused himself for having such authority. "The House, he said, had stood in his way in carrying out the laws against the Nonconformists, and upon it, not upon the Crown, must rest the blame of all unconstitutional proceedings. [Such a] document was shrewdly constructed to catch the sympathy of the High Church party, and it succeeded."[52] As later references show:

[Nonconformists] were able to hold scarcely any meetings . . . between the August of that year [1684] and the month of December 1686. [During this time, some] were driven from their homes, ruined by fines, or shut up in jail. And in these stern experiences they were not alone. In some places, matters proceeded to such extremity that at last humane magistrates refused to grant any more convictions, resorting on the bench to all sorts of evasions of the law for the purpose of saving men who were too resolute to save themselves. This leniency, however, was, only partial. In the parish of Hackney fifty distress warrants, amounting to £1,400, were issued in one month and two hundred in the town of Uxbridge. In Southwark, Nathaniel Vincent was dragged from his pulpit by the hair of his head, while in the city of London, John Wesley's grandfather, Dr. Annesley, had his house broken into, his meeting-place forced, and its fittings destroyed.[53]

In between the time we have traipsed heavenward with Christian in 1678, reflected on the *Life and Death of Mr. Badman* in 1680, and turned back heavenward with Christiana in 1684, there was a period of two years where Bunyan, the prolific author that he was, produced no books.

However, in 1682, he brought before the public *The Holy War* in its dramatic form as one of life's great battle literatures – the powers of light against the powers of darkness – in which we also find the doctrine of salvation by grace so distinctly displayed. From the reader's first acquain-

---

[51] J. A. Froude, *English Men of Letters*, pp.112-113, in Brown, *John Bunyan: His Life, Times and Work*, 319

[52] Brown, *John Bunyan: His Life, Times and Work*, 326

[53] Brown, *John Bunyan: His Life, Times and Work*, 343

tance with it and on into a more serious reading of it, the reader pursues the great Biblical drama of sin, the fall, the struggle with evil, God's undaunted love, so great a salvation, and the outcome of redemption from Genesis to Revelation.

Looking back on Bunyan's early life as a soldier through the eyes of this great salvation battle story, Alexander Whyte, at the opening of his lecture on "Five Pickt Men" – Captains Credence, Good-hope, Charity, Innocent and Patience – offers a pertinent reflection:

> John Bunyan never lost his early love for a soldier's life any more than he ever forgot the rare delights of his bell-ringing days. John Bunyan, all his days, never saw a bell-rope that his fingers did not tingle, and he never saw a soldier in uniform without instinctively shouldering his youthful musket. Bunyan was one of those rare men who are of imagination all compact; and consequently, it is that all his books are full of the scenes, the occupations, and the experiences of his early days. Not that he says very much, in as many words, about what happened to him in the days when he was a soldier; it is only once in all his many books that he says that when he was a soldier such and such a thing happened to him. At the same time, all his books bear the impress of his early days upon them; and as for this special book of Bunyan's now open before us, it is full from board to board of the strife and din of his early battles. The *Holy War* is just John Bunyan's soldierly life spiritualised – spiritualised and so worked up into this fine English Classic.[54]

Over the years between the publication of *The Holy War* in 1682 and the death of King Charles II in 1685, Bunyan authored several other pieces which included the *Barren Fig-tree* in 1682; *Greatness of the Soul* and *A Case of Conscience Resolved* in 1683; *Seasonable Counsel* or *Advice to Sufferers*; *A Holy Life the Beauty of Christianity*; and *A Caution to stir up to Watch against Sin* (Broadside on a half sheet of paper) as well as *The Pilgrim's Progress: Part 2* – Christiana's journey – in 1684.

On January 14, 1685, the Earl of Ailesbury presided at a meeting of the Bedfordshire justices in Ampthill, at which was extended a severe order against the Nonconformists of the county. It was an order John How called unreasonable and unchristian. On February 6, 1685, Ailesbury's son stood in the bedchamber with other royalty present when the King gave out a sharp cry, staggered and fell into his arms, stricken dead. Within the same year the Earl himself died, to which biographer John Brown expressed a

---

[54] Alexander Whyte, *Bunyan Characters – Third Series* [Public Domain] (Astounding-Stories.com, 2015), 59-60

grim obituary: "In the midst of all this lawlessness came the shadow of death among the persecutors themselves."[55]

The same day that King Charles II died, his brother, James II, met with the Privy Council to become his successor. As the king was now deeply intent on re-establishing Roman Catholicism in England, it was said:

> He had even less love for constitutional government and religious freedom than his easy-going brother; but these principles were in less danger now than before, for the simple reason that he was more daring in his attempt to subvert them. Happily, for the liberties of England, the new monarch was one of those narrow, obstinate men who, when they happen to take up an evil cause, bring it to ruin by the very precipitancy of their haste to serve it.[56]

As the Duke of York, James would hear mass behind closed doors. On becoming King James II, he featured Popish divines preaching the Lenten services at the palace that year. Easter was quite a regal fanfare. Then, by the autumn, the Nonconformists from one locality to another endured a gamut of petty, trite, and seriously painful and deadly disruptions. Those seeking to avoid detection often shifted meeting places.

Ministers approached pulpits through trapdoors or along garden paths. The rich suffered heavy fines. The poor paid with their persons. Richard Baxter, the notable Puritan divine, an old man at the time, was jailed for two years. Authorities even invaded a prayer service held in a gravel pit. Military butchery and judicial murders were common.

The King who seemed to be a stranger to human compassion and pity ruled English soil, with crusade after crusade, at a time compared with the worst days of cruel Archbishop Laud earlier in the century. Even so more, some people viewed their sufferings as extreme as early Christians endured under the Roman Emperor Diocletian. For a wrap, Bunyan's biographer laid out a heart-searching insight:

> It is unfortunately but too true that indulgence in cruelty makes men more relentlessly cruel. Happily, on the other hand, the darkest things become the foil of things that are the noblest, bring out patient endurance, brave resistance, and firm fidelity to conscience.[57]

At this time, Bunyan as tinker, preacher, pastor, and author kept extending care as best as he could. In 1685, he authored *Questions about the*

---

[55] Brown, *John Bunyan: His Life, Times and Work*, 344
[56] Brown, *John Bunyan: His Life, Times and Work*, 345
[57] Brown, *John Bunyan: His Life, Times and Work*, 349

Nature and Perpetuity of the Seventh-day Sabbath – affirming Sunday for Christian worship – as well as a discourse on *The Pharisee and Publican*; and then, in 1686, *A Book for Boys and Girls, or Country Rhymes for Children* in verse on seventy-four things. In this attempt to reach out to children, Bunyan makes a few spiritual applications by turning their attention to an egg, the bee, the sun's reflection upon the clouds, a mole, the cuckoo, a fruitful tree, the rose bush, a sheet of white paper, the going down of the sun, and other visual images.

However, one of Bunyan's the object lessons gets somewhat lengthy as it picks up an engaging conversation between a sinner and a spider. Here the spider confronts the sinner who is proud of being made in God's image, blessed with a soul, and possessing reason.

> Spider says: I know thou art a creature far above me,
>
> Therefore I shun, I fear, and also love thee.
>
> But tho' thy God hath made thee such a creature,
>
> Thou hast against him often play'd the traitor.
>
> Thy sin has fetch'd thee down: leave off to boast;
>
> Nature thou hast defiled, God's image lost.
>
> Yea, thou thyself a very beast hast made,
>
> And art become like grass, which soon doth fade,
>
> Thy soul, thy reason, yea, thy spotless state,
>
> Sin has subjected to th' most dreadful fate;
>
> But I retain my primitive condition;
>
> I've all but lost by thy ambition.

In somewhat of a tongue-in-cheek fashion, turning some people's self-righteous boasts into a lesson, he delivers a word "On the Cackling of a Hen."

> The hen, so soon as she an egg doth lay,
>
> Spreads the fame of her doing what she may;
>
> About the yard a cackling she doth go,
>
> To tell what 'twas she at her nest did do.

Just thus it is with some professing men:

If they do aught that's good, they, like our hen

Cannot but cackle on't where'er they go,

And what their right had doth their left must know.[58]

From 1686 until 1688, Bunyan produced no additional writings, once again, possibly because of the heightened persecution throughout the land. A few months after his *Country Rhymes*, there came a strange twist upon the political scene. On April 4, 1687, the king re-issued the notable Declaration of Indulgence, which suspended the penal laws against Catholics and Dissenters.

Suddenly the Nonconformists who suffered so much under the present king as well as under previous monarchs had now become a respectable people. Not only was this a new twist, but it had also come from a teeter-tottering of treatments Bunyan and the Dissenters felt they could not trust.

On one occasion, "a great man," probably Thomas Lord Bruce, who succeeded his father as Earl of Ailesbury at Houghton House, came to Bedford seeking a chance to talk with Bunyan. Previously the man had been no friend to Nonconformists. Any gifts anticipated in dialogue with such a person were enough to make one leery! Subsequently, Bunyan communicated he was unavailable. Such political ploys characteristic of Sir Thomas Bruce would resemble what Diabolus would try upon Emmanuel and Mansoul in Bunyan's *The Holy War*.

Some individuals conscientiously changed their views from previous positions. Consider Sir George Blundell's response to King James II's Test of Loyalty and the re-instatement of the Declaration of Indulgence as a pertinent example. Many years before, in 1660, Blundell was among the magistrates who sent Bunyan, the Dissenter, to jail. By this later time, in 1687, when the issue of Nonconformism arose again, Blundell's response, as evidenced by documents in the Bodleian, was that of a humbler and more thoughtful person "sincerely willing to live peaceably with such who are of other persuasions, having no animosity to the person of any man for difference of opinion."[59]

On the other hand, Dr. William Foster, Doctor of Laws, the gentleman who held a candle to Bunyan's face at Harlington House with a syrupy

---

[58] *The Complete Works of John Bunyan* with an Introduction by Rev. John P. Gulliver, *Divine Emblems; Temporal Things Spiritualized: Fitted for the Use of Boys and Girls* (Philadelphia: Bradley, Garretson and Co., 1872), 1006, 1012

[59] Brown, *John Bunyan: His Life, Times and Work*, 360

sweet guise after Bunyan had been cross-examined and sentenced to jail, seemed just as slippery years later. At any time, Foster could have played By-ends of Fair-speech as kindred to Facing-both-ways and Anything in *The Pilgrim's Progress*, or Captain Anything among Diabolus's notables in *The Holy War* who was placed in command over three surfacy shifters: Mr. Tradition, Mr. Human-Wisdom, and Mr. Man's-Invention.

On April 27, 1688, King James II put forward a Second Declaration of Indulgence and commanded the clergy to read it in their parishes. By this time in British history, the action was variously received. Sometimes among the clergy it was by misgiving, sometimes by compliance, sometimes by stout resistance, and sometime by clever evasion. One priest told his people he was required to read the document. They didn't have to listen. In fact, they could go and do something else while he read the document to empty pews.

With such a superficially friendly legislation coming forth from the government, it would seem people such as Bunyan would have welcomed it. For nearly a quarter of a century, though, the Nonconformists suffered under the opposite of any accommodation and leniency. Now, how could they blindly and gullibly welcome such and be left without wondering regarding the motives behind the officials bringing it about?

Be that as it may, the winds of change were blowing, and things were going on behind the scenes leading into a new day whether Bunyan would fully embrace or even experience it. While the King's authoritarian plan was being defeated, Lord William Russell, behind the scenes, was in transit back and forth to the Hague, negotiating with the Prince of Orange regarding a change in the monarchy.

Meanwhile in 1688, between March 25 and August 31, when John Bunyan passed away, Bunyan published five books and a sixth one appeared within a month of his death:

- *The Jerusalem Sinner Saved*
- *The Work of Jesus Christ as an Advocate*
- *The House of God*
- *The Water of Life*
- *Solomon's Temple Spiritualized*
- *The Acceptable Sacrifice.*

The first of these six books, The Jerusalem Sinner Saved, was a welcoming call to those outside the kingdom of God. "Come, man; Stand away, devil, Christ calls me; stand away, unbelief; stand away, discouraging apprehensions . . . It is because Christ shows mercy to the vilest that Satan rages so strongly."[60]

With this, among Bunyan's last writings, we may set a tone for the drama of salvation as we scroll back a few years to Bunyan's battle allegory, *The Holy War*, which was published in 1682.

---

[60] John Brown, *John Bunyan: His Life, Times and Work* (London: Wm. Isbister Limited, 1885), 374

Martin Luther's Hymn

"A Mighty Fortress Is Our God"
Martin Luther, 1529

1. A mighty fortress is our God,
a bulwark never failing;
our helper he, amid the flood
of mortal ills prevailing.
For still our ancient foe
does seek to work us woe;
his craft and power are great,
and armed with cruel hate,
on earth is not his equal.

2. Did we in our own strength confide,
our striving would be losing,
were not the right Man on our side,
the Man of God's own choosing.
You ask who that may be?
Christ Jesus, it is he;
Lord Sabaoth his name,
from age to age the same;
and he must win the battle.

3. And though this world, with devils filled,
should threaten to undo us,
we will not fear, for God has willed
his truth to triumph through us.
The prince of darkness grim,
we tremble not for him;
his rage we can endure,
for lo! his doom is sure;
one little word shall fell him.

4. That Word above all earthly powers
no thanks to them abideth;
the Spirit and the gifts are ours

through him who with us sideth.
Let goods and kindred go,
this mortal life also;
the body they may kill:
God's truth abideth still;
his kingdom is forever!

F. H. Hedge, 1852
Translator

John Bunyan's *The Holy War*: A Reawakening

Spoiling Goodness

Be fober and watch: for your aduerfarie the deuil as a roaring lyon walketh about, feking whome he may deuoure (1 Peter 5:8 from a facsimile edition of the Geneva Bible of 1560, afterwards GEN) [clues: read "f" as s; "u" as v; "y" as i].

Be sober, and watch: for your adversary the devil as a roaring lion walketh about, seeking whom he may devour (1 Peter 5:8 from the Geneva Bible of 1599, afterwards GNV in *Bible Gateway*)

As a traveler passing through the regions and countries of life, I came upon the continent of Universe, a large and spacious country – well-watered, richly adorned with hills and valleys, and very, very fruitful.

What is more, its people were not of one fixed complexion, language, mode, or way of religion,[1] but differing as much from each other as the planets do from one another.

Some were of the right and some were of the wrong as happens in the lesser regions!

In this country, there was a town, Mansoul, whose founder was Shaddai.[2] Its buildings were spacious, and its people enjoyed many privileges. There was no place like it anywhere beneath all the heavens.[3]

It certainly was an excellent place to live!

---

[1] The word "*religion*" came from the Latin, *religionem*, which meant a sense of the right, a respect for what was sacred, conscientious, and holy. According to Cicero, it was derived from *relegere*, "go through again" (in reading or in thought) from *re* meaning "again" and *legere* meaning "read," as with a lecture. However, the later ancients (Servius, Lactantius, Augustine), felt the connection for "*religion*" was with *religare*, "to bind fast." A piece of the word comes across as *rely*, thus, *reliable*. Another possible root was *religiens*, "careful," the opposite of *negligens* (content gleaned from *Online Etymology Dictionary*).

[2] Shaddai – Hebrew for God, the one of the mountains; God Almighty: all-sufficient God used in Job

[3] Genesis 1:26; Ecclesiastes 3:11

Amid Mansoul, there was a stately palace. It was as imposing as a castle. It was pleasant like paradise. It was so expansive. Why, it embraced the whole world! It was Shaddai's design – and herein lay the wisdom – that the walls of Mansoul could not be breached by even the most mighty and antagonistic potentate unless, I must tell you, its townspeople opened their doors to it. Quite clearly, Shaddai had every intent that no intruder would be able to come upon the Mansoulian people with an ill will.[4]

Oh, for a world free from heartache, misunderstanding, rancor, and destruction; and blessed knowing that all its people needed was provided with loving care! Such at first was Mansoul!

Now, Mansoul had five gates which, like its walls, were unassailable and carried such names as Ear-gate, Eye-gate, Mouth-gate, Nose-gate, and Feel-gate. Furthermore, Mansoul was held together with the best, most wholesome – indeed, most excellent – principles in the world. There was not a rascal, rogue or treacherous person allowed within its walls. What is more, if the Mansoulian people kept devoted to the laws Shaddai laid out,[5] the town would persist as God's sheer delight.[6]

There was a giant, though, Diabolus, king of the dark regions, a raving presence, who sought to make an assault on Mansoul.[7]

---

[4] "Just as Christian makes continual decisions to hold to the path in *The Pilgrim's Progress*, and because of such decisions is continually helped by divine agency, so the inhabitants of Mansoul are far from puppets—indeed, they become more puppet-like under the tyranny of Diabolus. None other than Emanuel is capable of realizing their salvation, yet they continually choose to either disobey or obey him, and when they obey, he goes to work on their behalf" Daniel V. Runyon, "John Bunyan's Master Story: The Holy War as Battle Allegory in Religious and Biblical Context" (Published version of Ph.D. dissertation, Lampeter, Wales: Edwin Mellen Press, 2007), 118.

[5] The Greek word for law, νόμος (nomos), and the Greek word for pasture, νομή (nomé), stem from the same root. As a pasture is to keep the farmer's livestock in a wholesome landscape for good grazing, hopefully keeping at bay the incursion of any predator, so also the intent of a law is in maintaining its people's well-being and safekeeping, as well.

[6] Proverbs 11:19-20

[7] Diabolus – The Devil, the slanderer, the calumniator, is the one set out to thwart God's plans by destroying the relationship between God and humanity (P.L. Hammer in *The Interpreter's Dictionary of the Bible* [hereafter TIDB], Nashville: Abington, 1962). In New Testament Greek, the word διεβλήθη appears once, as in Luke 16:1, but numerous times in classical Greek and Greek translations of the Old Testament, where it carries the ideas of "separating," "to set in opposition," "accuse," "misrepresent," "give false information" – hence, easily fitting into a courtroom context (see Werner Foerster and Gerhard von Rad in *The Theological Dictionary of the New Testament*, vol. 2, edited by Gerhard Kittel and Gerhard Friedrich, translated by Geoffrey Bromiley [Grand Rapids, Michigan: Wm. B. Eerdmans, 1964], 71-81). The more common Biblical Greek word "Satan," which appears thirty-six times in the New Testament, meaning "adversary," refers to both transcendent and human beings. In Latin, the word "diabolus" has roots back in Greek διά (dia)

And yet, that was not how it all started. Initially poor and beggarly, Diabolus rose to become one of Shaddai's most honored servants, even applauded as 'the son of the morning,'[8] but later, he strove to rise to a power just beneath Shaddai himself – a place reserved for Shaddai's Son![9]

Way back sometime in the far distant past, Diabolus and his rebels – for there were many engrossed in his prideful and wicked schemes – rendezvoused and attempted an assault upon Shaddai's place and power.[10] However, the King and his Son, always and ever with an eye upon things, realized what was taking place and cast the raging insurrectionists out of their heavenly place of benefit, honor, and preferment.[11]

Knowing they had forever lost their Prince's good favor, Diabolus and his evil entourage, roving and raging from place to place, set out to find a way to spoil something dear to Shaddai to revenge themselves.[12] Con-

---

"through" and βάλλω (ballo) "throw." Here, we have come to a directional word coupled with a word of propelling force, wherein God had lain out something good – Bunyan's Mansoul – and something unwholesome, slanderous, and destructive thrusts itself upon and through it! This is quite a contrast to the image of Paraclete, which in Greek refers to the Holy Spirit. In Greek, the word is an interesting combination of "para" and "kaleo." *Para* in English means "alongside of" and *kaleo* provides the root for the word "called." The *"Paraclete"* is "the One called alongside of" - the Advocate, Encourager – a rendering of the Holy Spirit (John 16:7-11). In *The Holy War*, Bunyan depicts Diabolus, this bramble (an image drawn from Judges 9:14-15), in various ways. He is a giant, king of the dark regions, raving presence, lion, liar, deceiver, beast, cunning fox, prince of the infernal cave, wicked tyrant, runagate (vagabond) slave, murderer, abominable one, boiling pot of iniquity, malice and rage, master of the den, enemy to all that is good, demon prince, and devouring tyrant – altogether a piling up of evocative words describing evil! [Compare with information expressed in Appendix One regarding Narcissistic Personality Disorder (hereafter NPD) and Borderline Personality Disorder (hereafter BPD), supplied by Wellness Counselor Abby Manzella.]

[8] Isaiah 14:12-15 (J. N. Oswalt citing Reformation expositors understands this conveys human, not angelic pride.) See John N. Oswalt, *The Book of Isaiah*, Chapters 1-39 (Grand Rapids, Michigan: Eerdmans, 1986), 320-321.

[9] Philippians 2:9-11

[10] "Inasmuch as demons are certainly to be traced back to the fall of Satan and the angels, which the Book of Genesis assumes as background material in the same way it assumes the existence of God as background material (Gen. 1:1), it cannot validly be charged that there are no demons in the opening book of the Bible. In any event or upon any possible inference based on revealed facts, they are there, whether as fallen angels, or as the disembodied spirits of a pre-Adamite race (Gen. 1:2), or as the result of the cohabitation of angelic beings with antediluvian women (Gen. 6:1-4). In the Book of Genesis the author assumes the existence of demons just as plainly as he assumes the existence of God or the fall of Satan and his angels" Merrill F. Unger, *Biblical Demonology* (Wheaton, Illinois: Scripture Press Publications, Inc., 1952), 20.

[11] Luke 10:18; 2 Peter 2:4; Jude 6; Revelation 12:8-9 (Early Church fathers view this as Satan cast out of heaven)

[12] 1 Peter 5:8

sequently, they set their sights upon the spacious country of Universe and centered upon the town of Mansoul.[13]

With gravest intentions, Diabolus and his infamous assembly of evil notables – namely, Alecto, Apollyon, Beelzebub, Lucifer, Legion, and others – came together in conference to discuss by what means they could win the lustrous town of Mansoul.

It was Diabolus who drew attention to the reality that it would not be possible for their whole company to rush in upon the place to conquer it. "Therefore, let it be a few," Diabolus brought forward; "No, just one of us. Better yet, let it be me!"

A second matter pertained to how they in their currently ragged and rascally appearance could approach Mansoul without being suspected as up to no good. The fierce Alecto[14] acknowledged that Mansoul had not yet seen them in so sorry a shape, a realization Apollyon[15] affirmed and with which Beelzebub[16] concurred.

The Mansoulian people had a sense of what these demons were once upon a time, but they had no sense of what these demons had become of late![17] Thus, these evil connivers' approach should be in a guise to which the people would be the most accustomed.

It was Lucifer[18] who put forward the beguiling idea of how it would be best for Diabolus to assume the body of a creature familiar to the citizens

---

[13] "From the time that they shook off their allegiance to God they shook off all goodness and contracted all those tempers which are most hateful to him, and most opposite to his nature. And ever since they are full of pride, arrogance, haughtiness, exalting themselves above measure; and although so deeply depraved through their inmost frame, yet admiring their own perfections . . . They are full of cruelty, of rage, against all the children of men, whom they long to inspire with the same wickedness with themselves, and to involve in the same misery" John Wesley's "Of Evil Angels" (Sermon 72), edited by Albert C. Outler, Volume 3, *The Works of John Wesley* (Nashville: Abingdon Press, 1986), I.5.

[14] Alecto – In Greek mythology a Fury, daughter of Gaea and sister of Tisiphone; also, appears in Dante's *Inferno*

[15] Apollyon – Greek name for the angel of the bottomless pit whose Hebrew name, according to Revelation 9:11, was Abaddon (B.H. Throckmorton, Jr. in TIDB)

[16] Beelzebub – In various periods of time and cultural contexts the word could be: Lord of Dung, Lord of the Abode (a shrine) or the Evil One (T.H. Gaster in TIDB)

[17] "From Homer down to New Testament times the sense of *daimon* and *daimonion* is seen thus to have increased gradually in its inferiority to *theos* [Greek for God], and to have gathered around it more and more the sense of evil, until it reached its precise and invariable New Testament meaning of an 'evil spirit' or 'messenger and minister of the devil.' As spiritual beings, demons are intelligent, vicious, unclean, with power to afflict man with physical hurt, and moral and spiritual contamination" Merrill F. Unger, *Biblical Demonology* (Wheaton, Illinois: Scripture Press Publications, Inc., 1952), 61.

[18] Isaiah 14:12 KJV (Day Star – Venus still showing in the sky after sunrise)

of Mansoul. Say, one over which the people had dominion![19] And yet, a creature that bore an impressive guise! One deemed wiser than all the other creatures! In this way the Mansoulian people would not be wary that an attempt was being made upon their souls.[20]

The group then discussed how best to convey the guise in which they were coming to Mansoul. It was Legion[21] who came up with the plan. "Let us assault them in all pretended fairness, covering our intentions with all kinds of lies, flatteries, delusive words – pretending what never would be, and promising what never could become. These people of Mansoul, every one of them, are so simple and innocent. They do not yet know what it is to be assaulted with fraud, guile, and hypocrisy. They are strangers to lying and dissembling lips.[22] What we promise they will surely believe, especially if, in all that we say, it bears a masquerade of abundant love."[23]

By the time the group came to a fourth consideration, whether they should shoot one or more of the principal Mansoulian townspeople, it was decided to target Captain Resistance, and that Tisiphone,[24] a fury of the lake, should be the one to fire upon him.

On concluding their plan of attack, the whole group marched toward the town of Mansoul in a guise of invisibility,[25] except one, Diabolus, who approached the town in the disguise of a dragon.[26]

Drawing up to Ear-gate, the place of hearing, Diabolus edged close to the wall and called for an audience. As in all the typically difficult matters, Ill-pause[27] served as Diabolus's orator. Thus, a cadre of Mansoulian

---

[19] Genesis 1:26-28; James 3:7

[20] Genesis 3:1-7

[21] Legion – Luke 8:30

[22] Psalm 26:4; 2 Corinthians 11:13-14

[23] Romans 12:9

[24] According to Greek and Roman mythology, Tisiphone ("avenger of murder") and her sisters Megaera ("jealous") and Alecto ("unceasing in anger") were furies of hell who, with whips made of serpents and with lighted torches, punished the wicked in Tartarus for crimes of murder, parricide, fratricide, and homicide. According to Hesiod the sisters sprang from the blood of Gaea's mutilated spouse Uranus. Sophocles referred to them as the daughters of darkness. Because they were so greatly feared, the Greeks used euphemistic names, Kindly and August, regarding them. Interestingly, in Bunyan, Tisiphone is not avenging a murder, she is engaging in murder (see *Britannica* and Runyon's *The Holy War Annotated Companion*, 13, 15).

[25] "Bunyan has called this conflict a holy war, and the spiritual battle he allegorizes is carried out largely against an invisible enemy, and one that when seen is well disguised" Daniel V. Runyon, "John Bunyan's Master Story: The Holy War as Battle Allegory in Religious and Biblical Context" (Published version of Ph.D. dissertation, Lampeter, Wales: Edwin Mellen Press, 2007), 124.

[26] Genesis 3:1, 4

[27] Ill-pause: Psalm 140:3; Romans 3:13

leaders, to wit, Lord Innocent,[28] Lord Willbewill, the Lord Mayor, Mr. Recorder, and Captain Resistance,[29] appeared in response.

"Why are you calling us?" the leaders wanted to know.

Diabolus, as if he had been a lamb,[30] began to speak through his orator Ill-pause. "I am," he said, "no far dweller from you. I am so concerned about something I must tell you. I have come to show you how you may obtain a great and ample deliverance from a bondage that, unawares to yourselves, is greatly enslaving you.[31]

At this, the Mansoulian officials began to prick up their ears.

So, Diabolus continued: "I know your King is a great potentate. However, the stuff he has told you is not true nor for your own advantage. It regards what he has forbidden you. Yes, it is something so trivial as eating a little fruit. There is such a great disproportion between your life and an apple, isn't there! He said you may eat of all and yet he forbids you the eating of one.[32]

"Shaddai is holding back some knowledge of a great good you might obtain. Why should you be pinned down in ignorance and blindness? You are not a free people! He is keeping you enchained! Is it not so sad that the very thing you're forbidden to do might yield you wisdom and honor?[33] You are made sheer underlings and wrapped up in momentous inconveniences. What a bondage is greater than this to be shut up in such a dark and stinking cave?[34]

---

[28] Innocent: Psalm 24:4

[29] James 4:7; 1 Peter 5:9

[30] Matthew 7:15-16

[31] Genesis 3:4-5

[32] Genesis 2:16-17

[33] David Wilkinson, a research astrophysicist: "Although human beings are encouraged to pursue wisdom, there is a wisdom that belongs only to God. The pursuit of wisdom without reference to God is the temptation here. It will be a hard wisdom for Adam and Eve [Mansoul], as it is for all of us. Do we make moral decisions without reference to the Lord, or are we prepared to seek and follow his guidance?" David Wilkinson, *The Message of Creation: Encountering the Lord of the Universe*, in Bible Themes Series, ed. Derek Tidball (Downers Grove, Illinois: InterVarsity Press, 2002), 55.

[34] Though Bunyan may not have been aware of it, this thought bears a semblance to Plato's Analogy of the Cave. And yet, there is a difference, as Suzanne Noffke points out: "Plato, building on the work of his master Socrates, argued that the soul (psyche) as the principle of life is both pre-existent and immortal. He described the soul as simple, spiritual and divine, though imprisoned for a time in a material body. This soul knows spiritual things (the forms) only through memory from its spiritual pre-existence. It is destined to be released from the material through death and subsequent rebirths and deaths, eventually to become one again with God, with the eternal and unchanging good, true and beautiful" (Sheldrake, 592). Not necessarily as Bunyan would unravel it!

Pen and Ink Drawing Depicting Diabolus
by Kaitlyn E. Priset, artist

Just as Diabolus was speaking, Tisiphone fired upon Captain Resistance, the only man of war in the town, and mortally wounded him, and he fell over the wall dead.[35]

Then, Ill-pause, the orator, addressed the town. "It is my master Diabolus's happiness he has this day a quiet and teachable audience. Look on the tree and its promising fruit. Remember that you yet know but little, and that this is the way for you to know so much amazingly more."[36]

When the townsfolk saw that the tree was good for food, pleasant to the eye, and desired to make one wise, they did as old Ill-pause advised.[37]

As Ill-pause was making his speech, Lord Innocent – whether by some shot from camp, or some sinking qualm that suddenly took him, or the stinking breath of that treacherous old villain Ill-pause – sank down in the very place where he stood and could not be brought back to life.[38]

PRAYER STARTER: *Gracious God, there are times when what might seem simple attractions are crafty deceptions. In times like these, help us to step back and draw upon insights you have already provided. Grant us discernment. Help us not become drawn off into enticements that bring us to lose sight of your abundant and loving care.* [From here on continue in your own prayerful words.] *In Jesus' name, Amen.*

The Grave Subjection

Judges 9:14-15: Thé faid all the trees vnto the bramble, Come thou and reign ouer us. And the bramble faid vnto the trees, If ye wil in dede anoint me King ouer you, come, & put your truft vnder my fhadow: and if not, the fire fhal come out of the bramble, and confume the cedres of Lebanon (GEN, 1560).

---

[35] C. S. Lewis, in his *The Magician's Nephew,* weaves an interesting parallel story regarding the headway evil made upon Creation. In the chapter, "Digory and His Uncle Are Both in Trouble," the lion Aslan – the Christ figure – confronts the matter of Narnia falling prey to Jadis's wicked presence. "You see, friends" he said, "that before the new, clean world I gave you is seven hours old; a force of evil has already entered it; waked and brought hither by this son of Adam." Consequently, with this genesis, we have the whole unraveling of redemption's saga through Lewis's Narnia set of children's literatures!

[36] "There are many . . . bewitched by the tricky devil who can make a lie look like the truth. Since the devil has this uncanny ability to make us believe a lie until we would swear a thousand times it was the truth, we must not be proud, but walk in fear and humility, and call upon the Lord Jesus to save us from temptation . . . ¶The spiritual witchery of the devil creates in the heart a wrong idea of Christ" Martin Luther, *Commentary on Galatians,* trans. by Theodore Graebner (Digireads.com Publishing, 2019), Galatians 3:1; p. 60.

[37] Genesis 3:6

[38] Innocent: Exodus 23:7; Deuteronomy 27:25; Psalm 10:8

Then said all the trees unto the bramble, Come thou, and reign over us. And the bramble said unto the trees, if ye will indeed anoint me king over you, come, and put your trust under my shadow: and if not, the fire shall come out of the bramble and consume the Cedars of Lebanon (GNV, 1599).

A serious line of demarcation had been crossed. Captain Resistance and Lord Innocent were dead! The townsfolk, now inheriting a fool's paradise, had opened their lives to Diabolus's tricks. Crafty Ill-pause had excelled as Diabolus's spokesperson. In their grave misfortunes the Mansoulian people had been drawn into a snare. The bait came through Ear-gate, the place of hearing, and Eye-gate, the place of perspection,[39] Thus, Diabolus, the giant, marched up into the midst of the town, took over the place, and made his conquest as secure as he could.

Discovering the affections of the people warmly inclined to him, Diabolus took another step in his ruse. "Alas, poor Mansoul, I have done you great service," he pointed out. "But now, you need something else. Seriously! You need a defender! Once Shaddai finds out what has happened, he will sweep right in upon you roaring like a lion and do all he can to rip you out of your newly-found privileges."[40]

Diabolus, this lowly and prickly bramble sort of character,[41] moved in to take possession of the castle, the citadel of strength and put his notables into place.[42]

He dealt early on with the Lord Mayor, whose name was Lord Understanding,[43] and the Recorder, whose name was Mr. Conscience.[44] It is true that the Lord Mayor had played a part in admitting the giant into Mansoul, and so did the Recorder, and yet Diabolus was a bit uneasy with

---

[39] Perspection – a rare word originating in the mid-16th century and meaning "contemplation, regard, scrutiny, inspection" (Oxford English and Spanish Dictionary)

[40] "The devil describes Christ [Shaddai's Son] as an exacting and cruel judge who condemns and punishes men . . . ¶Paul calls this present world evil because everything in it is subject to the malice of the devil, who reigns over the whole world as his domain and fills the air with ignorance, contempt, hatred, and disobedience of God. In this devil's kingdom we live" Martin Luther, *Commentary on Galatians*, trans. by Theodore Graebner (Digireads.com Publishing, 2019), content on Galatians 1:4; pp. 15, 16.

[41] Bramble: Judges 9:14-15

[42] "At this point *The Holy War* is not so much a story about guilty humanity and its fall from grace as it is about Diabolus and his revolution against the Creator. The revolution instigated by Diabolus becomes internalized and personified in the person of Lord Willbewill" Daniel V. Runyon, "John Bunyan's Master Story: The Holy War as Battle Allegory in Religious and Biblical Context" (Published version of Ph.D. dissertation, Lampeter, Wales: Edwin Mellen Press, 2007), 127.

[43] Job 12:12; Psalm 119:130; Proverbs 9:10; 24:3; Ephesians 1:18; Philippians 4:7

[44] Proverbs 20:27 (Compare Geneva Bible, 1599, to The Living Bible, 1971, where a person's conscience is called the Lord's searchlight)

how it would go once the two realized they would not be basking in their former luster.

You see, Lord Understanding was a seeing sort of person! Consequently, Diabolus built a high and strong tower whose walls fit in between the sun shining and the Mayor's palace windows. In this place that felt like a prison, the dragon Diabolus, by installing such a blind, would be shading him from the light.[45] Point blank, this Mr. Understanding was an uneasy person to keep around in any place of leadership or authority.[46]

Mr. Conscience, the Recorder, a person of courage and faithfulness and well versed in the laws of Mansoul, was one Diabolus feared more than he feared the Lord Mayor. The Recorder had a tongue bravely hung and a head filled with judgment. It is true, he, too, had been taken in by the giant's schemes; however, he was another Mansoulian that Diabolus could not trust. So, Diabolus had to do all he could to debauch the old man by seeing if he could harden his heart, stupefy his mind, and draw him past the prick of his conscience.[47] Nonetheless, there remained the fear that the Recorder would think of Shaddai, have a dread of the law, and raise a voice against Diabolus which would break out into the lion's roar.

Consequently, Diabolus had a plan. It related to times Mr. Recorder would slip into one of his notorious fits. Diabolus would convince the townsfolk that the Recorder had gone mad and was not to be taken seriously. Little by little, Diabolus got Mansoul to slight, neglect, and despise whatever the Recorder would say, even to the extent of making the old gent, especially when merry, unsay and deny what he had cried out before.[48]

Nevertheless, there came times Mansoul got so unnerved by the Recorder that Diabolus felt he had to speak to the people: "O Mansoul, it is nothing but the old codger's foolish prattle. He loves to do that! Notwithstanding the rage and rattle of his high and thundering voice, Shaddai pays him no attention. Shaddai hangs silent. It is because Shaddai knows you belong to me. Just look how much good I have done you. You now have freedom. Before I came to your rescue, you were a penned-up people.

---

[45] "Satan hates the light of the Gospel. When it begins to shine a little, he fights against it with might and main" Martin Luther, *Commentary on Galatians*, trans. by Theodore Graebner (Digireads.com Publishing, 2019), content on Galatians 5:1; p. 131.

[46] Job 28:28; Psalm 111:10; Isaiah 11:2; 2 Corinthians 4:4-5; Ephesians 4:18-19; Philippians 4:7; Colossians 2:2; 2 Timothy 2:7 [many other references in Job, Psalms, Proverbs and Ecclesiastes]

[47] 1 Corinthians 15:33

[48] Ephesians 4:14

But now, look at the chances without limit I have given you to live like princes!"

Liar and deceiver as he was, Diabolus would do all he could to frame and re-frame every outcry the Recorder would raise as though it had nothing to do with their hearing the voice of Shaddai through him.[49] In such a way Diabolus would quiet the town when the Recorder would molest them with his cursed orations, which would set the town in such a rage they wished he, the Recorder, were living a thousand miles away.

But he was not! He was right there! For all the bother he seemed to be, it was amazing he even survived. Nonetheless, his house was as strong as a castle and, if, at any time, some rabble attempted to put him away, he would pull up the sluices, and let out such a flood as would drown everything round about him. Quite simply, it was Shaddai's very providence which preserved this fellow remaining among them.[50]

There was another townsman, Lord Willbewill, a high-born person of substantial strength who enjoyed many privileges peculiar to himself. However much or not his lofty estate played into his pride, Willbewill plain and simply was quite full of himself! Thus, he set out to get in step with the new day and hoped for an advancement under Diabolus, even if he could become a petty ruler or governor.[51]

So, Diabolus sent for Willbewill one day and took him into confidence by making him captain of the castle, governor of the wall, and keeper of the gates – no trivial a position! The only stipulation was that Willbewill should do nothing aside from the awareness and sanction of Diabolus. What is more, Mr. Mind,[52] a man who would speak in every way as his master, would serve as Willbewill's clerk.

As he rose into his position, Willbewill would badmouth Mr. Recorder. Quite bluntly, he could not endure him! He hated to see him out and about. He would even stop up his ears should he come within hearing distance! In sort of a paper chase, Willbewill did all he could to purge every fragment of Shaddai's law which might surface in the community, although Mr. Recorder had some records of the law squirreled away in his study which Willbewill could not put his hands on.

---

[49] 2 Chronicles 24:19; 36:16; Isaiah 30:10; Jeremiah 29:19; Matthew 5:12; Luke 11:47, 49-50; 2 Peter 1:19

[50] Psalm 27:1-2, 12-14

[51] Willbewill: Colossians 2:18; 1 Timothy 3:6-7; 6:3-5

[52] Ephesians 2:3

Moreover, Willbewill thought there was too much light coming through the windows of the old Lord Mayor's house. The light of a single candle was not even endured.[53]

All in all, there was no one like Willbewill to trumpet the brave nature, wise conduct, and great glory of Diabolus – his new and illustrious lord and valiant prince – as he traipsed about Mansoul.[54]

Lord Willbewill had a deputy who served under him whose name was Mr. Affection,[55] a person greatly debauched and given to the flesh, more honestly called Vile-Affection, who fell in love and made quite a marriage with Carnal-Lust,[56] the daughter of Mr. Mind, who parented three sons – Impudent,[57] Blackmouth,[58] and Hate-Reproof[59] – and three daughters – Scorn-Truth,[60] Slight-God[61] and Revenge.[62]

By the time Diabolus engarrisoned[63] himself in the town and put down any individuals who would appear to be against him, he set about to demolishing the statues and statutes he felt were a grave distraction to his place and power. For example, the image of Shaddai engraved in gold first had to be defaced. Mr. Mind was accorded with the task. An image of Diabolus had to be raised high in its place. Then, any remaining laws and statutes affording a hint of Shaddai were to be done away with, as well.

Consequently, there was nothing good remaining in Mansoul which Mind and Willbewill did not seek to destroy, for in their plan, they, with the help of No-Truth, would be turning Mansoul into a brute and making her like a sensual sow.[64]

Ultimately, the edicts, statutes, and commandments in all places of resort or concourse were to give liberty to the lusts of the flesh, the lusts of the eyes, and the pride of life, which were of the world.[65]

---

[53] Nehemiah 9:26; John 3:20

[54] Psalm 50:16-23

[55] Affection / Vile-Affection: Romans 1:26; 6:19-20

[56] Carnal-Lust: Leviticus 18:20

[57] Impudent: Ezekiel 2:4; 3:7

[58] Blackmouth: A pejorative term for liars, slanderers, foul-mouthed political radicals; or Ulster Scots refusing to take the "Black Oath" imposed in 1639; or Covenanters eating blackberries while hiding in the wilds during the Killing Time, roughly 1679-1688

[59] Hate-Reproof: Proverbs 1:22, 27-31

[60] Scorn-Truth: Psalms 10:4; 50:17, 21

[61] Revenge: Luke 9:51-56; Romans 12:19

[62] Slight-God: Psalm 14:1

[63] Military for setting up a garrison (simple past tense and past participle of engarrison)

[64] No-Truth: 2 Peter 2:12

[65] 1 John 2:16

With Mansoul being wholly at Diabolus's beck, and brought wholly to his bow, nothing was heard or seen but what tended to promote his diabolical schemes.

PRAYER STARTER: *Enlightening God, there are times we feel enveloped by darkness. Shine into our hearts with the warmth of your love. Help clarify our direction. No matter how dim that light in this moment may seem, keep us glued upon it as your guiding star.* [From here on continue with your own prayerful words.] *In Jesus' name, Amen.*

A Dis-establishment

Matthew 18:7: Wo be vnto the worlde becaufe of offences: for it muft nedes be that offences fhal com, but wo be to that má, by whome the offence cometh (GEN, 1560).

Woe be unto the world because of offences, for it must needs be that offences shall come, but woe be to that man by whom the offence cometh (GNV, 1599).

Thinking about a new modeling[66] of the town, Diabolus set out to remove anyone who would get in his way. Significantly, Diabolus drew upon those he deemed would be his yes-people.

To start with, Diabolus raised a new Lord Mayor and a new Recorder to their respective positions. Lord Lustings,[67] who had neither the eyes nor the ears for people's good – an evil user-type-of-guy / a beast – became the new Mayor. Forget-Good,[68] a sorry sort of fellow, became the Recorder. His talent for mischief and his sick sense of humor distinguished him greatly. None of these diabolical assignments were commonsensical at all! Sadly, when such vile individuals move into key positions, they model a corruption that sets a tone and draws the public downward. In a crisp manner of putting it, this new modeling was what satisfied the Diabolonians and pleased Diabolus wondrously well!

---

[66] In modern language, a new modeling is Bunyan's wording for what would be a remodeling. On the dark side, Diabolus is not "re"-doing anything. He is setting out to erase any evidence of Shaddai and configure something totally different than what was before. Similar imagery appears when Emmanuel regains Mansoul. He too is going to do a new modeling. See the concluding part of "A Beauty for Ashes" and opening part of "A Serious Relational Drift."

[67] Lustings: Galatians 5:16-17, 24; Ephesians 4:22; 2 Timothy 4:3; 2 Peter 3:3; Jude 1:16, 18

[68] Forget-Good: Hebrews 13:16

Additionally, Diabolus brought forward several burgesses and aldermen – creating a pool from which officers, governors, and magistrates could be selected. Chief among them were Mr. Incredulity,[69] Mr. Haughty,[70] Mr. Swearing,[71] Mr. Whoring,[72] Mr. Hard-Heart,[73] Mr. Pitiless,[74] Mr. Fury,[75] Mr. No-Truth,[76] Mr. Stand-to-Lies,[77] Mr. False-Peace,[78] Mr. Drunkenness,[79] Mr. Cheating,[80] and Mr. Atheism[81] – thirteen in all.

There was also an election of common councilmen and others as bailiffs, sergeants, constables, and so on – all relatives to those in the higher positions.[82]

Diabolus then set out to fortify the town with several strongholds. The first he called the Hold of Defiance,[83] which was built close to Eye-gate to shut out as much light as possible, thus keeping the town from any awareness of its ancient King. The second, Midnight Hold,[84] was positioned hard by the castle to keep the town from an authentic knowledge of itself. The third, Sweet-Sin Hold,[85] stood in the marketplace, the center of daily life and commerce, thus crowding against any desires for the good of Mansoul.

Spite-God,[86] a most blasphemous wretch who accompanied the rabble that first came against Mansoul, was made governor of the Hold of Defiance. Love-no-Light,[87] also among those first-comers, was made governor of Midnight Hold. Then, Love-Flesh,[88] a very lewd fellow who could find

---

[69] Incredulity: Deuteronomy 1:32-36 (topical reference)

[70] Haughty: Proverbs 6:17

[71] Swearing: Hosea 4:2; 10:4

[72] Whoring: Leviticus 17:7; Deuteronomy 31:16; Ezekiel 6:9

[73] Hard-Heart: Exodus 7:13, 22; 8:15, 32; 9:34-35; 13:15; Deuteronomy 15:7; Psalm 95:8; Proverbs 28:14; Mark 3:4-6; 6:52; 8:17; 16:14; John 12:40; Ephesians 4:18; Hebrews 3:8, 15

[74] Pitiless: Psalm 69:20; Jonah 4:9-11; Matthew 18:33

[75] Fury: Deuteronomy 32:26-28; 2 Kings 19:20-34

[76] No-Truth: Proverbs 3:3; Jeremiah 7:28; 9:3; Hosea 4:1; John 8:43-45

[77] Stand-to-Lies: Proverbs 6:17, 19; Hosea 4:2

[78] False-Peace: Jeremiah 6:14; 8:11

[79] Drunkenness: Ecclesiastes 10:17; Isaiah 5:11; Hosea 4:18; Luke 21:34; Romans 13:13; Galatians 5:21-23

[80] Cheating: Proverbs 11:1, 26; 16:11; 20:10, 14, 23

[81] Atheism: Psalms 14:1; 53:1; Romans 1:21-22, 25

[82] Seems like nepotism

[83] Hold of Defiance - Romans 13:1-3

[84] Midnight Hold - Judges 16:3; Acts 16:24-26; 27:26-28; 28:1

[85] Sweet-Sin Hold - Isaiah 43:24-25

[86] Spite-God: Ezekiel 25:15-16

[87] Love-no-Light: Isaiah 9:2; Matthew 4:15-16; John 3:19

[88] Love-Flesh: Galatians 2:20; 5:12-17

more sweetness in lust than he did in the paradise of God, was made governor of Sweet-Sin Hold.

You would think word had reached Shaddai about his runagate servant Diabolus and the loss of Mansoul. Significantly a tidings-teller did bring an account to Shaddai, not in private, but in open court. Present at that time were Emmanuel, Shaddai's Son, as well as the high lords, chief captains, and nobles, all of whom felt great sorrow and regret to think Mansoul was taken.[89]

Not surprisingly, Shaddai and his Son had already anticipated the matter. They knew Diabolus and the bent of his life. Nonetheless, it was in their divine plan that something profoundly better and more redemptive would unfold.[90] In their private chamber, they engaged in further discussion, positing Mansoul would suffer loss for a while and eventually recover in a way that would give both Shaddai and Emmanuel eternal fame and glory.[91] The understanding was that the King's Son should journey into the country of Universe and make war on Diabolus while he possessed the town. By his all-imposing strength, Emmanuel would drive Diabolus from his lair and take the place for himself.[92]

Subsequently, the Lord Chief Secretary[93] drew up a record of what was determined and posted it throughout the Universe. "Let it be known that the Son of Shaddai, the great King, through his matchless love, is engaged in a covenant with his Father to bring Mansoul back into his care and a better state than ever before."[94]

---

[89] Text and Song Interactional: Aaron Johnson, Evan John, Ryan Williams and Wesley Schrock, songwriters, "World Needs Jesus" by River Valley Worship, released 2014

[90] Colossians 1:26-27; 1 Peter 1:10-12

[91] "The Lord, being a discerner of hearts and foreknowing all things, perceived the weakness of men and the manifold wiles of the devil, how that he will be doing some mischief to the servants of God, and will deal wickedly with them. The Lord then, being very compassionate, had pity on His handiwork, and appointed this (opportunity of) repentance" *The Shepherd of Hermas*, trans. J. B. Lightfoot (London: Macmillan, 1891; reprint, CrossReach Publications, 2017), Mandate 4, p. 34.

[92] Daniel V. Runyon unveils *The Holy War* in a succinct and helpful way: "If creation was the perfect miracle, then the fall was the perfect crime, and the struggle toward restoration and perfection makes for the perfect universal narrative. This is the master story of the loss of identity and the quest to regain it. The details of this master story involve an ideal creation that is alienated from its creator through revolution, growing self-awareness, rising action with ever-increasing conflict between good and evil, a climax where gridlock can only be broken by superhuman strength, and a resolution that anticipates a better world" Daniel V. Runyon, "John Bunyan's Master Story: The Holy War as Battle Allegory in Religious and Biblical Context" (Published version of Ph.D. dissertation, Lampeter, Wales: Edwin Mellen Press, 2007), 6.

[93] The Lord Chief Secretary represents the Holy Spirit

[94] Isaiah 49:5; Hosea 13:14; 1 Timothy 1:15

It was all but a happy matter for Diabolus who caught wind of the scheme. Fretfully he muttered, "I shall be molested, and my habitation taken!"

On the other hand, when Shaddai and his Son aired the news in and about their court, there was a great stir in an opposite way. At first, the high lords, chief captains, and noble princes whispered it to one another and the sound of it swelled throughout the palace with everyone talking about the King and his Son and their marvelous intentions.

After a few casts of mind, Diabolus was not without a bevy of schemes himself. From the first, he resolved, the news of Shaddai must be kept from the townspeople. If the people heard that their former master intended good for them it might occasion a revolt! Diabolus then renewed his flattery with Lord Willbewill and gave strict orders that he should keep a careful watch at all the gates by day and by night – especially Ear-gate and Eye-gate – and if rumors of any attempted intrusion should arise, he must cut them off! Then, he should put spies walking up and down the town to suppress and destroy anybody they perceived plotting against him.

Secondly, the dragon Diabolus imposed a new oath upon the folk. It was what could be called the horrible covenant. In short, they should not desert him nor his government under any circumstances. No one should ever betray him nor seek to alter his laws. Instead, they should own, acknowledge, confess, and stand by Diabolus as the one and only rightful king and discountenance anybody who would side with another claimant.

Once this was conveyed, silly Mansoul didn't balk, but swallowed it whole without chewing as if it had been a sprat in the mouth of a whale.[95]

Thirdly, there was a push drawn up by Mr. Filth and promoted at the castle gates to lure the people into beastly behavior. By this Diabolus gave the people license to do anything on the dark side they may have ever wanted. All this lay shrouded in Diabolus's frame of mind to weaken the Mansoulian against believing that Shaddai had the best for people's lives in heart and mind and would redeem the sinners they had eventually become. Thus, the more Mansoul was absorbed in sin, the lesser the stake they would have in Shaddai's grace and mercy.

Consider, for instance, the time Shaddai cast Diabolus away. So, Diabolus was banking on a scheme that Shaddai would do the same with the Mansoulian people. In this manner, there would be no redemption for the depraved and the fallen![96]

---

[95] Isaiah 28:14-17, Sprat are highly active, small, oily forage fish
[96] Job 15:16; Proverbs 30:12; Isaiah 64:1, 6

For a fourth point, Diabolus sought to enflame the people's concern Shaddai was raising an army to come and destroy Mansoul. If Diabolus could convince the people about this, he could mute any message of Shaddai's intent to deliver them. Therefore, calling the whole town to gather in the marketplace, he addressed the group.

"My good friends, you know what liberties and great privileges you have enjoyed under my government from the very first. Now! I so greatly care about you that I must not refrain from telling you something. A noise of trouble is coming upon you! I received a post from Lord Lucifer. Your old king, Shaddai is coming to destroy you root, branch, and all.[97]

"For my part, I am but one, and I can with ease shift for myself, but my heart is so firmly united to you that I am willing to stand and fall with you.

"What do you say, O my Mansoul? Will you desert me, your old friend, or will you stand by me? It is vain to believe Shaddai will grant you any quarter.[98] Perhaps, at his first sitting down, he will pretend to be merciful and, thereby, with the more ease and less trouble, speak of taking you back to himself. Whatever he may say, do not believe a bit of it. By such language, he intends to overcome you and make you wallow in your blood to become trophies of his unmerciful victory.

"Suppose he should get you to yield and save some lives, but what would that do for you who hold office about town? What if he even granted quarter to all of you? Be sure, though, that he will bring you back into bondage.

"Listen, I'm for you, if you're for me. It is better to die valiantly than live as pitiful slaves. Blood, blood, it is nothing but blood in every blast of Shaddai's trumpet.

"Pray, raise the alarm. He is coming. Stand to your arms while you have the liberty. I can teach you war. I have armor for you. I can gird you from top to toe and fasten it all about you."

The soldiers would be clad with helmets to keep off many a blow, so that no arrow, dart, sword, or shield could hurt them. The breastplate of iron, forged in Diabolus's own country, was a hard heart, a stone past any sense of feeling – thus sparing the weak from the fear of judgment, or the temptation to extend mercy.[99] The sword was a tongue burning with the

---

[97] Poignant, twisted misapplication of John 15:1-8, 16

[98] The difference of one letter "s" in spelling a word: *Quarter* means the showing mercy or pity to a defeated opponent, whereas *Quarters* indicates a place of accommodation

[99] Revelation 9:9

fire of hell. It could bend itself to speak evil of Shaddai, his Son Emmanuel, and their people. By making effective use of it one could not be conquered.[100] Diabolus's shield was a piece of armor to ward against the pitfall of belief, thus fitting one to call into question the truth of any of Shaddai's words and judgments.[101] Another piece (a very important one) was a dumb and prayerless spirit – a spirit that could heap scorn on anyone crying for mercy. In addition to all this, there were mauls,[102] firebrands, arrows, and death – all good hand-to-hand weapons![103]

On fitting the Mansoulian people with such armor and arms, the dragon lord Diabolus wrapped up his talk by reminding them what a kind, accommodating, and honorable leader he was for them.

Then, doubling the guards, he took himself to the stronghold of his castle while his military kept exercising daily and learning the ways of war.

PRAYER STARTER: *We spend so much energy devising that which would serve us ourselves. Help us to sort out the good from the not so good. Guard us against easy rationalizations and crafty deceptions. Strengthen us to face the challenges of each day. In whatever we strive to do, help it to be for the betterment and not diminishment of others.* [From here on continue in your own prayerful words.] *In Jesus' name, Amen.*

Under Diabolus's Control

Revelation 3:19-20a: As manie as I loue, I rebuke and chaſté: be zealous therefore and amende. Beholde, I ſtand at the dore, and knocke. If anie man heare my voice & opé the dore, I will come in . . . (GEN, 1560).

As many as I love, I rebuke and chasten: be zealous therefore and amend. Behold, I stand at the door, and knock, if any man hear my voice, and open the door, I will come in . . . (GNV, 1599).

---

[100] Psalms 57:4; 64:3; James 3:6

[101] Job 15:26; Psalm 76:3; Mark 6:5-6

[102] A maul is a tool that has a heavy head and handle that is used for ramming, crushing, and driving wedges

[103] Regarding Diabolus's parody on the Armor of God as found in Paul's letter to the Ephesians 6:10-18, Spring Arbor University professor, Dr. Daniel V. Runyon points to the humor lodged in this passage. "Diabolus modeling his armor after the armor of God in Ephesians six reflects a view of sin as twisted righteousness and Satan's best innovations as mere imitation of God's genuine creativity. The enemy is to be laughed at as much as feared" Daniel V. Runyon, "John   Bunyan's Master Story: The Holy War as Battle Allegory in Religious and Biblical Context" (Published version of Ph.D. dissertation, Lampeter, Wales: Edwin Mellen Press, 2007), 144.

As King Shaddai prepared to approach Mansoul, now held under Diabolus's tyranny, he thought first of sending his servants, rather than his Son.[104] The crucial question was whether the Mansoulians would be brought back into relationship with the King. The captains sent to regain Mansoul totaled four: Captain Boanerges, Captain Conviction, Captain Judgment and Captain Execution – all stout and rough-hewn leaders[105] fit to break through the battlements and make a way by the sword.[106] To each of them Shaddai gave a banner displaying the goodness of his cause.

Captain Boanerges,[107] chief of the four, had ten thousand men. Mr. Thunder[108] was his ensign.[109] He bore black colors and his scutcheon[110] bore three burning thunderbolts.[111] To Captain Conviction[112] were given ten thousand men. His ensign was Mr. Sorrow.[113] He bore pale colors and his scutcheon bore the book of the law laid wide open, from whence came a flame of fire.[114] To Captain Judgment[115] were given ten thousand men. His ensign was Mr. Terror.[116] He bore the red colors. His scutcheon bore a burning fiery furnace.[117] To Captain Execution[118] were given ten thousand men. His ensign was Mr. Justice.[119] He also bore the red colors. His scutcheon bore a fruitless tree, with an axe lying at the root.[120] All were people of exceptional faith and military action fit to break through the ice and swiftly wield the sword.

---

[104] Matthew 21:33-45; Mark 12:1-12

[105] Various suggestions have arisen regarding who these four captains might signify: The four Horsemen of the Apocalypse (Revelation 6:2-8); four Nonconformist preachers (John Owen, George Cokayne, George Griffith, and Anthony Palmer); four Old Testament prophets (Moses or Elijah, Hosea, Isaiah or Jeremiah, and Joel); or the four Gospels. See John Bunyan, *The Holy War* Annotated Companion to *The Pilgrim's Progress*, ed. Daniel V. Runyon, (Eugene, Oregon: Pickwick Publications, 2012), p. 42, note 88, p. 43, note 90.

[106] Ezekiel 21:1-32

[107] Boanerges from the Hebrew "sons of thunder" referring to James and John, Jesus' disciples, in Mark 3:17

[108] Thunder: 2 Samuel 22:14; Job 37:5; Psalm 46:6; Revelation 19:6

[109] An officer in the military of what was formerly the lowest commissioned rank

[110] A shield often displaying a coat of arms or, in this case, a poignant symbol

[111] Psalm 78:47-49

[112] Conviction: Deuteronomy 33:2; 2 Kings 22:9-13; 2 Chronicles 17:7-10; John 8:9

[113] Sorrow: Psalm 32:10; Isaiah 53:3-4; 2 Corinthians 7:10; Revelation 21:4

[114] Exodus 19:16-19; 20:1-18

[115] Judgment: Jeremiah 4:2; 9:24; 10:24; 23:5; John 16:8-11; Jude 1:15

[116] Terror: Job 6:4; Psalms 55:4; 88:15; Ezekiel 21:12; 2 Corinthians 5:11

[117] Psalm 21:1, 7-11; Daniel 3:13-30

[118] Execution: Matthew 3:10; Romans 13:4

[119] Justice: Job 8:3; Psalms 72:3; 94:15; Proverbs 14:34; 21:3; Ecclesiastes 3:16

[120] Luke 13:6-8

From the very beginning, King Shaddai commissioned Captain Boanerges with the task of first offering conditions of peace.[121]

> "Do not hurt the least native that moves or breathes therein,[122] hoping they will but submit to me.[123] Treat them as if they were your friend or family. Let them know I love them all. They are dear to me. Tell them that in time I will come to them. Let them know I am merciful.[124]

> "However, if they stand out, resist, and rebel against you, I command you to make use of all your cunning, power, might, and force, to bring them under by strength of hand."[125]

When the commanders had been provided their instructions, the day was appointed, and the place of rendezvous fixed, for each commander to appear in such gallantry as became his cause and calling.

Bearing further orders and encouragements from Shaddai, they set off in a forward march toward the famous town of Mansoul. Captain Boanerges led the van. Captain Conviction and Captain Judgment made up the main body. And Captain Execution brought up the rear. Having a great way to go, for the town of Mansoul was far away, they marched through the many regions and countries of people, not abusing anyone along the way, but blessing those in whatever places they passed through.[126]

After many days, they came within the sight of Mansoul. When they saw how prostrate the Mansoulian people were to the will of Diabolus, they, with heavy hearts, could do no less than bewail the serious condition of the town. To get on with the task, the captains marched up to Ear-gate, entrenched themselves, and addressed the people. The townsfolk, seeing so gallant a force, so bravely accoutered, and so excellently disciplined could not help but come out of their houses and gaze. However, Diabolus, the cunning fox, fearing that the people were wowed by the sight and would open the gates, came down with haste to speak with them.

"Gentlefolk," he said, "though you are my beloved friends, I must chide

---

[121] At various times throughout the story, Shaddai's and Emmanuel's directive seems like the just-war tactic, as originating in the work of St. Augustine (4th century), which "requires that the object of war be peace and that every expedient for reconciliation shall have been exhausted prior to the declaration of hostilities" (Roland H. Bainton, *Christian Attitudes Toward War and Peace* [Nashville: Abingdon Press, 1960], p. 128).

[122] Matthew 10:11; 25:40; Luke 16:10; Ephesians 3:8; Hebrews 8:11

[123] Luke 10:5; 1 Thessalonians 2:7-11; James 4:7

[124] Numbers 6:25; Deuteronomy 4:31; 2 Chronicles 7:14; Psalms 111:4; 145:8; Joel 2:13; Matthew 5:7; Luke 6:36

[125] Exodus 15:13; Isaiah 1:4, 16-20; 40:26; Luke 9:1

[126] Ephesians 2:13-17

you for your uncircumspect action. Do you know who these are? They are the ones I told you about. They have come to destroy this town. They are the ones with whom I at great cost have armed you *cap-a-pie.*[127] At their first appearance, why didn't you raise the alarm and cry out, 'Fire the beacons!' What have you done? You've made me half afraid! Did I not double the guards? Have I not endeavored to make your hearts as a piece of the nether millstone?[128] Fie, fie! Stiffen your back for defense. Beat the drum. Gather for war.

"I will stop chiding you now. I will rebuke you no further. I charge you from here on out to let me see no more such actions. Let no one so much as show his head over the wall of the town of Mansoul without an order obtained from me!"

A great change came over the townspeople. Stricken with a panic fear, they ran back and forth along the streets crying for help.

"The destroyers of our peace have come upon us. Those who had turned the world upside down have come upon us."[129]

"Ah, this is where I like it!" gloated Diabolus. "Just as I would have it! Now, they'll obey me. Let Shaddai's forces of this so-called prince take the world if they can!"

Before three days passed, Captain Boanerges commanded his trumpeter,[130] Take-heed-what-you-hear,[131] to go down to Ear-gate and in

---

[127] Middle French meaning "from head to foot"

[128] Dr. Janis Gibbs points out an interesting analogy. "The thing about the bottom (nether) millstone is that it is stationary – immobile. The top one moves, but the bottom can't."

[129] Acts 17:6

[130] Isaiah 58:1: The trumpet or cornetto, the trumpeter, and the drum appear often throughout Bunyan's *The Holy War*. In various contexts, the trumpet was used to gather people together, to mark the step for an advancement of troops, or as calvary trumpet signals, or to strike fear and frustration in a community under siege. During Bunyan's lifetime the trumpet emerged from its traditional military and ceremonial role and entered the mainstream of composed art music, according to Peter Downey in "On sounding the trumpet and beating the drum in 17th-century England." Dr. Hsuan Wen Chen, a scholar and performer in Baroque Era music, also points out that Purcell, a contemporary of Bunyan, wrote a good amount of music for the trumpet. Most was on the Baroque trumpet or natural trumpet. A slide trumpet (flatt trumpet) was used during this time as well. On the music score, the part for the trumpet was often indicated "tromba" which meant trumpet in Italian. One would need to know the harmonic series for the instrument, however, to clarify which instrument was meant for use. Moreover, "trumpeters and kettledrummers," according to Caldwell Titcomb, in "Baroque Court and Military Trumpets and Kettledrums," performed "for the nobility and at the express order of the sovereign or noble who had jurisdiction over them. They were specifically forbidden to provide music at such affairs as middle-class and peasant weddings, annual fairs, festivals, public dances and theatre performances, and the like."

[131] Mark 4:24; Luke 8:18

the name of Shaddai sound his trumpet for a hearing. The trumpeter did so, but no one responded. It was as Diabolus had commanded. The trumpeter returned to Captain Boanerges and gave his report, which grieved the captain, who then sent him to his tent.

A little afterwards, though, Boanerges directed the trumpeter to head out to Ear-gate again, which he did, and just as before he came back with no response.

After Shaddai's captains and field officers held a council of war, they agreed to have the trumpeter approach the gate a third time and if the community still refused to respond, they could use force to bring Mansoul into submission.[132]

At this point, though, the apostate Lord Willbewill, governor of the town and keeper of the gates, approached him and with big and ruffling words demanded the trumpeter declare who he was, where he came from, and what was the cause for all this insufferable noise!

"I am a servant to the most noble Captain Boanerges, general of the forces of the great King Shaddai, with a message for you and the town of Mansoul for lifting your heel against Shaddai. If you keep refusing to peaceably cooperate, you will have to take what is about to follow!"

In response, Lord Willbewill, a truly evasive diplomat, said he would carry the words to Lord Diabolus.

However, the trumpeter replied: "Our message is not for Diabolus. It is for the miserable town of Mansoul. We have no interest in what Diabolus might want us to hear. We have come to recover the town from his cruel tyranny and submit, as formerly, to the most excellent King Shaddai."

Being greatly hemmed into a tight spot, Lord Willbewill then replied he would carry the errand to the town.

"Sir do not deceive us," the trumpeter replied. "If you do, you are deceiving yourselves. If you do not submit to us, we will make war upon you. Our black flag, with its hot, burning thunderbolts is a token of our defiance against your intruder prince. We are here to reclaim Mansoul for your Lord and rightful King."

Willbewill returned to Mansoul and provided Diabolus – yes, Diabolus – with his report and the trumpeter returned to the camp and provided Boanerges with his report. In response, Boanerges said, "Let us lie still in our trenches for a while and see what these rebels will do."

Meanwhile, when those in Mansoul heard the trumpets sounding throughout Shaddai's camp and thought they were making ready to storm

---

[132] Isaiah 58:1

the corporation,[133] the Mansoulians fell into a fearful spirit, which, after a little while, subsided as they themselves started with what seemed the closest task at hand and make ready for war.[134]

After some further time had passed, though, Boanerges resolved to reach for an answer. He sent the trumpeter to summon Mansoul to another hearing. It was not the Lord Mayor that Captain Boanerges had hoped for, but Lord Incredulity, one of Diabolus's other leaders, who showed himself over the wall. This greatly incensed the captain.

"This is not who we expected!" Boanerges exclaimed. "Where is Lord Understanding, the ancient Lord Mayor of Mansoul who we have known previously? I will speak to him!"

By this time, Diabolus felt compelled to approach the gate. "Mr. Captain, I do not know why you think you have the authority to come here. What are all these carryings-on?"

Boanerges did not want to talk with the dragon. His address was intended for Mansoul. Most critically, Shaddai's forces needed the Mansoulian people to comprehend the serious choice they were facing in submitting to Shaddai or fostering a rebellion!

In tandem with this discourse between Captain Boanerges and Diabolus, Captain Conviction approached the people.

"O, Mansoul, once you were so innocent but now you have fallen for such lies and deceit. You would benefit greatly by just responding to Shaddai. No one can stand once his anger is aroused. If you say you have done nothing wrong, the whole of your doings since the day you cast him off speaks woefully against you.[135] Why have you listened to Diabolus? He is a tyrant. Don't be blinded by his flattering wiles. It will run you into a thousand miseries.[136]

"Perhaps with deceit Diabolus may attempt to make you believe we seek our own profit. That is not so. Know it is our call for your obedience to King Shaddai and his love for your happiness that bring us here.[137]

"O Mansoul, consider the amazing grace that King Shaddai should humble himself in making such a sweet persuasion. Does he have that need of you that we are certain you have of him?

---

[133] In the 17th century, a reference to a corporation meant a town that was larger than a thinly populated country village (see John Brown, *John Bunyan: His Life, Times and Work* [London: Wm. Isbister, Ltd., 1885], p. 220).

[134] Zechariah 7:11

[135] 1 John 1:10

[136] Psalm 130:1

[137] 2 Chronicles 36:15-16; Psalm 50:21-22; Romans 3:10-19, 23; 16:17-18

"No! but he is merciful and does not want the Mansoulians to die. He wants you to turn to him and live."[138]

Adding another word to what his fellow captains stressed, Captain Judgment underscored the seriousness behind their reaching out to Mansoul.

"O Mansoul, we have not come with something of our own devising. We have not come to even out some petty quarrel. We have come in a peaceable way, but on a very serious note. Do not let Diabolus keep deceiving you. Shaddai is the founder and creator of all that is. Know a chance for the King's clemency will not always stand open. A day will come that shall burn like an oven.[139] Yes, it hastens; it does not slumber.[140]

"Is it so little in your eyes that our King offers you mercy and that, after so many provocations? He still holds his golden scepter out to you. Now is the time![141] Will you lose that gate of opportunity and provoke him any further? Beware, lest he take you away with a stroke and provide no ransom to deliver you. Does the King care about your riches? No, not even for your gold. Nor for what you presume your strength to be. Seriously, the time is coming for justice and judgment to take its hold!"[142]

While Captain Judgment was making this oration, some noticed that Diabolus trembled. However, the captain continued.

"O woeful town of Mansoul, won't you open your gate? We are deputies of your King. Can your heart endure? Can your hands be strong? Must you, as well, drink the sea of wrath your King has prepared for Diabolus and his angels? How we would so exceedingly rejoice to see you live!"[143]

Eventually, the fourth captain, Captain Execution addressed the townsfolk and added his poignant concern to their present circumstances.

"O once famous Mansoul, but now a fruitless bough; once the delight of the high ones, but now a den for Diabolus: listen to me in the name of the great Shaddai. Behold, the axe is laid to the root of the tree. Every tree that does not bring good fruit is hewn down and cast into the fire.[144]

"Yes, Mansoul, you have been a fruitless tree. You now bear nothing but thorns and briars. Your grapes are grapes of gall and your clusters are so

---

[138] 2 Corinthians 5:18-21; 2 Peter 3:8-10
[139] Psalm 104:31-32; Malachi 4:1; 2 Peter 2:3
[140] Isaiah 55:6-7
[141] 2 Corinthians 6:2
[142] Job 35:14; 36:18; Psalm 9:7; Isaiah 66:15
[143] Isaiah 66:5
[144] Matthew 3:7-10

bitter.[145] You have rebelled against the King and we, by the power and force of Shaddai, are the axe laid close to your root. What will you say now? How will you turn? For what then are you fit if mercy does not prevent your being hewn down and cast into the fire?[146]

"Patience and forbearance may be for a year, or two, or three, but not forever. Do you think these are only threatening words and the King has no power to act?[147]

"You have cumbered[148] to the ground too long. Will you keep on doing the same? Your sin brought this army to your walls and it shall bring about your judgment, as well."[149]

PRAYER STARTER: *You keep on persisting with us, God. You keep holding out before us so many chances to respond. Yet, there remain such a tangle of voices that keeps drawing us aside. The deceptions are many. We keep misconstruing your love. Forgive us, Lord. Come be our deliverance.* [From here on continue with your own prayerful words.] *In Jesus' name, we pray. Amen.*

Summer Battles and Winter Assaults

2 Corinthians 10:3-5: Neuertheles, thogh we walke in the flefh, yet we do not warre after the flefh, (For the weapons of our warrefare are not carnal but mightie through God, to cast downe holdes) Cafting downe the imaginations, and euerie high thing that is exalted againft the knowledge of God, and bringing into captiuitie euerie thought to the obedience of Chrift (GEN, 1560).

Nevertheless, though we walk in the flesh, yet we do not war after the flesh. (For the weapons of our warfare are not carnal, but mighty through God, to cast down holds.) Casting down the imaginations, and every high thing that is exalted against the knowledge of God, and bringing into captivity every thought to the obedience of Christ (GNV, 1599).

While Shaddai's four captains declared their message, their voices beat hard against Ear-gate. Yet, they could not stir any significant response. So,

---

[145] Deuteronomy 32:32e

[146] Matthew 3:10; Luke 3:9; 13:9

[147] 2 Peter 3:9-10

[148] Cumber, a verb declining in use since the late-19th century, meaning to *hamper* or *hinder* (someone or something), *obstruct* (a path or space)

[149] Ezekiel 18:21

they commanded Mansoul to get Ill-pause out of the way, but if not, they would provide the Mansoulians no more time. "We know," the captains cried out, "that so long as Ill-pause draws breath, all good considerations will be confounded."[150]

In response, Diabolus was loath to lose Ill-pause and consequently set out to provide the besieging army an answer by himself. But then, changing his mind, he commanded the Lord Incredulity, who by this time had become the Mayor, to engage the invaders.

"Gentlemen," Incredulity began, "you tell us in your terrible speech you have authority from Shaddai, but by what right he commands that, we are ignorant. You have summoned this town to desert her lord and, for protection, yield to Shaddai, with flattery telling her, if she does it, he will not charge her past offences against her. Further, you've threatened to punish this corporation if she doesn't cooperate.[151]

"Now, you captains, from whencesoever you have come, our brave Mansoul does not regard your person, your message, or your King! As for the war you threaten, we must defend ourselves. In short, we believe you to be some vagabond runagate crew, ranging from place to place to see if, through rage, flattery, and threats, you can frighten us or any other silly town, city, or country to desert their place and leave it all to you.[152] We do not dread you. We do not fear you. We will not obey you. Our gates are shut. Keep out! Let our people live quiet lives. Be gone or we will fly against you from our walls!"[153]

Incredulity's oratory was seconded by Willbewill, "Gentlemen, we have heard you – lots of noise that is – and we do not regard your threats. Get away from here. We remain as you found us.[154] You do not want to rouse the lion Diabolus!"

The new Diabolonian Recorder, whose name was Forget-Good, contributed his remarks, too. "As you must see, my Mansoulian lords have answered enough of your rough and angry speeches with such mild and gentle words.

"Hey, we love quiet and ease. We don't want to hurt or molest anybody. So, leave – I say, leave! Do it quietly. Take advantage of our kindness. Depart! Or we shall come out in force and you shall feel the dint of our swords."

---

[150] Psalm 140:1-3; Romans 3:13
[151] John 5:24
[152] Proverbs 14:16
[153] Luke 11:21
[154] Exodus 32:9

After all these words, the whole town of Mansoul shouted for joy, rang the bells, made merry, and danced upon the walls. Diabolus returned to the castle. The Lord Mayor and the Recorder returned to their places. Lord Willbewill took special care to secure the gates with double guards, double bolts and double locks and bars.

Then, Willbewill commissioned an angry and ill-conditioned old fellow, Mr. Prejudice,[155] to be captain of the ward at Ear-gate, putting sixty deaf men under his power. In a pathetic way, it was a condescending attempt to hamper any undesired communication breakthroughs from invaders![156]

As Shaddai's forces saw Mansoul persisting with defiance and preparing for battle, the King's army sent more assault forces against Ear-gate, for they knew if they could not penetrate Ear-gate, they could do Mansoul no good. So, after Shaddai's captains sounded their trumpet[157] and spoke their word, "You must be born again,"[158] the battle began.

In addition to the small weaponry, Mansoul placed two great guns upon the tower over Ear-gate. One of them was called High-mind;[159] the other, Heady.[160] These mischievous pieces had been cast in the castle by Mr. Puff-up,[161] who supervised Diabolus's foundry. Yet, how effective these warheads were was dubious. The guns did nothing worse than send shots whizzing past the soldiers' ears – thus, becoming more annoyance than anything else.

With as much valor as they could muster, Shaddai's forces realized that unless they could break open Ear-gate, getting beyond the wall would be in vain. Yet, with several slings to assail the townspeople in their homes and two or three battering-rams to crash through the wall, Shaddai's forces kept up their assault.

After a number of skirmishes and brisk encounters, with many brave attempts to break open and beat down the tower, the captains realized the great charge and expense of carrying on this summertime war and, consequently made a fair retreat and entrenched themselves in their winter quarters.

While heading back across the countryside, Shaddai's army happened upon three fellows, proper men of courage and skill (at least by appear-

---

[155] Proverbs 24:13; John 7:24; 13:34; James 2:1, 4; 1 John 2:11
[156] 2 Chronicles 24:19
[157] Numbers 10:9
[158] John 3:3, 7
[159] High-mind: 2 Timothy 3:4
[160] Heady: 2 Timothy 3:4
[161] 1 Corinthians 8:1-3

ance) – Mr. Tradition,[162] Mr. Human-Wisdom,[163] and Mr. Man's-Invention[164] – who had a mind to do some soldiering. Consequently, the captains cautioned these young applicants against being rash in what they were craving to do. Soldiering was more dangerous and demanding than they had been imagining. Nonetheless, considering they were men of courage they were permitted to join Shaddai's army.

As the war ratcheted up again, a company of Lord Willbewill's men sallied out of the castle through the sally port[165] and fell upon the rear of Captain's Boanerges' men, where the three new recruits were situated. Willbewill captured them and took them back into Mansoul as prisoners of war. Consequently, it was noised about in Mansoul, even reaching Diabolus himself, what three notabilities lay in captivity.

After some days, Diabolus sent for them and learned they were willing to serve under his command against their former captains. "Of course, we must let you know," they piped in response, "we do not live by religion so much as by the fates of fortune."

Taking advantage of their availability and shifting commitments, Diabolus directed them to Captain Anything.[166] Now, Anything, recognizing their value, made Mr. Tradition and Mr. Human-Wisdom sergeants and Mr. Man's-Invention his ancient-bearer.[167]

Bivouacked in their winter quarters, though, Shaddai's forces carried out a maneuver or two in which they crashed through the roof of the Lord Mayor Incredulity's house, thus making him more vulnerable than before. With a sling, they nearly slew Lord Willbewill, who made shift to recover. With one shot, they cut down six aldermen – Swearing, Whoring, Fury, Stand-to-Lies, Drunkenness, and Cheating – inattentive hotheads as they were. And they dismounted the two guns, High-mind and Heady, which stood upon the tower over Ear-gate.

Subsequently, Mansoul could not sleep as quietly as before. People could not go out and about so easily to their former debaucheries. With unpredictable military maneuvers springing from Shaddai's encampments,

---

[162] Tradition: Matthew 15:3, 6; Mark 7:13; Colossians 2:8; 1 Peter 1:18

[163] Human-Wisdom: Deuteronomy 12:8; Proverbs 3:5; 14:12; 2 Corinthians 1:12

[164] Man's-Invention: Judges 2:19; Psalms 28:4; 99:8; 106:29, 39; 119:113; Ecclesiastes 7:31; Jeremiah 4:4, 18; 23:22; 25:5; 44:22; Hosea 7:2; 9:15; Micah 7:13

[165] Sally Ports: The strength in castles built in medieval times resided in their defensive and holding abilities – thus, the hold – as opposed to their offensive maneuvers carried out in the field. Ideally, a sally port was situated in some obscure, hidden, or less noticed part of the castle to enable a contingent of soldiers to sneak out to forward communications or carry-on offensive maneuvers against vulnerable attack forces or valuable siege equipment.

[166] Anything: 2 Timothy 3:1-5

[167] Standard-bearer

Mansoul suffered terrifying alarms and, at those very times when the nights were long and weather cold, they could hardly maintain any peace of heart – in effect, a winter within a winter itself!

There were times Shaddai's trumpets would blare out. There were times Shaddai's slings would whirl stones into the town. Sometimes ten thousand of the King's soldiers would be running around the walls at midnight, shouting and lifting the voice for the battle. What clamorous, unsettling, and terrifying disturbances!

There were times some of the townsfolk themselves were wounded and cried out with such anguishing sounds that that would pile molestation on molestation to the presently languishing town. Even Diabolus had his own rest broken. Poor guy!

With their confidence so continually unraveled, some townsfolk would say: "We cannot keep living this way." Others would reply, "This will soon be over." A third would remark, "Let us turn to Shaddai and put an end to these troubles. A fourth would bristle with fear, "He will not receive us." The old gentleman, the (previous) Recorder – that is, the one that Diabolus removed from office – started crying out so loudly, as would be expected, that his voice came across like claps of thunder.

Everyone inside and outside of the town were caught in the very depths of winter. What seemed the valuables of so long ago took on such a tarnish. Common and ordinary necessities were growing scarce. The lusts that people once thought they enjoyed were no longer the same. All things that once were so beautiful were losing their luster, bearing a semblance of the shadows of death.[168]

Shaddai's captains extended a call, by way of Boanerges's trumpeter, for Mansoul to admit defeat. As far as could be gathered, the town would have given up before this, had it not been for crusty old Incredulity and fickle Lord Willbewill. Even diabolical Diabolus began wringing his hands in rage. More and more, Mansoul was in great distress, suffering under a mountain of perplexing fears.

The first time the trumpeter went out he extended words of peace, telling Mansoul the captains bewailed and did pity their misery, if only they would humble themselves and turn from their notorious and rebellious treasons.[169] The second time, he approached them more roughly, telling them bluntly their rebellion did chafe and heat up the captains.[170] The third time out the approach came across with more roughness still. At this point,

---

[168] Luke 15:14-15
[169] 2 Chronicles 7:14
[170] Jeremiah 25:7

the trumpeter did not know whether the captains would extend mercy or judgment. "Just open your gates!" he cried.

The last two summonses distressed the town so greatly that they called for a consultation, which resulted in Lord Willbewill's going up to Eargate and requesting a parley. Consequently, the townsfolk would reach an agreement upon certain terms:

1. That their current Lord Mayor and Mr. Forget-Good, with brave Willbewill, would remain as the governors of their town, castle, and its gates.

2. That no one currently serving under Diabolus be cast by Shaddai out of the harbor, house, or freedom they currently enjoy.

3. That they of the town of Mansoul continue enjoying the rights and privileges as had been granted under Diabolus.

4. That no law, officer, or executioner of law or office shall have power over them without their own choice and consent.

In effect, there would not be much of any change. So, when the captains heard this pathetic offer couched in its rebelliously audacious demands, Captain Boanerges made the following rejoinder:

"O, you that inhabit Mansoul, when I heard your trumpet, I can truly say I was so glad. And when you said you were willing to submit to our kind allowance, I was even happier. And yet, when you made your silly provisions and foolish cavils, you laid a stumbling-block before your very own feet and turned my gladness into sorrow.[171]

"Give yourselves into our hands, which means placing yourselves into Shaddai's hands. Entrust yourselves to Shaddai and we'll be at peace with you.[172]

"I suspect that old Ill-pause, the ancient enemy of Mansoul, drew up those proposals that do not deserve to be admitted to the hearing of anyone who pretends to serve Shaddai."

---

[171] Ezekiel 14:3
[172] 2 Timothy 2:19

Pen and Ink Drawing Depicting Ill-pause
by Kaitlyn E. Priset, artist

In response, old Incredulity, the Lord Mayor, cried out in exasperation: "Who would be so foolish as to put the staff out of their own hands into the hands of whom they know not? For my part, I will never yield to such an unlimited proposition. It is said by some individuals that he will be angry with his subjects if even by the breadth of a hair they chance to step out of the way. It is said by others he requires much more than they can ever perform.

"This is incredulous! Once you give yourselves to another, you're no longer your own. To give yourselves up to such an unlimited power is the greatest folly in the world! Don't you realize that when you are his, so many questions will arise: which of you will he kill, which of you will he save, or whether or not he will cut every one of you off?"

Following this sour venting which seemed to undo everything, Lord Incredulity went to Diabolus's chamber and, with a low congee,[173] told him the whole of the matter which Diabolus was glad to hear.

"My good and faithful Incredulity," Diabolus said, "I've had confidence in your fidelity more than ten times already and I have never found you false.

"I promise you, as we get through this, I'll make you my universal deputy – a position of honor far better than your being Lord Mayor of Mansoul – and you will have, next to me, all nations under your hand."[174]

PRAYER STARTER: *At times, God, your call gets muffled by a mangling of many distractions. Amidst the various disturbances – come summer, come winter, come anytime – help us to home in on your call for the reconciliation, hope, and healing it offers! Help us, Lord God, to better listen so that we might better hear.* [From here on continue in your own prayerful words.] *In Jesus' name, we pray. Amen.*

The People in an Uproar

Romans 16:17: Now I befeche you brethren, marke them diligently which caufe diuifion and offences, contrarie to the doctrine which ye have learned and auoide them (GEN, 1560).

Now I beseech you brethren, mark them diligently which cause division and offenses, contrary to the doctrine which ye have learned, and avoid them (GNV, 1599).

---

[173] A congee, an archaic word, suggested a bow, curtsey, or other gesture, which originally was made at a departure, but came to include a greeting in obeisance or respect.

[174] Proverbs 16:18; Matthew 4:8-10

The Lord Mayor's and Diabolus's response repulsed Shaddai's captains and put Mansoul into a mutiny. Meanwhile, the Lord Understanding, who was Lord Mayor before Diabolus took over control of Mansoul, and the old Recorder, namely Mr. Conscience, drew some of the town's people together, hoping to bring them to their senses.

So serious was this matter of neglecting Shaddai's demands, while being sucked into Incredulity's craftiness, a few townsfolk were becoming concerned regarding the evil Incredulity had been fostering throughout the town and around every corner.[175]

First, people started to mutter, then to talk openly, and after that, to run to and fro,[176] crying frantically as they ran.[177]

When Incredulity realized Mansoul was in such an uproar, he came down to appease the people and thought he could quash their heat with a show of his own importance. However, once they saw him, the people came running upon him, and doubtless would have done him grave mischief, had he not be-taken himself to his house. Even so, the people were in such a frenzy that they would have pulled the house down about his ears, had the place not been so strong.

After seizing a measure of protection for himself, though, the Mayor addressed the people from an open window, "Gentlemen, why such an uproar?"

In response, Lord Understanding pointed out: "It is because you and your master have not carried us rightly. You would not let Mr. Conscience and myself be at the hearing of your discourse. You propounded such terms of peace that by no means could ever be granted. After Shaddai's captains graced us with what would have granted mercy, you came at them with a crooked, unsavory, unseasonable, and ungodly speech."[178]

When old Incredulity heard this, he was repulsed: "Treason! Treason! To arms! O you trusty friends of Diabolus."

Nonetheless, Lord Understanding wouldn't back down: "Sir, you may place what meaning you want upon my words. I am sure the captains of such a high lord as theirs deserved a better treatment than what you have given."

Then, old Incredulity chafed: "What I said I said for my prince, for his government, and the quieting of his people, whom by your unlawful actions you have this day brought into mutiny."

---

[175] Text and Song Interactional: "Remind Me Who I Am" by Jason Gray, released 2011
[176] Archaic word from the Old Norse into Middle English meaning "from"
[177] Proverbs 16:27-29
[178] Isaiah 59:4, 8

At this point, Mr. Conscience replied: "Sir, you should not contradict what my good Lord Understanding said. It is obvious he has spoken the truth and you are an enemy to Mansoul. Realize the evil behind your saucy and malapert[179] language. Comprehend the grief you have caused to Shaddai's captains. Recognize the damages to which you have subjected Mansoul. Had you accepted their terms for peace, the sound of the trumpet and the alarm of war would have come to a quiet."

"Sir," old Incredulity said in frustration, "If I live, I will do your errand to Diabolus and bring you an answer. Meanwhile, we seek the good of the town."

However, old Understanding would not lower the heat: "You and Diabolus are intruders. You are not natives of Mansoul. You are not one of us! Who can tell, but what you would try to maneuver us into tighter straits? We know we can't depend on you. If all falls apart, you may leave us to shift for ourselves or set us on fire and go away in a smoke. Certainly, it'll come to ruining us!"

Nettled by such biting remarks, Incredulity responded: "You forget that you are under a governor, and ought to humble yourself like a subject. Know that when my lord, the king, shall hear of this day's work, he will give you but little thanks – and that is to put it mildly!"

While these men kept bantering back and forth, Lord Willbewill, Mr. Prejudice, old Ill-pause, and several of the newly inducted aldermen and burgesses descended from the walls and gates upon the place and asked why the hubbub.

It all got so noisy, with everyone butting in with their own notions, nothing could be distinctly heard.

Still, it was quite intriguing that that old fox Incredulity stepped in again and, finally, was able to bring them all into a silence.

"These are a couple peevish gentlemen who, I fear, through Mr. Discontent's advice,[180] have, as a fruit of their own bad dispositions, tumultuously gathered this company together and attempted to bring this town into rebellion."

Consequently, all the Diabolonians who were present stood up and affirmed that these things were all very, very true.

Then, there arose such a rift among the people that both sides came to blows. One party sided with the Diabolonians, old Incredulity, Forget-Good, the new aldermen, and Diabolus. The other cried up Shaddai, his

---

[179] Being malapert (an archaic word) is to render bold disrespect to a person of higher standing

[180] Philippians 4:11-13 (Content in contrast with Discontent)

laws, the captains, their mercifulness, and applauded their conditions and ways. The wrangling surged as the words passed into blows.

Old Mr. Conscience was knocked down twice by Mr. Benumbing.[181] Another assailant nearly finished Lord Understanding with an arquebuse.[182] He didn't, however, have a good aim. Mr. Rashhead,[183] a Diabolonian, had his brains beaten out by Mr. Mind, Lord Willbewill's servant. It was very funny to see old Mr. Prejudice getting kicked about and tumbled in the dirt. Mr. Anything, too, became quite brisk in the broil, and yet, both sides bashed him about because he was true to nothing. And yet, for all his impertinence, Mr. Anything suffered no more than a broken leg, while the person having done it wished he had broken his neck.

To put it blankly, both sides suffered harm. It even got to the point that the party lines became so blurred that some of the blows fell upon people belonging to their own camp. "Friendly fire" is what some might call it – quite an oxymoron!

Notwithstanding, it was a wonder to see Lord Willbewill becoming so indifferent to all the goings on. He did not seem like the same guy. It looked like he was bearing no concern for one side or the other. It even seemed as if he found amusement as old Prejudice got tumbled around in the dirt; then, while Anything came halting up before him, it appeared as if he had taken no notice.

By the time the uproar reached a lull, Diabolus apprehended Lord Understanding and Mr. Conscience and clapped them both in prison for a while as the ringleaders behind the heavy, riotous rout throughout the town.

Meanwhile, Shaddai's captains, having gone back from the gate to their camp, called a council of war to deliberate what to do next. Some said they should fall upon the town again, but the greater number thought it would be better to give them the chance of another summons. Possibly the town could be quieted into a more inclinable mode. Thus, the trumpeter set out for Ear-gate once again and sounded his trumpet as he was commanded.

"O hard-hearted Mansoul, how long will you love your sinful simplicity?"[184] declared the trumpeter. "You keep despising offers of peace and deliverance. Do you think your carriages toward Shaddai will yield

---

[181] Ephesians 4:19; also, according to the freedictionary.com, one understanding of benumbing is to render senseless or inactive, as from shock or boredom

[182] An arquebuse (**aar·kwuh·buhs**) is an early type of portable gun supported on a tripod or a forked rest

[183] Ecclesiastes 5:1; Colossians 2:17-19

[184] Proverbs 1:22

you peace and comfort and make him afraid as a grasshopper? Do you think you are stronger than Shaddai?

"Look to the heavens. Behold and consider the stars. How high are they? Can you stop the sun from running its course? Can you hinder the moon from giving its light? Can you stay the bottles of heaven? Can you behold every one that is proud, and abase them? Nevertheless, these are works of our King, in whose name we come to you, that you might be brought under his authority."[185]

At this point, the Mansoulian people were once again at a stand and did not know how to respond. Therefore, Diabolus took it upon himself to address the people.

"My faithful subjects, if you cave into Shaddai's demands, he'll be a terror to you. As for now he is at a distance. Who could endure it if you were in his presence?

"Look at me. I, your prince, am familiar with you. You may play with me as you would with a grasshopper.[186] Consider how you have profited from me. Remember the immunities I have granted you.

"Further, if all this be true that that one has said, how does it come to pass that Shaddai's subjects are so enslaved in other places?

"None in the universe are so unhappy as they. None are so trampled upon as they. Look at what sourpusses Shaddai's people are! It is a bum ride to submit to this Shaddai."

On this speech, Mansoul hardened her heart again. The thoughts of Shaddai's greatness quite quashed them, and the thoughts of his holiness sank them into despair.

After a brief consultation, they of the Diabolonian party sent back a "no thanks" by the trumpeter. They were resolved to stick with their own diabolical prince. They would not yield to Shaddai. Indeed, they would rather die than submit.[187]

Even though Mansoul seemed out of reach, Shaddai's captains knew what they could do. They were not beat out of heart. They thus sent an-

---

[185] Job 38:1-42:6

[186] The grasshopper is an interesting image drawn from Job 39:20 with which Diabolus - twisting scripture, of course - identifies himself in a pretentiously playful way. However, a grasshopper is not the pleasant and playful creature in the Hebrew Bible that Diabolus makes himself out to be: See, Exodus 10:14; Numbers 13:34; Deuteronomy 28:38, 42; Ecclesiastes 12:5; Nahum 3:17 and others

[187] Isaiah 1:4; Hosea 11:2, 7; Galatians 4:9

other summons, more sharp and severe than the last. However, the oftener they reached out to Mansoul, the further off the town's people seemed to drift. In a jam as to how to continue despite Mansoul's resistance, Captain Conviction came forward with the suggestion of sending a message to Shaddai acknowledging the limitation of their efforts, but also their hopes for Shaddai to send a gallant and well-spoken commander who would come forth with reinforcements to complete what they had already started to accomplish.[188]

The petition was drawn up. Mr. Love-to-Mansoul was the one honored to carry it. When it reached the palace of King Shaddai to whom should it be delivered but Shaddai's Son, Emmanuel himself. It had pleased Emmanuel so much that, upon mending it some, he carried it to his Father, as well.

On seeing the petition, Shaddai was so pleased that his servants besieging Mansoul remained so steadfast in their resolve and had already seen some success.

What was more, Shaddai was ready to commission his Son Emmanuel to prepare himself to go to the town of Mansoul and engage in the great war to win them away from the power of evil Diabolus.[189]

PRAYER STARTER: *Gracious God, you are so patient despite our repetitive turnings away. Help us, Lord. Our hearts are so hard. Soften us, center us, receive us. Help us comprehend those voices calling us in response to your love and mercy.* [From here on continue with your own prayerful words.] *In Jesus' name, we pray. Amen.*

---

[188] Dr. Daniel V. Runyon points out: "Here is the root of Bunyan's covenant theology. Both narratives—Bunyan's and the Bible's—illustrate the moral frailty of humanity and the patience of God. Both the captains and the prophets feel more should be done than they are able to do, and both turn to God for help. A new covenant will result." Runyon also points out the great significance of prayer embodied in this part of the story. "Captains turning to prayer move the narrative from the Old to the New Testament, from the works of the law as a hopeless means of salvation to the grace of God in the form of a Savior who can redeem all who respond to him" Daniel V. Runyon, "John Bunyan's Master Story: The Holy War as Battle Allegory in Religious and Biblical Context" (Published version of Ph.D. dissertation, Lampeter, Wales: Edwin Mellen Press, 2007), 139, 154.

[189] Text and Song Interactional: Phil Wickham and Brian Mark Johnson, songwriters, "Battle Belongs," sung by Phil Wickham, released 2021.

The Coming of the Prince Emmanuel

John 1:11-12: He came vnto his owne, and his owne receiued him not. But as many as receiued him, to them he gaue power to be the fonnes of God, euen to them that beleue in his Name (GEN, 1560).

He came unto his own, and his own received him not. But as many as received him, to them gave he gave power to be the sons of God, even to them that believe on his Name (GNV, 1599).

By this time, the coming of Emmanuel, the King's Son, to Mansoul raised the hopes of a new attempt, which had been in the heart of Shaddai from the beginning.[190]

"Your law is within my heart," Emmanuel exclaimed. "I delight to do your will. This is the day I have longed for. This is the work I have waited for.[191] Grant me what power you, in your wisdom, think meet. I will go and deliver this perishing town of Mansoul from the power of Diabolus. I have not thought there was anything else too dear for Mansoul. Vengeance is in my heart for you, my Mansoul.[192] I am glad my Father has made me the Captain of their salvation."

When the King's Son said this, it became the talk all around about the court. You cannot imagine how the courtiers were so taken with news.

"Someone should go and carry the glad tidings to the camp!"

When they at the camp heard the wonderful news, there was a shout that made the whole earth shake throughout the camp.

You need to know that even though Mansoul herself was not concerned (alas for them! They were so woefully besotted,[193] so tied up in their own pleasures and lusts),[194] Diabolus, their governor was duly shaken. Indeed, there was no one in the kingdom Diabolus feared so greatly as Prince Emmanuel![195]

As the time arrived for the King's Son to set out in his chariot at the head of the army, the five noble captains and their forces, each one ten

---

[190] John 1:1; Hebrews 10:7

[191] John 6:39-40

[192] Isaiah 63:4; Romans 12:19

[193] Strongly infatuated; intoxicated, drunk (late 16th century)

[194] Proverbs 19:3

[195] For reflection and discussion throughout the next three chapters, "The Coming of the Prince Emmanuel," "The Battle for Mansoul, "and "The Conquest," contrasting the nature of Diabolus with the nature of Emmanuel, engage the information found in Appendix One by Abby Manzella, LMSW, 227-229.

thousand strong, accompanied him.[196] First, there was Captain Credence.[197] His colors were red. Mr. Promise[198] was his standard bearer. For his scutcheon[199] Credence had the holy lamb upon a golden shield. Then, there was Captain Good-Hope,[200] his colors being blue, his standard-bearer was Mr. Expectation,[201] and on his scutcheon he had three golden anchors. The third was Captain Charity.[202] His standard-bearer was Mr. Pitiful.[203] His colors were green. For his scutcheon he had three naked orphans embraced in the bosom. Then fourth, there was Captain Innocent.[204] His standard-bearer was Mr. Harmless,[205] his colors were white, and for his scutcheon he had three golden doves. The fifth captain was Captain Patience.[206] His standard-bearer was Mr. Suffer-Long.[207] His colors were black. For a scutcheon he had three arrows through the golden heart. As it was with the Prince at the very front, Captain Credence led the van while Captain Patience brought up the rear. The other captains made up the main body.[208]

---

[196] Some scholars suggest these five Captains personify various attributes of God, or what becomes possible for those who accept the Messiah, or along the line of a Paul's listing of spiritual qualities in Galatians 5:22-23. See Daniel V. Runyon, "John Bunyan's Master Story: The Holy War as Battle Allegory in Religious and Biblical Context." (Published version of Ph.D. dissertation, Lampeter, Wales: Edwin Mellen Press, 2007), 161-162.

[197] Captain Credence: Isaiah 43:10; John 1:29; Galatians 5:22-23 (faith); Ephesians 6:16

[198] Promise: 2 Peter 3:9

[199] A scutcheon is a shield; especially one displaying a coat of arms

[200] Captain Good-Hope: Proverbs 11:23; Galatians 5:22-23 (goodness); 2 Thessalonians 2:16; Hebrews 6:19

[201] Expectation: Psalm 62:5; Romans 8:19-21

[202] Captain Charity: Romans 13:10; 1 Corinthians 13:1-13; Galatians 5:22-23 (love)

[203] Pitiful: Jonah 4:10; Zechariah 10:6; Matthew 18:33

[204] Captain Innocence: Psalm 24:4; Matthew 10:16; Galatians 5:22-23 (meekness)

[205] Harmless: Matthew 10:16 KJV; Philippians 2:15 KJV

[206] Captain Patience: Luke 8:15; 21:19; 2 Corinthians 6:4; Galatians 5:22-23 (longsuffering); 1 Thessalonians 1:3

[207] Suffer-Long: 2 Corinthians 6:6; Ephesians 4:2; James 5:10; 2 Peter 3:14-15

[208] According to Daniel V. Runyon, the following colors traditionally symbolized: "red for faith, blue for hope, green for youth, white for innocence, black for suffering." According to George Ferguson, gold signified "pure light, the heavenly element in which God lives." Regarding other symbols, according to Ferguson: a lamb symbolized Christ; an anchor - hope; nudity [a naked orphan] - purity and innocence; a dove - purity and peace; the heart- the source of understanding, love, courage, devotion, sorrow, and joy; while the number three, according to Pythagoras, was the number of completion and in Christian art signified the Trinity and the three days that Jesus spent in the tomb. See John Bunyan, *The Holy War* Annotated Companion to *The Pilgrim's Progress*, ed. Daniel V. Runyon (Eugene, Oregon: Pickwick Publications, 2012), 78, footnote 142 and George Ferguson, *Signs & Symbols in Christian Art* (New York: Oxford University Press, 1954; reprint, 1972), 15, 20, 42, 48, 49, 154.

As Emmanuel's troops advanced upon Mansoul, O, how the trumpets sounded, soldiers' armor glittered, and colors waved in the wind! The Prince's armor was all of gold. It shone like the sun in the firmament. The captains' armor, of proof, bore the appearance of glittering stars. There were some from the court who would ride as reformades[209] for the love that they had for King Shaddai and for the happy deliverance of Mansoul.

In setting out to regain Mansoul, Emmanuel, at the command of the Father, took fifty-four battering-rams and twelve slings to whirl stones[210] — every one of them made of purest gold.

By the time Emmanuel's armies neared Mansoul and the old soldiers in the camp saw the reinforcements coming, they gave such a shout it threw Diabolus into another fright.

Emmanuel's armies positioned themselves not just at the gates but surrounded the whole town. Whichever way Mansoul would look, they saw a great force lying in siege. There was Mount Gracious[211] on the one side and there was Mount Justice[212] on the other side. There were several small banks and advance-grounds as Plain-Truth Hill[213] and No-Sin Banks,[214] where many slings were poised against the enemy. Five of the best battering-rams were placed upon Mount Hearken[215] hard by Ear-gate.

---

[209] According to the *Dictionary of Nautical Terms*, the reformades were "the sons of nobility and gentry who served in the navy under letters from Charles II and were allowed table-money and other encouragements to raise the character of the service."

[210] Among military weaponry, slingshots appeared with the Roman Legions as an instrument of war in Scotland nearly 2,000 years ago. An easy find even earlier on ancient battlefields in the Middle East, sling stones the size of tennis balls have surfaced at archaeological digs. In Judges 20:15-17, among the troops of Benjamin, there were seven hundred left-handed warriors from Gibeah who could sling stones within a hair's breadth of accuracy. There, too, is the famous Bible story in 1 Samuel 17:40, featuring David felling Goliath with a sling shot. In 2 Chronicles 26:13-15, King Uzziah equipped an army of over three hundred thousand troops with slings and stones as well as devices that could hurl large stones over a wall. Sling stones in Job 41:19 and Zechariah 9:15, however, were no match for Leviathan and the Lord of Hosts. As a deadly form of ammunition, sling stones have been tested to have a penetrating / stopping power like a bullet fired from a .44 magnum handgun. As to exactness, stones fired from twenty-five feet away have been known to split a pencil in two. Moreover, in present-day technological development, the slingshot remains among serious weaponry. No surprise Bunyan imagined Emmanuel's army slinging stones as a grim aggravation to Diabolus's forces! Also see: Judges 20:15-16.

[211] Mt. Gracious: Exodus 34:6; 2 Chronicles 30:9; Psalms 25:8; 34:8; 68:9; 145:8; Joel 2:13; Luke 4:22

[212] Mt. Justice: Psalm 72:3; Proverbs 14:34; 21:3; Isaiah 33:5; 41:10; 46:13; Jeremiah 23:5

[213] Plain-Truth Hill: Deuteronomy 32:4; John 3:21; 2 Corinthians 4:2

[214] No-Sin Banks: Acts 16:19-40; 1 John 3:1-11

[215] Mt. Hearken: Deuteronomy 11:12-14; 26:17; Psalms 66:16; 81:13; Proverbs 15:31;

All of this bore a peculiar effect. When the townsfolk took in the sight, they were forced to shift, and to shift, and to shift again, and hardly shifted their thoughts to something stouter. Rather, their thoughts became feebler. At one point, they thought they were sufficiently guarded. At another point, no one knew what their hap would be. Confusion reigned!

In the first placement on Mount Gracious, Emmanuel displayed the white flag bearing an image of the three golden doves among the golden slings. By this Emmanuel was trying to convey he'd be gracious if they'd turn back to him.[216]

After two days and sensing no evidence of response, the Prince directed the raising of the red flag on Mount Justice. This one displaying a burning fiery furnace for several days attracted no response.[217] Finally, he directed the hanging of the black flag of defiance with its three burning thunderbolts. And yet, no matter what flag was raised, Prince Emmanuel sorrowfully resolved no response for mercy or judgment was coming from Mansoul.[218]

"Possibly these strange carriages arise more from their ignorance of our manner and feats of war than from any defiance of us," Emmanuel graciously pondered. "Or, they may understand the ways and means of their own wars, but not the rites and ceremonies of this war."[219]

Consequently, the Prince directed a message to Mansoul to let them know the weight of what they were facing, grace and mercy or the execution of judgment, all by the way in which they managed their gates.

Finally, the townsmen responded: "Great Sir, we are bound by the law and custom of this place and can give you no answer. What you are asking is against the law, government, and the prerogative royal of our king regarding making war or peace. We can only ask our prince to come down to the wall and express as he thinks fit and most profitable."

When Prince Emmanuel heard this response and saw how terrible the slavery and bondage in which the people were contented to abide, it grieved him deeply.[220]

At first, Diabolus refused to approach the invaders and huffed about, but in his heart, he was sorely afraid. However, he finally said that he would go

---

Jeremiah 26:3
[216] Acts 10:43
[217] Romans 2:2
[218] Jeremiah 8:18
[219] Ephesians 4:18
[220] Psalm 95:10

down to the gates and give an answer as he would see fit. However, it on purpose was in a language the townsfolk would not comprehend.[221]

> "O Emmanuel, I know who you are,"[222] Diabolus stormed. "Why have you come to torment me?[223] As you know, this town of Mansoul is mine. First, it is mine by conquest. I won it in the open field. Shall the prey be taken from the mighty or the lawful captive be delivered?[224] Further, this town is mine by their subjection. They opened their gates to me. They have sworn fidelity to me. They have openly chosen me as their king and have given their castle into my hands.

> "Not only that, Mansoul has disavowed you! They have cast away your law, your name, your image, and all that is yours. However, they have committed themselves to my law, my name, my image, and all that is mine. Ask your captains how they've responded to your summons. Ask them how they've shown love and loyalty to me, but disdain, spite, contempt, and scorn for you. Go away! Leave us in peace. This is my justly-achieved inheritance!"[225]

As indicated previously, the oration came in the language peculiar to Diabolus. Although the dragon could speak to every person in his/her own language, else he couldn't draw them into temptation; however, he had a language proper to himself – that of the infernal cave, or the dark pit.

Sadly, Mansoul did not understand what their prince Diabolus was saying, nor could they see how Diabolus crouched and cringed while he stood before Emmanuel. Instead, the people were in such awe of their diabolical prince's seeming magnificent power!

> "You deceiver," Emmanuel fired back. "I have, in my Father's name, a will for the good on behalf of this wretched town. You, on the other hand, pretend to have a right to Mansoul, which you obtained through lying, falsehood and deceit.[226]

> "Now, if lying, wiliness, sinful craft, and all manner of horrible hypocrisy, will go in my Father's court, I will confess you have made a lawful conquest. But alas! what thief, what tyrant, what devil may conquer as you have done? You, O Diabolus, in all your pretenses have nothing truthful to say.

---

[221] 2 Kings 18:25-27
[222] James 2:19
[223] Matthew 8:29
[224] Isaiah 49:24
[225] 1 Peter 2:22-23
[226] Proverbs 21:6

"Do you think it is right to lie regarding my Father and frame him as being the greatest deluder of all time? What do you have to say about your perverting the right purport and intent of the law? Was it for good that you made a prey of the innocence and simplicity of this now miserable town? You overcame Mansoul by promising them happiness by transgressing my Father's laws. You knew you could not do that! By your own experience you comprehended that! If not enough, you, O master of enmity, defaced my Father's image in Mansoul. Then, you set up your own image in place of it, all wreaking damage upon this perishing town!

"By deluding and undoing this place by your lies and fraudulent carriages, you've set the people against their own deliverance. You have stirred them up against the voices that had been reaching out to deliver them. All this and much more! You have even worked against the light you once enjoyed. You have inspired contempt against my Father and his laws. O Diabolus, you prince of the infernal cave, I have come as the lawful power and am here to take this town out of your blistering fingers. This town of Mansoul is mine by an undoubtable right. All one needs to do is search the most ancient records to certify my title to it.[227]

"First, my Father built this town and fashioned it with his own hand. The palace amid the town he built for his own delight. Thus, by the best of titles, Mansoul is my Father's and he that gainsays the truth must lie against his soul.

"Secondly, Mansoul is mine! I am my Father's heir. I have a right and title to Mansoul.[228] His it was, and he gave it to me. Nor have I been forced, by playing bankrupt, to sell it to you. Mansoul is my desire, my delight, the joy of my heart.[229]

"Third, when this Mansoul sinned by hearkening to your lie, I put in and I became a surety to my Father that I would make amends for Mansoul's transgressions, and my Father accepted it.[230] When the time appointed was come, I gave body for body, soul for soul, life for life, blood for blood, so redeeming beloved Mansoul.[231]

---

[227] Throughout this dialogue between Emmanuel and Diabolus there are points and patterns so close in sounding to themes C.S. Lewis brings out while engaging Aslan and the White Witch in "Deep Magic from the Dawn of Time" and "Deeper Magic from before the Dawn of Time," chapters 13 and 14, respectively, in *The Lion, the Witch and the Wardrobe*, of Lewis's children's literature series: The Chronicles of Narnia.

[228] John 16:15; Hebrews 1:2

[229] Isaiah 50:1; John 17:6

[230] Ephesians 1:13-14; Hebrews 7:22

[231] Matthew 5:18; 1 Peter 3:18

"Fourth, it was not halfway done. My Father's law and justice were both concerned. They both are now satisfied and very well content that Mansoul should be delivered.

"Fifth, I am come out against you, O Diabolus, you fountain of deceit, by command of my Father as he was the one who said to me, 'Go down and deliver Mansoul.'"

At this point of time, the golden-headed Prince, Emmanuel, turned with a word to Mansoul. But hardly before he started, the gates were double-guarded, and the people commanded to give no audience. And so, anything said was relegated to soliloquy:

"O unhappy town of Mansoul," Prince Emmanuel mused, "I cannot but be touched with pity for you. You have accepted Diabolus as your king. You have opened your gates wide to him and shut them fast against me. I am come to you bringing salvation, but you pay me no regard.[232] What shall I do? Shall I save you? Shall I make you a monument of the richest grace? Yes, what shall I do? Hearken to my word and find life. Don't shut me out of your gates. I am merciful. You will find me so.[233]

"I am not inclined to hurt you. Why fly away so fast from your friend and stick so close to your enemy? Indeed, I would have you as it becomes you to be sorry for your sin. Do not despair of life. This great force is not here to hurt you, but to deliver you.[234]

"My commission is to make war upon Diabolus and all Diabolonians who commit themselves to him. He may be that strong man who is armed that keeps the house. But I will drive him out of his hold. I will divide his spoils. His armor I will take.[235] Diabolus will come to a painful realization that when he is compelled to follow me in chains Mansoul will rejoice to see it so!

"At the time I put forth my might, I could compel him to leave, but I have it in my heart to deal with him in a way all may see. He has taken Mansoul by fraud and he keeps it by deceit. I will strip him naked and bare in the eyes of all his observers!"

Although the words were intended for Mansoul, they could hear none of it! So horribly had Diabolus enchanted them to ignore their rightful

---

[232] John 1:11; Titus 2:11
[233] Song of Solomon 5:2; John 12:47; Revelation 3:20
[234] Luke 9:56
[235] Mark 3:27

Lord and Prince, they shut up Ear-gate,[236] kept it locked and bolted, and set a guard at it. The command was as hard as granite. No Mansoulian should go out![237]

PRAYER STARTER: *Emmanuel, God with us! How blessed we are with your coming. But how blinded at times we are to see it. Still be the call that reaches into our hearts. Still be the light with which God shines from above. Be the nurturing voice and the guiding star beckoning us to a greater future under the canopy of your love.* [From here on continue in your own prayerful words.] *In Jesus' name, we pray. Amen.*

The Battle for Mansoul

2 Peter 3:9: The Lord is not flacke concerning his promes (as fome men count flackenes) but is pacient towarde vs, and wolde haue no man to perifh, but wolde all men to come to repentance (GEN, 1560).

The Lord of that promise is not slack concerning his promise (as some men count slackness) but is patient toward us, and would have no man to perish, but would all men to come to repentance (GNV, 1599).

As Emmanuel neared the extent of offering Mansoul any more prospects of a peaceful response, he sent word for his host to stand poised to attack. As there was no way to take the town except through the gates, the captains and commanders were to bring the battering rams, slings,[238] and soldiers before Eye-gate and Ear-gate.

Thus, with Shaddai's armies visibly poised for attack, Emmanuel held off a little longer to see if Mansoul would yield peaceably.

On the other hand, Diabolus called the Mansoulian officials to a war council. At this conference, they resolved upon certain propositions that should be offered to Emmanuel.

They commissioned an old man by the name of Mr. Loth-to-stoop,[239] a stiff sort of fellow and a prodigious doer for Diabolus, to approach Emmanuel's camp with a proposition.

---

[236] Zechariah 7:11

[237] Galatians 3:1

[238] Judges 20:16

[239] Loth-to-stoop [reluctant, unwilling to humble oneself]: see Luke 20:46. Loth is more commonly rendered loath in Britain and the United States although both loth and loath are appropriate spellings. As a verb, loathe means "to dislike greatly." As an adjective, loath means "not willing."

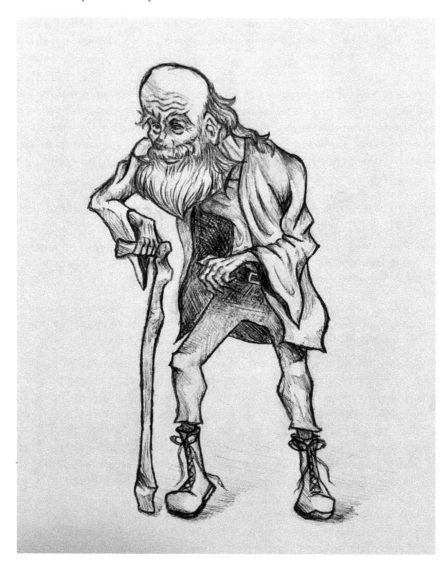

Pen and Ink Drawing Depicting Loth-to-stoop
by Kaitlyn E. Priset, artist

Mr. Loth-to-stoop began, "Great sir, my master really is a good-natured prince. He has sent me to tell you, he is willing, rather than going to war, to deliver one half of the town of Mansoul into your hands if your Mightiness would just accept the proposition."[240]

"Nothing about this 'half's' kind of stuff," Emmanuel rebutted, "The whole is mine by gift and by purchase."[241]

"Sir," said Loth-to-stoop, "my master said he would be content for you to be the nominal and titular Lord of all, if he may possess but a part."[242]

"The whole is mine," Emmanuel responded, "Not just in name and word. I only will be Lord and Possessor of all or none."

"But sir," Mr. Loth-to-stoop said, "Behold the condescension of my master! He says he would be content if only he had a private living space in Mansoul, and you could be the Lord of all the rest."[243]

"All that the Father gives me shall come to me,"[244] responded the golden Prince. "I will lose nothing – no, not a hoof nor a hair.[245] I will not grant Diabolus the least corner of Mansoul for a dwelling place."

Then, Loth-to-stoop said again, "But, sir, suppose my Lord should resign the whole town to you, only with this proviso, that he sometimes, when he comes into this country, may, for old acquaintances' sake, be entertained as a wayfaring man for two days, or ten days, or a month, or so. Such a small matter! Couldn't this be granted?"

Then, Emmanuel said, "One came as a wayfaring man to David. He did not stay long. It nearly cost David his soul. I will not consent he should ever find any such harbor here."[246]

"But, Sir," Loth-to-stoop muttered, "You seem so hard. Suppose my master should yield all that your lordship has said, provided his friends and kindred in Mansoul may have liberty to trade in the town, and enjoy their present dwellings?"

"No," Emmanuel kept pressing, "that is contrary to my Father's will. All Diabolonians found living in Mansoul at any time shall lose not only their lands and liberties, but also their lives."[247]

---

[240] Titus 1:16

[241] John 10:27-29

[242] Luke 13:25

[243] Acts 5:1-5

[244] John 6:37

[245] 2 Samuel 14:11; Daniel 3:27; Acts 27:34

[246] 2 Samuel 12:1-5

[247] Romans 6:13; Colossians 3:5; Galatians 5:24

Not content to give up, Mr. Loth-to-stoop persisted, "But, sir, mayn't my great lord and master by letters, passengers, accidental opportunities, and the like maintain some kind of friendship with Mansoul?"[248]

"No, I say, by no means! Any such fellowship, friendship, intimacy, or acquaintance in whatever way it is maintained will tend to the corrupting of Mansoul, the alienating of their affections from me, and the endangering of their peace with my Father."[249]

"But great sir," Mr. Loth-to-stoop kept pressing on, "Since my master has many friends, may he not, while departing from them, bestow upon them, as he sees fit, some tokens of his love and kindness to the end that Mansoul may remember him and the merry times they sometimes enjoyed with one another?"

Then, Emmanuel said, "No, not the least scrap, shred, or dust Diabolus left as gifts shall be permitted as a call into remembrance the horrible communion between them and him."

"Well, sir," said Loth-to-stoop, "I have one thing more to propound. Suppose that there is someone in the town that has some business of high concern with which nobody can help except my master. May not my master be sent for upon so urgent an occasion as this? Or, if not admitted into the town, what would be against him and the person concerned meeting in some village near Mansoul for his help?"[250]

To this last of Loth-to-stoop's ensnaring propositions, Emmanuel emphasized that there would be no case, or thing, or matter that may not be solved by the Father, for in everything, by prayer and supplication, the folk were to let their requests be made known to God.[251] What is more, if anything be granted as Diabolus would want, a door would be set open for him to slip in, plot, hatch, and bring to pass some treasonable designs.[252]

Coming through what went on between Prince Emmanuel and Loth-to-stoop in the ruse of a negotiation, it became clear that there was no way to responsibly reconcile even a smidgen of an agreement between Diabolus and Emmanuel except by force.

Consequently, Emmanuel commanded Captain Boanerges, Captain Conviction, Captain Judgment, Captain Execution as well as Captain Credence to approach Ear-gate with trumpets sounding, colors flying, and soldiers crying out. Then, Emmanuel directed Captain Good-Hope and Captain Charity to draw themselves up before Eye-gate. The rest of the

---

[248] John 10:8
[249] 2 Corinthians 6:17
[250] 2 Kings 1:3, 6-7
[251] Philippians 4:6-7
[252] 1 Samuel 28:15; 2 Kings 1:2-3

captains and their soldiers should place themselves for their best advantage round about the town. At the battle cry of "Emmanuel," the fighting began, the battering-rams played, and the sling-shooters whirled stones into the town.[253]

Captain Boanerges made three of the fiercest assaults, one after another, upon Ear-gate, with Captain Conviction moving up fast for backup. As they sensed the gate beginning to yield, the captains commanded the battering rams to be played hard against it. Notwithstanding, Captain Conviction, having got up close and receiving three wounds in the mouth, was driven back.

For the valor of these two captains, the Prince directed both to his pavilion for rest and refreshment. Likewise, care was extended to Captain Conviction so he should be healed of his wounds.[254]

On another front, however, Captain Good-Hope and Captain Charity did not fall behind in the conflict but behaved so well at Eye-gate that they had nearly broken through it.

Several of Diabolus's officers were slain in battle. There was Captain Boasting,[255] who thought no one could shake the posts of Ear-Gate. There was Captain Secure,[256] who used to boast the blind and lame were able to hold the gates against Emmanuel. There was Captain Bragman,[257] a very desperate fellow, who was captain over a band that threw firebrands, arrows, and death, and then was mortally wounded by Captain Good-Hope. Still another casualty was Mr. Feeling,[258] not a captain, but a great stickler encouraging Mansoul to rebellion. And there was Willbewill who from this point on seemed woefully daunted and unable to do as he used to do. Some said he received a wound in the leg. Some in the Prince's army saw him limping as afterwards he walked on the wall.

There was no accounting of the soldiers slain in the town. Many were maimed, wounded, and slain. When people saw the posts at Ear-gate shaken and Eye-gate nearly broken open, and that their captains were slain, it took away the hearts of many Diabolonians.

Many fell by shot sent by the golden slings into the midst of the town. Of the townsmen, one Love-no-Good[259] received a mortal wound and died soon afterward.

---

[253] Ephesians 6:17

[254] Psalms 27:14; 127:2; Isaiah 14:3

[255] Boasting: Psalm 10:2-4; Proverbs 27:1; James 4:16-17

[256] Secure: Psalm 52:1-9; Isaiah 36:6

[257] Bragman: Proverbs 27:1-3

[258] Feeling: 1 Samuel 18:5-9

[259] Love-no-Good: 2 Timothy 3:3

There, too, was Mr. Ill-pause who received a grievous wound in the head, some saying his brainpan was cracked. He was not the same afterwards. Moreover, old Prejudice and Mr. Anything fled.

When the battle was over, the Prince commanded that once more the white flag should be set upon Mount Gracious in sight of the town of Mansoul, to show that, even so, Emmanuel had grace for the wretched town.[260]

However, when Diabolus saw the flag, realizing it was not for him, he cast in his mind to play another prank to see if Emmanuel would lift his siege and begone on Diabolus's promise of reformation. One evening, while the sun was gone down, Diabolus went down to the gate and called out to Emmanuel.

"Forasmuch as you are given to peace, I want you to know we are ready to accept your terms. I know you are given to devotion. I know that holiness pleases you. Yes, and the great end to making war upon Mansoul is that it may be your holy habitation. Draw off your forces and I will bend Mansoul to your bow. I will lay down all acts of hostility. I am even willing to become your deputy. More particularly, I will persuade Mansoul to receive you as Lord. I will show them where they have erred. I will show them the holy law to which they must conform. I will press on them the necessity of a reformation according to your laws. That none of these things may fail, I, at my own cost, will set up and maintain a sufficient ministry, besides lectures, in Mansoul for their care and edification. Then, year by year, we shall provide you with a token of our subjection to you – whatever you think fit!"[261]

"O Diabolus, full of deceit, I have no need of your help!" Emmanuel exclaimed, "how movable are your ways![262] How often you keep changing and changing and changing just to keep possession of Mansoul! I am the rightful heir! Each time you make a proposal none is better than the last.

"You think you can get somewhere by transforming yourself into an angel of light?"[263] Emmanuel parried. "You the head of a reformation? You the corrector of vice? You the consummate tutor? Is this the last card

---

[260] Ephesians 2:8-9

[261] "Note the resourcefulness of the devil. Heretics do not advertise their errors . . . So, the devil masquerades all his devices and activities. He puts on white to make himself look like an angel of light. He is astoundingly clever to sell his patent poison for the Gospel of Christ . . . ¶The devil knows better than to appear ugly . . . He prefers to carry on his nefarious activities in the name of God. Hence the German proverb: 'All mischief begins in the name of God'" Martin Luther, *Commentary on Galatians*, trans. by Theodore Graebner (Digireads.com Publishing, 2019), content on Galatians 1:7; p. 20.

[262] Psalm 10:7

[263] 2 Corinthians 11:14

you must play? Eventually all will come to know you as the one with the cloven foot![264]

"No way with my Mansoul, O Diabolus," Emmanuel exclaimed. "I do love my Mansoul! I haven't come just to put Mansoul through some works to live by. I am come that they may be reconciled to my Father.[265]

"You talk of subjecting this town to good. Really, none desire it at your hands. I am sent to possess it myself and to guide it by the skillfulness of my hands.

"I will set up mine own standard amid them. I will govern them by new laws, new officers, new motives, and new ways. I will pull down this town and build it again; it shall be as though it had not been, and it shall then be the glory of the whole universe."[266]

PRAYER STARTER: *Almighty God, be with us in times we are taunted and tempted by conniving voices. Be with us through the petty struggles of daily life which, like grains of sand, would wear us down. There is such a play of voices that would possess us at whatever level they can. Help us in you to know a wise and discerning hope for a tattered and tottering world.* [From here on continue with your own prayerful words.] *In Jesus' name, we pray. Amen.*

The Conquest

1 Corinthians 13:6-7: It reioyceth not in iniquitie, but reioyceth in the trueth: It Suffreth all things: it beleueth all things: it hopeth all things: it endureth all things (GEN, 1560).

It rejoiceth not in iniquity, but rejoiceth in the truth: It suffereth all things: it believeth all things: it hopeth all things: it endureth all things (GNV, 1599).

Realizing he was caught in his deceits, Diabolus became utterly befuddled. However, this boiling pot of iniquity, malice, and rage set out to strengthen himself afresh for battle and to do whatever mischief possible. It was not the health and happiness of Mansoul he designed.[267] It was its ut-

---

[264] Leviticus 11:26

[265] 2 Corinthians 5:18

[266] Jeremiah 30:1-31:40 [The Book of Consolation]; Romans 12:2

[267] Ephesians 6:11 – "Satan, in destroying humanity, may not think that he can *still* ascend God's throne in battle. He may be fighting as many of God's creatures as possible before going down in the end" Walter Martin, Jill Martin Rische and Kurt Van Gorden, *The Kingdom of the Occult* (Nashville, Tennessee: Thomas Nelson, 2008), 5.

ter overthrow and ruination. Consequently, he commanded his officers to deliver whatever harm they could.[268] Then, if they got to a position where they could not hold onto Mansoul, they were to leave it in utter ruin.[269]

On another flank of the battlefield, Emmanuel turned to his officers, high captains, and men of war, advising them to show themselves strong against Diabolus and the Diabolonians, yet favorable, merciful, and meek to the old inhabitants of Mansoul.[270]

As the day of battle came and the command was given, the Prince's army bravely stood to their arms and bent their main force against Ear-gate and Eye-gate with the battle cry: "Mansoul is won!"

Diabolus displayed incredible resistance from within the walls while his high lords and chief captains hammered away against the Prince's army with disconcerting cruelty. After three or four notable charges, though, the Prince and his captains broke through Ear-gate, its bars and bolts splintered into a thousand pieces, which drove Diabolus further back into his hold. The Prince then established his throne onsite and placed his standard upon Mount Hear-well[271] and, from that vantage point, commanded the golden slings to keep playing on the town, especially against the castle.

For the meantime, Prince Emmanuel directed Captain Boanerges, Captain Conviction and Captain Judgment to head down a street to the house of Mr. Conscience, who was the Recorder before Diabolus took Mansoul, his house being nearly as strong as the castle. When they came to the house and demanded entrance, the old gentleman, so frightened and confused, kept the gates fast shut. Then, despite one strike of the battering ram after another, the fellow, seriously shaken and trembling, did not dare to open his gate. Be as it may, he came down and, with quivering lips, asked who was there.

"We are the captains and commanders of the great Shaddai and the blessed Emmanuel," Boanerges responded. "We demand possession of

---

[268] Text and Song Interactional: Jeff Pardo, Matthew Joseph West and Anne Wilson, songwriters, "I Still Believe in Christmas," by Anne Wilson, released 2021

[269] John Wesley on Evil Angels: "It is well for mankind that God hath set them their bounds which they cannot pass. He hath said to the fiercest and strongest of the apostate spirits, 'Hitherto shalt thou come, and no farther.' Otherwise, how easily and how quickly might one of them overturn the whole frame of nature! How soon would they involve all in one common ruin, or at least destroy man from the face of the earth. And they are indefatigable in their bad work" upon Ephesians 6:12 in Wesley's "Of Evil Angels" (Sermon 72), edited by Albert C. Outler, Volume 3, *The Works of John Wesley* series (Nashville: Abingdon Press, 1986), I.5.

[270] Matthew 5:5, 7

[271] Mt. Hear-well: Deuteronomy 12:28; Ezekiel 44:4-6; Luke 6:27

your house for our noble Prince's use." With that, the battering-ram struck at the gate once again, which made the old gentleman tremble even more.

Strategically, the Recorder's house was a most convenient nerve and assault center for Emmanuel's communication and military intelligence. It fronted the castle. It was strong. It was large. The Mansoulian people easily knew its whereabouts. Stricken by such thundering beginnings, though, the Recorder was trembling still – hardly comprehending what Emmanuel was trying to convey.[272]

Lay upon this his own guilt feeling for the hand he did not play previously opposing Diabolus, Mr. Recorder moaned: "I had been silent when I should have spoken openly. True, I have suffered because of Diabolus. But alas! what now shall I do? Can there be anything to make compensation for these rebellions and treasons I committed?[273]

While things were happening in and around the old Recorder's house, Captain Execution was busy in other parts of the town, securing the back streets and the walls. Most specifically, he hunted Lord Willbewill sorely. Suffering him not to rest in any corner, the Captain pursued him so hard that it spun Willbewill's men off from him and got Willbewill himself to thrust his head into a hole.[274] Meanwhile, Captain Execution cut three of Lord Willbewill's officers down to the ground. One was old Mr. Prejudice who had his crown cracked in the mutiny. Another was Mr. Backward-to-all-but-naught,[275] an officer and captain of the two guns once mounted atop Ear-gate. Still another was Captain Treacherous,[276] an awfully vile man, with whom Willbewill had placed vast confidence. Furthermore, there was a great slaughter among Lord Willbewill's soldiers, all Diabolonians, but not one Mansoulian native was hurt.

Other feats of war were accomplished by other captains, as at Eye-gate, where Captain Good-Hope and Captain Charity were in charge. For instance, Captain Good-Hope slew Captain Blindfold,[277] the keeper of the gate, who led more than thousand men who fought with mauls. Captain Good-Hope's troops pursued Blindfold's men, slew many, wounded more, and made the rest hide their heads in corners. Among the casualties, there was old Ill-pause who had a beard that reached down to his waste – easily remembered as the orator for Diabolus who did much mischief in Mansoul – who fell by the hand of Captain Good-Hope.

---

[272] Ephesians 2:14-16
[273] Daniel 9:5
[274] Isaiah 2:19; 42:21-23
[275] Backward-to-all-but-naught: Psalm 70:1-3; Isaiah 1:4
[276] Treacherous: Psalm 25:3; Isaiah 21:2
[277] Blindfold: Luke 22:63-65

What shall I say? In these three days alone, there were many Diabolonians who died because of the war although many remained alive in Mansoul.

Now, the old Recorder, Lord Understanding and other notables around Mansoul came together with a petition confessing their sins to send to Emmanuel. They were awfully regretful they had offended his Majesty. They prayed that the Prince would spare their lives.[278] However, there came no answer from Emmanuel and the people, greatly troubled, continued feeling no relief.[279]

At some time during the siege, the castle gate which was called Impregnable was broken through and a way made up into Diabolus's hold. The tidings of such were sent down to Ear-gate and, oh, how the trumpets sounded, for at this time it seemed the war was nearing an end and Mansoul was about to be set free.

Emmanuel rose from his place, took his men of war who were in the most fit condition and marched up to the old Recorder's house. He held his countenance in such reserve that the people could not tell whether he was radiating love or hatred by his looks.[280] Certainly, if Emmanuel were bearing love for them, they would see it by the way he was carrying himself. As best as they could see, the Mansoulian people would talk of the comeliness of the Prince's person and how much in glory and valor he had outstripped the great ones of the world.[281] It seemed surface talk at this point, though. Alas, the poor hearts, their thoughts would chance upon all extremes like being tossed or whipped around by a whirlwind.[282]

On coming to the castle gates, Emmanuel commanded Diabolus to surrender. How loath was the beast when he came out into the open! How he shrank! How he cringed! And yet, how could he do otherwise? Next, at Emmanuel's command, Diabolus was fast bound in chains while he would be awaiting judgment, but Diabolus pled for Emmanuel not to send him into the deep but allow him to depart in peace. However, as Emmanuel led him into the marketplace and stripped Diabolus of his armor, the trumpets of the golden Prince kept sounding, the captains kept shouting, and the soldiers kept singing for joy. Consequently, Mansoul beheld the beginning of Emmanuel's triumph!

The wicked tyrant, Diabolus, stripped naked before the crowd, intentionally humiliated, was bound with chains to his chariot wheels. Still, the

---

[278] Psalm 38:17-18
[279] Amos 8:11
[280] Genesis 43:1-45:28; 50:15-21
[281] Hebrews 1:1-3
[282] James 1:6

atmosphere was so intense throughout the town no one could dismiss the fact that a violent resistance could erupt on Diabolus's behalf and storm the town.

The townsfolk, in their own quandary, spirits teetering back and forth between the heavens and earth, could not tell the outcome of their own lives. For now, as the brave Prince finished this phase of the conquest, Diabolus was driven away from the camp to inherit the parched places in a salt land, seeking rest, but finding none.[283]

After the battle, Captain Boanerges and Captain Conviction, both impressive men with faces like lions and voices like the roaring sea, stayed in Mr. Conscience's house. However, the town in continual hearts-aching kept wondering about their own future. The restless people neither knew what being at rest or ease, peace or hope, at all might mean.

What is more, the Prince did not stay in Mansoul. He went out to his royal pavilion in the camp, amid his Father's forces. At a fitting time, he sent orders to Captain Boanerges to call the townspeople to gather in the castle-yard to watch as Lord Understanding, Mr. Conscience and Lord Willbewill were taken, put into ward, and placed under strong guard, awaiting the time of Prince Emmanuel's pleasure concerning them would be known.

Daily life continued at an unsettled pace for Mansoul during this time in that the people did not know how Emmanuel would be dealing with any of them.

Were their former fears of Mansoul's ruin going to be confirmed? What death would they die? How long would they be in their dying? They even feared that Emmanuel would direct them into the deep, you know, the place of which Diabolus was so afraid of going.

Quite frankly, if the town notables were cut off, they were certain that their execution would be the beginning of others. Therefore, together with the men in prison they, pleading for clemency, prepared a petition to be carried by Mr. Would-live for the Prince and to read as follows:

"Great and wonderful Potentate, victor over Diabolus, and conqueror of the town of Mansoul, we, your miserable inhabitants of this most woeful corporation, do humbly beg that we may find favor in your sight and be spared according to the greatness of your mercy.[284]

Please do not let us die. Let us live in your sight. We are most willing to be your mere servants and, if you think proper, would gather our meat from

---

[283] Matthew 12:43-45
[284] Psalm 123:3

under your table."[285]

Mr. Would-live as the carrier handed the petition to the Prince, who then took it into his hand, and sent the petitioner away in silence. The lack of any response from the Prince affected Mansoul so greatly that they decided to prepare another petition.

Wondering if the deportment of the first petitioner had offended Emmanuel in one way or another, the people hoped to have Captain Conviction, instead of Mr. Would-live, carry the other.

Instead, the captain said that he did not dare petition Emmanuel for traitors. Nor would he advocate for rebels.

"Yet withal," said he, "our Prince is good, and you may adventure to send it by the hand of one of your town, provided he went with a rope about his head, and pleaded nothing but mercy."[286]

PRAYER STARTER: *All-knowing God, it seems we have been through so much and we have so greatly gone astray. Every day seems like a battle – indeed, is a battle. The ends we expected to see have suddenly shifted. Confusion reigns. We think we have known patience and longsuffering. What does all that mean anymore? Come, do come, to help, gracious God.* [From here on continue in your own prayerful words.] *In Jesus' name, we pray. Amen.*

The Awakening

Matthew 5:3-5: Bleffed are the poore in fpirit, for theirs is the kingdome of heauen. Bleffed are they that mourne: for they fhal be comforted. Bleffed are the meke: for they fhal inherite the earth (GEN, 1560).

Blessed are the poor in spirit, for theirs is the kingdom of heaven. Blessed are they that mourn: for they shall be comforted. Blessed are the meek: for they shall inherit the earth (GNV, 1599).

The Mansoulian citizens were in a jam. They hung on through fear amidst the delays if they could. Who next could they call upon to carry a

---

[285] Matthew 15:21-28

[286] 1 Kings 20:31-32; John Gray draws attention to "the gesture [regarding the ropes] in the light of the Bedouin custom whereby, in the negotiations for commutation in the convention of blood-revenge, the representative (wakīl) of the homicide appears before the avenger of blood in the attitude of a suppliant over whom he has the power of life and death, bareheaded, with the rope of his Bedouin headdress around his neck" John Gray, *I & II Kings* Commentary, 2nd Edition, The Old Testament Library, (Philadelphia: The Westminster Press, 1964, 1970), 429-430.

petition to Emmanuel? Almost everything up to this point seemed a fruit-less hope. The first messenger garnered no explicable response. Their second messenger simply bowed out. The Mansoulian people had to settle on someone. Reluctantly, they turned toward a neighbor's suggestion of Mr. Desires-awake[287] who lived in a humble cottage in town. Quite nicely his response came with no hesitation. "Why shouldn't I do something to save our town?"[288]

Briefed with instructions regarding how he should present himself, Mr. Desires-awake hurried off to the Prince's pavilion and asked to speak to his Majesty. Now Emmanuel appeared. Mr. Desires-awake fell face forward to the ground and cried out, "Oh that Mansoul might live before you!" and then presented the petition.

Upon reading it, the Prince – presumably moved – turned away and wept.[289] Then, he turned back to the man who all the time lay at his feet and, holding back his feelings, said, "Go to your place. I'll consider your requests."

Although besieged with a barrage of questions by the townspeople upon his return, Mr. Desires-awake insisted he must first go to the prison and report to the Lord Mayor, Lord Willbewill, and Mr. Recorder. Not content to be left hanging, a multitude flocked after him to catch whatever the messenger might have for the three imprisoned notables. At first sight, one could hardly help but notice the Lord Mayor's turning white as a cloud and Mr. Recorder's quaking.

Delivering the account of how he carried himself in Emmanuel's presence, Mr. Desires-awake concluded with something not much more than what the first messenger brought back: "Go your way. I will consider," said Emmanuel. Then, the messenger went on to tell how he was so moved by the Prince's beauty and glory. "Whoever appears in his presence must love him and fear him greatly."[290] Then, he tacked on a word: "I do not

---

[287] Desires-awake: Song of Solomon 8:4; Romans 13:11; Ephesians 5:14; Revelation 16:15

[288] "You do not need any book of instructions to teach you how to love your neighbor. All you have to do is to look into your own heart, and it will tell you how you ought to love your neighbor as yourself. ¶My neighbor is every person, especially those who need my help" Martin Luther, *Commentary on Galatians*, trans. by Theodore Graebner (Digireads. com Publishing, 2019), Galatians 5:14; p. 148.

[289] Genesis 42:24; 43:29-31; John 11:35

[290] John 1:14. John Bunyan's character Desires-awake's impression of Emmanuel, "love him" and "fear him," is an image similar to how C. S. Lewis depicts the Lion Aslan's not being safe, but good, in his Narnia children's series. The context from which I draw is C. S. Lewis's "What Happened after Dinner," in *The Lion, the Witch and the Wardrobe* as the children were discussing the nature of Aslan [the Christ figure] in the home of the

know how this will come out." Thus, the Mansoulian people were at a stand.

After the prisoners of note started mulling over the message, they started commenting on Emmanuel's words. The Lord Mayor suspected the answer did not take on a rugged face.[291] Willbewill said it betokened evil.[292] The Recorder insisted the message was one of death.[293]

In hopes of trying to sort everything out, some people could not hear much of anything clearly. Some caught one piece of a sentence and others caught another. Some latched onto what the messenger said while others laid onto the prisoners' remarks. All in all, no one had an accurate understanding of anything. Whatever anyone thought they had heard flew as a cacophony of jumbled voices in and about the town!

One would remark, "We must all be killed"; another, "We must all be saved"; and a third believed the Prince could bear no concern for Mansoul; while a fourth was certain that the prisoners would suddenly be put to death. Everyone stood upon the point that his or her take was the rightest of all others. Thus, no one knew what to rest the sole of his or her foot upon. With those who caught the story at its end, there was a blunt insistence the Prince would be putting Mansoul to the sword. Therefore, as the day wore on and it started getting dark, the Mansoulian people did not get much sleep that night, left to hang in sad bewilderment until the next morning.

As best as any could gather, all the hubbubs came through something the Recorder said, newsworthy as it may have seemed, that the Prince's response was a messenger of death. To put it bluntly, it was this that most fired up the town and instilled a fright in Mansoul. After all, in former times, people could count on Mr. Recorder. He was a seer and whatever he presented was equal to the best. But now, how to figure?

Increasingly so, Mansoul was beginning to feel the effects of their stubborn rebellion and unlawful resistance.[294] In fact, the effects of their guilt feelings and fear nearly swallowed them up. So, they drew up a third petition and, wow, did they pour their hearts out!

"Prince Emmanuel the Great, Lord of all worlds, and Master of mercy, we, your poor, wretched, miserable, dying town of Mansoul, confess unto your

---

beavers. "Ooh!" said Susan . . . "Is he – quite safe? I shall feel rather nervous about meeting a lion" . . . "Safe?" said Mr. Beaver . . . "'Course he isn't safe. But he's good. He's the King, I tell you."

[291] Ezekiel 3:7-9
[292] Revelation 2:4
[293] 2 Kings 1:15-17; Proverbs 16:14
[294] Isaiah 30:1

great and glorious Majesty we have sinned against your Father and you and are no more worthy to be called your Mansoul, but rather to be cast into the pit. If you will slay us, we have deserved it. If you will condemn us to the deep, we cannot but say you are righteous. We cannot complain whatever you may carry out toward us. But, oh! let mercy reign, and let it be extended to us! Let mercy take hold of us, and free us from our transgressions, and we will sing of your mercy and judgment. Amen."[295]

After the wording was fine-tuned and completed there came the perennial question of who should be the carrier?

On the suggestion there was an old man in the town, Mr. Good-Deed, who could carry the message to the Prince, the Recorder was quick to raise an objection that the old fellow was not the one who should go since he was a man who bore only the name of goodness but had nothing of its nature.[296]

"Just say, this guy is standing before the Prince and has to identify himself and the Prince cannot help but chafe, 'Send him back to where he came from and let what the people know of Good-Deed's trying to save them!'"

With old Good-Deed dropped from the picture,[297] the Mansoulian notables turned back to Mr. Desires-awake who asked they allow Mr. Wet-Eyes, a poor man of a broken spirit,[298] to accompany him to approach Emmanuel.

Mr. Desires-awake, with a rope drawn upon his head, and Mr. Wet-Eyes, wringing his hands – both hoping not to be a burden to anyone – trudged toward the Prince's pavilion. Plain from the start they did not want to trouble Emmanuel with any intrusion or surfacy talk, the two emphasized they were coming out of great necessity. They sincerely realized their people's transgressions against Shaddai were abundant. Desires-awake also apologized if he had come across improperly the last time which may have offended his Holiness. Thenceforth, casting himself prostrate upon the ground, he, with trembling hand, delivered the petition.[299]

As before, the Prince read the petition, turned aside awhile, then came back to the petitioner laying on the ground, and demanded his name and how he was so esteemed in the town of Mansoul that he, instead of any other, had been chosen to be the carrier of such a message.

---

[295] Psalms 100:5; 101:1

[296] Good-Deed: Ezekiel 36:30-32

[297] Titus 3:5

[298] Wet-Eyes: Psalm 51:17; Isaiah 61:1-3; Luke 4:17-19

[299] Matthew 5:3

"Oh! please, let not my Lord be angry," Desires-awake pleaded. "Take no great notice of me. Why the townspeople chose me is best known to them. It cannot be that they thought I posed some great advantage with you. Indeed, there is such a great distance between who I am and who you are. Quite bluntly, the townsfolk and I are guilty of great transgressions. I have come in their name to beg my Lord for mercy."[300]

Then, at this point, Prince Emmanuel asked Desires-awake to state who his companion was in this weighty matter.

"He is poor Wet-Eyes, one of my neighbors. I know there are many of such a name who are nothing. Take some people. Tears come so showy. Not with Mr. Wet-Eyes! I hope there is no offence I have brought this, my poor neighbor, with me."

"My Lord," said Wet-Eyes, "whether some have deemed my name something pretended or true, I got it because Mr. Repentance[301] was my father. I know that good people have badly behaved children and the sincere, at times, beget hypocrites. However, my mother called me by this name from the cradle.

"I do not know if it were because of the moistness of my brain or the softness of my heart. I see dirt in my own tears and filthiness in the bottom of my prayers.[302] I pray that you will not remember our transgressions against us any longer, and please do not take offence at how unqualified we are. Be merciful to Mansoul. Please do not hold from us your grace any longer."[303]

At this moment, the Prince, Emmanuel, addressed the two messengers as they stood trembling before him:

"The town of Mansoul grievously rebelled against my Father and chose a liar, a murderer, and a runagate slave, Diabolus, for their captain. Though timely discovered, apprehended and, for his wickedness, bound in chains and separated to the pit with his companions,[304] he offered himself to you, and you received him. This was and for a long time has been an extraordinary affront to my Father, wherefore my Father sent a powerful army to reduce your people to obedience. You know how this army – their captains and their counsels – were esteemed by you. You rebelled against them, *you shut your gates upon them,*[305] you bid them to do battle, and you fought for Diabolus against them. So, they sent to my Father for more power, and

---

[300] Psalm 25:7; Romans 3:23
[301] Repentance: 2 Corinthians 7:10
[302] James 4:10
[303] Micah 7:18
[304] Revelation 20:2-3
[305] Matthew 13:15

I, with my men came, but as you treated the servants, so you treated the Lord.[306] *You shut up your gates against me,* turned the deaf ear to me, and resisted if you had hopes you might prevail. And yet, I have conquered you, and you now have come to me for a favor! Why didn't you cry to me when I hung the white, red, and black flags[307] before? Despite all, I will consider your petition and answer it to bring me glory."[308]

Prince Emmanuel then directed Captain Boanerges and Captain Conviction to bring the prisoners into the camp to him tomorrow and have Captain Judgment and Captain Execution to stay in the castle until hearing further from him.

After this audience with the Prince, the petitioners set out on their way back to Mansoul again. On the way, their thoughts began to work upon them that no mercy was intended by the Prince to Mansoul.

Upon reaching the town gates and being met by the Mansoulian citizens eager to hear the news, Desires-awake and Wet-Eyes resisted saying anything at all, like how it had been handled the time before, until they would first provide the prisoners an accounting. Once again, their report gave the prisoners – indeed, the whole town – no clear sense of what was going to happen.

In the group that had gathered, however, there was this notable, sharp-witted fellow, old Inquisitive, who sought to pry for more information. Often there is someone like him around when there is a hot item at bay! "Is there something you left out?" he pressed upon them. Therefore, it was clarified that the three prisoners were to appear before Emmanuel for a more definitive unveiling the next day.

When the time had come, the prisoners, accompanied by Captain Boanerges and Captain Conviction, were bound in chains and, with drooping spirits, taken down to appear before Emmanuel. Having put ropes upon themselves, smiting their breasts with their fists, and crying out, "O unhappy men! O wretched men of Mansoul!" it was such a sad and heart-wrenching processional to witness.[309]

The townspeople, too, appeared on the wall all clad in mourning weeds, hoping that the sight of that might touch the Prince with compassion.

As the prisoners arrived at the Prince's pavilion, they threw themselves down prostrate upon the ground. Then, one entered the pavilion to tell the Prince the prisoners were present. Emmanuel ascended his throne of

---

[306] Matthew 21:33-44

[307] The white flag of Emmanuel's mercy, the red flag of justice, and the black flag that threatened execution.

[308] Lamentations 3:22-23a

[309] 1 Kings 20:31-32

state and sent for the prisoners. They came trembling before him, covering their faces with shame.[310] At the time that they threw themselves at his feet, Prince Emmanuel instructed Captain Boanerges to bid the prisoners to stand.

"Are you the ones who once had been servants of Shaddai?" – to which they said, "Yes." "Did you suffer yourselves to be corrupted and defiled by that abominable one, Diabolus?" – to which they responded, "We did more than suffer it, Lord. We chose it in our own mind." The Prince asked further, "Could you have been contented your slavery should have continued under his tyranny as long as you had lived?" – to which the prisoners responded again, "Yes, Lord, yes, for his ways were pleasing to our flesh; and we were grown aliens to a better state." "Did you," said he, "when I came up against this town of Mansoul, heartily wish that I might not have the victory over you?" – "Yes, Lord, yes," they said. Then the Prince said, "what punishment do you think you deserve at my hand for these and other high and mighty sins?" – And they said, "Both death and the deep, Lord; for we have deserved no less." He asked again if they had anything else to say about the sentence they confessed they deserved to have passed onto them? – And they said, "We can say nothing, Lord, for you are just and we have sinned." Then, said the Prince, "And for what are those ropes about your heads?" – The prisoners answered, "These ropes are to bind us withal to the place of execution, if mercy be not pleasing in your sight." Moreover, he asked if all of Mansoul were resolved upon this confession as they were?" – They answered, "All the natives, Lord, except the Diabolonians who came into Mansoul when Diabolus gained possession of us, we can say nothing for them.[311]

At this point, the Prince commanded a herald to be called and to proclaim with the sound of the trumpet, that the Prince, the Son of Shaddai, in his Father's name and glory, had accomplished a perfect conquest and victory over Mansoul. The prisoners following him should say, "Amen."

Presently music in the upper region sounded melodiously, the captains shouted, the soldiers sang songs of triumph, the colors waved in the wind, and great joy was everywhere except in the hearts of the Mansoulian people.

At this point, Prince Emmanuel called for the prisoners to come and stand again before him and they did, trembling.

What came next, no one could have expected.[312]

---

[310] Psalm 119:120

[311] Proverbs 5:22

[312] Text and Song Interactional: Jason Ingram and Meredith Andrews, songwriters, "He

It started with Emmanuel's announcement: "For the sins, trespasses, and iniquities that you, with the whole town of Mansoul, have committed against my Father Shaddai and me, I have the power and commandment from my Father to forgive you and the town of Mansoul accordingly."[313]

So profoundly unsuspecting were they to hear the unbelievably gracious words!

Having proclaimed this the Prince gave the prisoners a large and general pardon, written on parchment and sealed with seven seals,[314] charging the Lord Mayor, Lord Willbewill and Mr. Recorder to proclaim the good news tomorrow, by the time the sun would be up, throughout the whole town of Mansoul.

PRAYER STARTER: *Lord, for too long, we have listened to the wrong voices. We've ignored you, resisted you, bolted against you? We have gone as far as we can down this dead-end street of deceptive promises. We now face the loneliness of not knowing what is next! How we yearn to understand your call upon our lives!* [From here on continue with your own prayerful words.] *In Jesus' name, we pray. Amen.*

A Beauty for Ashes

Isaiah 61:3: To appoint vnto thé that mourne in Zión, & to giue vnto thé beautie for afhes, the oyle of ioye for mourning, the garmét of gladnes for the fpirit of heauines, that thei might be called trees of righteoufnes, the planting of y Lord, that he might be glorified (GEN, 1560).

To appoint unto them that mourn in Zion, and to give unto them beauty for ashes, the oil of joy for mourning, the garment of gladness for the spirit of heaviness, that they might be called trees of righteousness, the planting of the Lord, that he might be glorified (GNV, 1599).

As the Lord Mayor, Lord Willbewill and Mr. Recorder were stripped of their mourning weeds, Emmanuel gave them beauty for ashes, the oil of

---

Has Come for Us (God Rest Ye Gentlemen)," a remake of a classic Christmas song, by Meredith Andrews, released 2017.

[313] "Did not Christ Himself say: 'I am the way, and the truth, and the life: no man cometh unto the Father, but by me'? Without Christ there is no access to the Father, but futile rambling; no truth, but hypocrisy; no life, but eternal death" Martin Luther, *Commentary on Galatians*, trans. by Theodore Graebner (Digireads.com Publishing, 2019), Galatians 1:3; p. 12.

[314] Revelation 5:1-10

joy for mourning, and the garment of praise for the spirit of heaviness.[315] He then bestowed on them jewels of gold and precious stones. He took away their ropes and put chains of gold about their necks and earrings in their ears.

When these three prisoners heard the gracious words and beheld all being done, they nearly fainted. The grace, the benefit, and the pardon were all so sudden, glorious, and expansive, they could not, without staggering, stand up under it. Lord Willbewill swooned outright.

The Prince stepped up to him, put his everlasting arms under him, embraced him, kissed him, and bid him be of good cheer.[316] He also kissed, embraced, and smiled upon the other two. Right before their faces, their fetters were broken into pieces which were flung into the air and their steps were enlarged.[317]

Accompanied by one playing the tabor and pipe, they were directed to rise and go into the town to tell everyone what the Prince had done.[318] Then was fulfilled that for which they had never looked as they came to possess what they had never dreamed.[319]

The Prince then called for Captain Credence and his officers to march with flying colors into the town. The Recorder was to read the general pardon aloud to the people. Captain Credence, with his ten thousand's, was to march into Mansoul through Eye-gate and, by way of high street to take possession of the castle for his Lord.

Meanwhile, as Mansoul was delivered from the terror of the first four captains,[320] Captain Judgment and Captain Execution were to leave the stronghold to Captain Credence, withdraw from Mansoul, and return to the camp.

On the other hand, the townspeople were severely absorbed with expecting judgment and death. The prickling of thorns, a wind blowing with great uncertainties, or a balance disquieted by a shaking hand were but a clumsy set of metaphors with which one might grasp their feelings. For so long, the Mansoulian people kept looking over the wall to catch a glimpse – even a peep – of someone (anyone!) coming from the Prince's camp. They then beheld something they in no way expected. As they watched the prisoners returning, it was hard to decipher the difference between what they had been awaiting and what they were now seeing.

---

[315] Psalm 30:11-12; Isaiah 61:2-4
[316] Deuteronomy 33:27
[317] Psalm 18:36
[318] John 4:28-30
[319] Ephesians 1:3-8
[320] Captains Boanerges, Conviction, Judgment, and Execution

The prisoners who had gone down to the camp dressed in black were now coming back dressed in white.[321] They had gone down to the camp in ropes. They were coming back in chains of gold. They had gone down scuffling with their feet in fetters. They were coming back with their footsteps enlarged beneath them.[322] They had gone down looking for death. They were coming back with the assurance of life.[323] They had gone down with heavy hearts. They were coming back to the sounds of the pipe and tabor.[324] As soon as they reached Eye-gate, the poor and tottering town of Mansoul ventured to give out a shout. Alas! for them, poor hearts! Who could blame them? Those they thought dead had come to life![325]

As the three prisoners went away to the judgment of Emmanuel expecting nothing but the axe and the block, something so different than what they had feared had now come to be – joy and gladness, comfort and consolation, the melodious notes of music attending them – sufficient to make the extremely sick well![326]

Upon their arrival, the people saluted each other. "Welcome, welcome! Blessed be the one who has spared you! We see it is well with you, but how must it go with Mansoul?"

The Recorder ready to respond exclaimed: "Oh! tidings! Glad tidings! Tidings of great joy to poor Mansoul!"[327]

They then gave a shout that made the earth ring.

"Tell us, tell us more, tell us more particularly," they pled.

As Mansoul was told all that had happened, the people at first were confounded regarding the wisdom and grace of the Prince.[328]

Nonetheless, how the people were exhilarated! "Pardon, Pardon, Pardon for Mansoul," they cried. This would be more fully expressed in the marketplace on the very next day!

Another sleepless night, but for wholly different reasons. There was no one in Mansoul who could sleep easily for the joy that the people felt. In every Mansoulian house, there was joy, music, singing, and making merry![329]

---

[321] Revelation 3:5

[322] 2 Samuel 22:37; Psalm 18:36

[323] Hebrews 10:22

[324] 1 Samuel 10:5

[325] Galatians 3:20

[326] Isaiah 33:24

[327] Psalm 98:4; Luke 2:10

[328] Luke 4:22

[329] Text and Song Interactional: Edward Mote, Eric Liljero, Jonas Myrin and Reuben Morgan, "Cornerstone" (a remake of a 19th-century Gospel Hymn, "My Hope Is Built," originally by Edward Mote and William B. Bradbury), currently sung by Hillsong Worship,

How yesterday would any have thought that tomorrow, at the rising of the sun, would become such a day?[330]

Who would have thought, upon seeing the prisoners go down to the camp in irons, they would be coming back with chains of gold? Who would have thought, upon their going down to face the Judge, they would be coming back acquitted, not because they were innocent, but because of the Prince's mercy?

Still, there was the wonderment: Was this the common custom of such princes?

No, but this was particular for this Prince Emmanuel and Shaddai!

As morning drew on apace, the Lord Mayor, the Lord Willbewill, and Mr. Recorder went down to the marketplace, the customary place for the reading of public matters, at the time the Prince had appointed and just where the people were eagerly waiting.

The Recorder beckoned with his hand for silence and then proceeded to read with a loud voice Emmanuel's pardon: "The Lord, the Lord God, merciful and gracious, pardons iniquity, transgressions, and sins; and to his people all manner of sin and blasphemy shall be forgiven."

Hardly able to contain themselves, the people could not forbear leaping and skipping for joy. "Let Emmanuel live forever!" they shouted.[331]

The young men were directed to go and ring the bells. So, the bells did ring, the people sang, and the music went in every house throughout Mansoul.

As the Recorder finished reading the pardon, all the trumpets in Emmanuel's camp sounded while the colors were boldly displayed – half of them upon Mount Gracious and half of them upon Mount Justice – all in accord with Emmanuel's direction.[332]

After this, Emmanuel, the Prince, commanded his captains and soldiers to show Mansoul some of their feats of war. But oh! with what agility, liveliness, nimbleness, quickness, and dexterity, did these warriors display their impressive skill before an awe-stricken town! The soldiers marched, counter-marched; opened to the right and left; divided and subdivided; closed, wheeled, made good their front and rear with their right and left wings, and twenty more things, with an aptness that ravished the hearts of the people beholding it.

Australia, released 2012.

[330] Psalm 143:8

[331] Exodus 34:6; Psalm 85:2; Mark 3:28

[332] Jeremiah 33:8

When this was over, Mansoul came out as one to the Prince to thank him and praise him and beg him to take up his quarters with them forever. If Emmanuel should withdraw, the people feared, who could say what mischief Diabolus and any remaining Diabolonians might wreak upon them. "O thou, the desire of our eyes and the strength of our lives, accept this motion we have made, and come and dwell in the midst of us, and let us be your people forever!"[333]

At this point, the Prince responded: "If I come into your town, will you keep with me to prosecute that which is against my heart and yours?"

"We do not know what we would do," the people responded with honesty. "We had no idea we would be such traitors to Shaddai in the beginning. What shall we say now? Please do come and dwell in our castle. Make our town a garrison. Let your noble captains and warlike soldiers be over us. Conquer us with your love. Overcome us by your grace. Be with us and help us.

"We do not know the depth of your wisdom, O Emmanuel. Who could have thought so much sweetness would have come through such bitter trials![334]

"Lord, let your light go before us. Let your love come after us. Take us by your hand and lead us by your counsels.[335] O, Lord, we are your servants; let all things be for the best. Do come to our Mansoul. Do what you will. Keep us from sinning and make us serviceable to your Majesty."

At this, Emmanuel responded: "Go, return to your houses in peace. I willingly comply with your desires. I will draw up my forces before Eye-gate tomorrow. I will possess your castle and set my soldiers over you. I will do in Mansoul things which cannot be paralleled in any nation, country or kingdom under heaven."[336]

The people of Mansoul gave out a shout and returned to their houses in peace. What is more, they told their families and friends what the good Emmanuel promised to do!

In preparation for the Prince's taking up residence, the inhabitants went out to the green trees in the meadows to gather boughs and flowers that they would strew upon the streets down which the Son of Shaddai should come. They also made garlands and other fine works to betoken how joyful they were. These were spread from the Eye-gate to the castle gate. Moreover, they prepared what music they might play before him.

---

[333] Psalm 73:25-26
[334] Isaiah 38:17
[335] Psalm 31:3-5
[336] Leviticus 26:11-12

As Emmanuel made his approach, the walls of Mansoul filled with the trampling of its inhabitants to view the approach of the blessed Prince. Also, the casements, windows, balconies, and tops of the houses filled with all sorts of people.

By the time Emmanuel reached the Recorder's house, he commanded one should go to Captain Credence to see whether the castle was prepared for Emmanuel's royal presence.

On the other hand, the townsfolk cared in their deliberating how the Prince's captains and soldiers might be quartered among them. To serve their Lord with gladness, nothing would grieve the people more than appearing as if there was not enough room.[337] They counted it their glory to be waiting upon them. Hospitality was lavish.

The results: Captain Innocency should quarter at Mr. Reason's. Captain Patience should quarter at Mr. Mind's. Captain Charity should quarter at Mr. Affection's. Captain Good-Hope should quarter at the Lord Mayor's. Captain Boanerges and Captain Conviction should take up their quarters with the Recorder as his house was next to the castle. Lord Willbewill would take Captain Judgment and Captain Execution in because he was to rule under the Prince for the good of the town.[338] The rest of the town would quarter Emmanuel's forces. Captain Credence and his men would abide in the castle.

Now, the ancients and elders of Mansoul raised the concern that they never would have enough of Prince Emmanuel. Although the castle was his place of residence, they prayed he would often visit their streets, houses, and people. For his presence, looks, smiles, and words would be the life, strength, and sinews of the town. Essentially, the people yearned to have continual access to him.

Now, at this time, Emmanuel made a feast for the whole town of Mansoul. When the day arrived, the townsfolk came to the castle to partake of all kinds of outlandish delights – produce that grew nowhere throughout any of the fields of Mansoul nor from anywhere else throughout the Kingdom of Universe. It was food that came from his Father's court. There was dish after dish set before them which they were welcomed freely to eat.[339] When a fresh dish was brought in, the people would whisperingly ask one another what it was, for they did not know what to call it.[340]

---

[337] Psalm 100:2-3
[338] Romans 6:19
[339] Luke 14:12-14
[340] Exodus 16:15

It is hard to imagine how scrumptious what they had experienced! The people drank of the water that was turned to wine.[341] They ate angels' food and enjoyed honey that came out of the rock.[342] They were merry with the food and drink peculiar to court.[343] There were musicians at this table. They were not of the country in or around Mansoul. They were masters of the songs which were sung at the court of Shaddai.[344]

After the banquet, Prince Emmanuel entertained the town with curious riddles – secrets drawn up by his Father's Secretary with the skill and wisdom of Shaddai. When speaking about their wars and doings for Mansoul, Emmanuel blessed the people with insights they never would have known. How the people were amazed such rarities could have been couched in so few and ordinary words! The words were a portraiture of Emmanuel himself and while looking into his face, it all dawned on them. "This is the lamb![345] This is the sacrifice![346] This is the rock![347] This is the red cow![348] This is the door![349] And this is the way with many other things!"[350]

Oh, how the people, upon turning toward home, were transported with joy, and drowned with wonderment, while they saw, understood, and considered what mysteries Emmanuel opened to them.[351] And yet, once home, they could not help but sing, even in their sleep, of him and what he did.

It was in Prince Emmanuel's heart to remodel the town of Mansoul, by putting it into a condition as would be most pleasing, profitable, and secure for all. Emmanuel also provided a system against insurrections at home and invasions from abroad, for such a love as he had for them.

Strengthening its defenses, Emmanuel commanded the great slings to be mounted upon some of the battlements of the castle. There was also an instrument invented by Emmanuel to cast stones out from Mouth-gate. It was a warhead that would not miss, nor could it be resisted. This was committed to the care of, and to be managed by Captain Credence in case of war. Lord Willbewill was to take care of the gates, wall, and towers, and, with the militia, withstand all insurrections and tumults that might rise

---

[341] John 2:1-11
[342] Deuteronomy 32:13; Psalm 81:16
[343] Exodus 16:15; Psalm 78:24-25
[344] Luke 15:22-25
[345] John 1:29; 1 Peter 1:18-20
[346] Hebrews 10:11-13
[347] Exodus 33:21-22; Deuteronomy 8:15; Psalms 27:5; 40:2; 105:41; Matthew 7:24-25; 16:18; 1 Corinthians 10:4
[348] Numbers 19:2
[349] John 10:7, 9
[350] John 14:6
[351] Proverbs 25:2; Matthew 13:52; Luke 8:10; Romans 1:19-20

against the King and the peace and tranquility of the people. Moreover, upon finding Diabolonians lurking in any corner of the town, he should apprehend and commit them to safe custody.

The old Lord Mayor, Lord Understanding, was reinstated to his former office. In fact, it became his lifelong appointment. Emmanuel directed him to build a palace near Eye-gate, fashioning it like a tower of defense. He, as well, should read in the Revelation of Mysteries all the days of his life, that he might know how to perform his office aright.[352]

Emmanuel made Mr. Knowledge[353] the new Recorder, not because of contempt for the old Mr. Conscience, but because he had other employment for him which the old gentleman eventually should know.

Then Emmanuel commanded the image of Diabolus to be taken down, destroyed, beat into powder, and cast to the wind,[354] while the image of Shaddai was to be set up again on the castle gates.

Consequently, Shaddai's image should be more fairly drawn than previously, since Emmanuel and his Father had come to the town of Mansoul in more grace and mercy.[355] Moreover, his name should be engraved on the face of the town, as well.[356]

PRAYER STARTER: *Oh, Lord, how often something great, wonderful, and beautiful springs up in unlikely ways. It is all your doing! Thank you, so much, gracious Lord. Stay with us forever. Guide us, direct us, protect us, as you already have redeemed and nourished us. Day by day, teach us the wonders of your love.* [From here on continue in your own prayerful words.] *In Jesus' name, we pray. Amen.*

A Day in Court

Proverbs 15:3; 23:23: The eyes of the Lord in euerie place beholde the euil and the good . . . Bye the trueth, but fel it not: likewife wifdome, and inftruction, and vnderftading (GEN, 1560).

The eyes of the Lord in every place behold the evil and the good . . . Buy the truth, but sell it not: likewise wisdom, instruction, and understanding

---

[352] Romans 16:25; Revelation 1:1-5, 20
[353] Exodus 31:3; Psalms 19:2; 49:3; Proverbs 1:7; 2:10-15; 3:20; 9:10; 18:5; Ecclesiastes 7:14; 12:9; Isaiah 7:15; Jeremiah 3:15; Habakkuk 2:14; Romans 11:33; 1 Corinthians 1:5; 12:8; 13:2, 8-12; 2 Corinthians 4:6
[354] Exodus 32:20
[355] Romans 5:20; Colossians 1:12-14
[356] Revelation 22:4

(GNV, 1599).

Emmanuel gave the command that three Diabolonians, e.g., the two Lords Mayor of late – to wit, Mr. Incredulity and Mr. Lustings – as well as Mr. Forget-Good, the Recorder, be tried in a court of law. What is more, there were several burgesses and aldermen that were to be brought before the court, too.

The aldermen facing trial were Atheism, Hard-Heart, and False-Peace and the burgesses facing trial were: No-Truth, Pitiless, and Haughty. The gaoler[357] commissioned to keep them in close custody was Mr. True-Man – a man brought from Shaddai's court when he at first made war upon Diabolus.

Therefore, those to come before the judge and facing the court for sentencing on that day appeared on the following list (all being intruders upon the town of Mansoul):

Incredulity	Lustings	Forget-Good
Atheism	False-Peace	Hard-Heart
Haughty	No-Truth	Pitiless

Meanwhile, Emmanuel gave the order that the three strongholds Diabolus had the Diabolonians build must be demolished and utterly cleared away – a rather formidable job because of the largeness of the place and the stones, timber, iron, and rubbish to be carried outside the town.

The day of the trial came. The court was set and Mr. True-Man, gaoler, was directed to bring the prisoners, pinioned, and chained together to the bar. Thence, they stood before the Lord Mayor, the Recorder, and the rest of the honorable bench. Mr. Do-Right[358] served as the Town-Clerk. The twelve jury members empaneled were Mr. Belief,[359] True-heart,[360] Upright,[361] Hate-Bad,[362] Love-God,[363] See-Truth,[364] Heavenly-Mind,[365]

---

[357] British for jailor

[358] Do-Right: Deuteronomy 6:18; 12:28; 13:18; 21:8-9; Psalms 82:3; 106:3; Revelation 22:14

[359] Belief: Romans 10:4, 9-11, 14, 16

[360] True-heart: Psalm 125:4; Hebrews 10:22

[361] Upright: Genesis 6:9; Deuteronomy 18:13; Psalm 119:80

[362] Hate-Bad: 2 Samuel 13:22; Psalm 119:113

[363] Love-God: 1 John 4:7-12, 16, 20-21; 5:2-3

[364] See-Truth: Psalm 98:3; John 6:14; 14:17; 2 Corinthians 12:5-7

[365] Heavenly-Mind: Psalms 42:1-4; 63:1; 143:6; Colossians 3:1-2

Moderate,[366] Thankful,[367] Good-Work,[368] Zeal-for-God,[369] and Humble.[370] The sworn witnesses were Mr. Know-All,[371] Tell-True,[372] and Hate-Lies;[373] Willbewill and his man would be witnesses, if needed. What follows summarizes the proceedings. [For contrasting observations from a respected, present-day trial attorney, see Appendix Two, for remarks by Lynda Ashbery Dodd, 229-230.]

At the direction of the Clerk, Mr. Atheism was sworn in. Questioned upon whether he perniciously and doltishly maintained there was no God,[374] Mr. Atheism blurted out: "Not guilty!"

He was a shifty soul! The Crier then summoned Mr. Know-All to come forward. "Yes, for many years, I have come to know Atheism as a pestilent fellow. There was even a time we were in Villain's Lane together. I could not help but notice how he could talk so briskly and pipe so many different opinions. Why! although he did not believe in God, he even said he could be religious, depending on the circumstances. Next, Mr. Tell-True stepped up to the bench and owned up to the fact he once had been one of Mr. Atheism's companions − "but I repented of that!" he quickly interjected. "There was a time in Blasphemer's Row[375] − and other places, too − I heard Atheism avow there was no God, angel or spirit. Clearly, Atheism is a Diabolonian, son of that Diabolonian, Never-be-good,[376] who had more children just like him." Wrapping up this round of the testimony, Mr. Hate-Lies came forward and added Mr. Atheism was one of the vilest wretches with whom he had ever been associated. "I've even heard him say that it was as good to go to a whore-house as to go to hear a sermon!" When asked where he heard this, he said: "On Drunkard's Row[377] just at end of Rascal-Lane, in Mr. Impiety's house."

After Mr. Atheism's sentencing, the Clerk of the court called Mr. Lustings to the bar, facing charges of devilishly and traitorously teaching it was

---

[366] Moderate: 1 Corinthians 6:12; Galatians 5:13; Philippians 4:5

[367] Thankful: Psalm 33:1; Ephesians 5:20; Colossians 3:15; Hebrews 11:13

[368] Good-Work: Psalms 73:28; 145:9; Matthew 5:16; Mark 14:6; Acts 9:36

[369] Zeal-for-God: Numbers 25:13; Psalm 146:1

[370] Humble: Leviticus 16:31; 2 Chronicles 7:14; Psalm 25:9; Proverbs 29:23; Micah 6:8; Matthew 18:4; 23:12; Luke 14:11; Philippians 2:8; James 4:6; 1 Peter 5:6

[371] Know-All: Psalm 67:2; Proverbs 8:8-10; 1 Corinthians 1:5; 2 Peter 1:5

[372] Tell-True: 1 Kings 22:16; John 8:14

[373] Hate-Lies: Proverbs 13:5; 2 John 1:3-9

[374] Psalm 14:1

[375] Blasphemer's Row: Psalm 119:41-43; 1 Timothy 1:13

[376] Never-be-good: Mark 14:21

[377] Drunkard's Row: Deuteronomy 21:20; Proverbs 23:20; 26:9; Nahum 1:10; 1 Corinthians 5:11; 6:10

lawful and profitable to give way to one's own carnal desires.[378] He was a man of high birth and very used to the pleasures and pastimes that came with his self-perceived greatness.

"I should be left alone," he exclaimed, "to follow my own will in whatever pleases me." And then, with a filthy expletive or two, as was normal with the man, he thought it strange he should have to face such interrogation. "Besides," he thought, "all men, either secretly or openly, love, do, and approve of such doings."

At this point, however, the Clerk responded, "Sir, we are not concerned with your sense of greatness, but about how you have been behaving.[379] Regarding the indictment brought against you: How say you? Guilty or not?" To which Mr. Lustings gave a customarily clipped response: "Not guilty!"

The court called Mr. Know-All forward as a witness. "Yes, my Lord, I know the fellow. He is Lustings, the son of Beastly,[380] whose mother, Evil-Concupiscence's daughter,[381] bore him in Flesh Street.[382] I knew the whole family. And, yes, as he said, he is a great man, but greater in wickedness than by pedigree. I know him to be a swearer, a liar, a Sabbath-breaker, as well as a fornicator. He is one guilty of an abundance of evils.[383] Quite bluntly – an extremely filthy man."[384] Asked to help with additional specifics, Tell-Truth, who concurred with Know-All, pointed out Mr. Lustings' wickedness was this and more – indeed, it was known throughout all of the town.

Given a chance to express himself, Mr. Lustings muttered: "I was ever of the estimation that the happiest man around was the one to keep back from nothing he desired in the whole world. I have lived in the love of my notions all my days. Nor was I ever coarse, having found such sweetness in them, as to reap the praises of others."

And with this, the court broke off any further cross-examination, saying it had enough – enough by Mr. Lustings's own mouth – and they needed to move on! Then, they brought Mr. Incredulity forward.

When addressed as an officer previously tied closely with Diabolus and fighting against King Shaddai, Incredulity with briskness pressed: "I do not know Shaddai. I love my old prince Diabolus. To be true, my trust,

---

[378] James 1:15
[379] Luke 12:48
[380] Ezekiel 21:31
[381] Evil-Concupiscence's daughter: Colossians 3:5
[382] Flesh Street: Galatians 5:16-17; 6:8
[383] Exodus 20:8; Hosea 4:2; 10:4; 1 Corinthians 5:9-11
[384] Colossians 3:5-6

my duty was to resist strangers and foreigners with might. Nor have I, nor shall I! through fear, change my view, though you presently hold the power in this place."[385]

It was a brusque moment. "The man," court resolved, "is an incorrigible unbeliever! Quite clearly, he is a villain – downright rebellious and with impudent confidence!"

Next, Forget-Good was brought before the court, charged with utterly forgetting to serve the people in what was good and, consequently, falling in with Diabolus against Shaddai.

"But, gentlemen," Forget-Good implored, "As to that of which I'm several times accused, I ask you please to attribute this so-called problem to my age and not my willfulness. I hope, by your charity, I may be excused from punishment, although you think I am guilty.

At this point, the court, not willing to buy into what Forget-Good was posing, laid out the case: "Your forgetfulness was not frailty. It was of purpose. Do not think you can blindside the court. You would not hesitate at wallowing in the bad when you could be pointing out the good. Your age and pretended craziness are a cloak to cover your knavery. To try to be fair, we'll listen to the witnesses."

Mr. Hate-bad came forward, saying he heard the accused say he could not abide thinking of goodness, not even for a quarter of an hour. He said he heard it in All-base Lane at the house next door to the sign of the conscience seared with a hot iron.[386] Stepping up with his testimony, Mr. Know-All pointed out that Mr. Forget-Good was just another Diabolonian, the son of a Diabolonian by the name of Love-Naught.[387] Moreover, Forget-Good at times would remark that any *thoughts of goodness were the most burdensome thing in the world* – outrageous words Mr. Know-All heard expressed in Flesh Lane,[388] right opposite to the church! Then, Mr. Tell-True chimed that the prisoner at hand often said he would rather *think of the vilest thing in the world* than anything contained in the Holy Book. Where spoken? In many places, but most particularly in Nauseous Street,[389] in the house of Shameless;[390] and in Filth Lane,[391] at the sign of

[385] 2 Peter 3:13
[386] 1 Timothy 3:9; 4:2; Titus 1:15
[387] Love-Naught: 1 John 3:10, 14; 4:8
[388] Flesh Lane: Romans 7:18; 8:1, 3-9, 12-13
[389] Nauseous Street: Isaiah 28:8; Revelation 3:15-16
[390] Shameless: Proverbs 7:11-27
[391] Filth Lane: 2 Chronicles 29:5; Proverbs 30:12; Isaiah 64:6; Ephesians 5:4; Colossians 3:8

the Reprobate,[392] next door to the Descent into the Pit.[393] All quite a string of incriminating remarks all expressed in quite a string of disreputable places! The testimonies confirmed, the Judge directed the gaoler to bring the next prisoner, Mr. Hard-Heart to the bar.

Mr. Hard-Heart, another intruder, was charged with desperately and wickedly possessing the town with impenitency and obdurateness,[394] thus, keeping the people from any remorse and sorrow for their evil-doings.[395]

Attempting some sort of a statement, Mr. Hard-Heart stated, "My lord, I never knew what remorse or sorrow meant in all my life. I cannot be penetrated. I care for no one. I love being a rock. I cannot be pierced with anyone's troubles. Life brings enough challenges. Anyone else's groans do not touch my heart. Whenever I run into one plagued with some mischief or wrong, it brings music to me.[396]

The decision of the court was obviously easy and quite clear. By his very words it was obvious Mr. Hard-Heart had condemned himself.

By this time, it had become quite a day in court as the gaoler brought Mr. False-Peace charged – to put it most poignantly – with the extremely serious crimes of wickedly and satanically bringing, holding, and keeping the town of Mansoul in a hellish rebellion of a false, groundless, and dangerous peace, thus, to the dishonoring of Shaddai, the transgression of his law, and the bringing about great damage to his town.[397]

In his own defense, Mr. False-Peace stressed his real identity was Mr. Peace. It was not False-Peace.[398] People could check with anyone who knew him. He could not respond to an indictment which did not use his real name. "I was always one who loved to live quietly, and I thought others deserved the same. If I saw any neighbors laboring under a disquieted mind, I endeavored to help in whatever way I could. When our town declined the ways of Shaddai and fell into disquieting reflections, I sought the means to bring them to a quiet. Even when the ways of the old world,

---

[392] Reprobate: Romans 1:28; Titus 1:6

[393] Descent into the Pit: Job 17:15-16; 33:30

[394] Exodus 7:3; Deuteronomy 2:30; Luke 5:32; 2 Corinthians 7:10; 2 Peter 3:9

[395] Psalms 38:2-6; 51:1-19

[396] Hebrew 4:2

[397] In Ezekiel 13:10-16, Matthew Henry describes "the most dangerous seducers [as those] who suggest to sinners that which tends to lessen their dread of sin and their fear of God. Now this is compared to the building of a slight rotten wall, or, according to our Saviour's similitude, which is to the same purport with this (Matt. vii. 26), the building of a house upon the sand, which seems to be a shelter and protection for a while but will fall when the storm comes [see Matthew Henry's Commentary].

[398] False-Peace: Jeremiah 6:14

say, of Sodom,[399] were in fashion, if anything happened to molest that state of life, I tried to bring them into an ease again. When war fell out between Shaddai and Diabolus, it was I who, by some way, device, or invention, sought to bring them to peace again.[400] Quite frankly, I do not deserve this inhumane treatment! I deserve the liberty and license to seek damage from those who have been my accusers."

At this point, the Clerk of the court directed the crier to make a proclamation: "Since the prisoner at the bar has denied that his name is False-Peace as mentioned in the indictment, the court asks if anyone in the place could come forward to bring forth any evidence that helps us clarify his name."

After he swore the oath, Mr. Search-Truth[401] said he had known the man since childhood. His father's name was Mr. Flatter.[402] His mother's name was Mrs. Soothe-Up. His parents gave him the name of False-Peace at birth. "I remember his mother calling him home from play, 'False-Peace, False-Peace, come home quickly, or I'll fetch you.' I even remember his mother sitting or playing with him in her arms and calling him, twenty times together, 'My little False-Peace! My pretty False-Peace! Oh! my sweet rogue, False-Peace!' and 'Oh! my little bird, False-Peace, and how I love you, child!' The gossips[403] around town could affirm the same."

Mr. Vouch-Truth then came forward with a similar testimony, saying that all conveyed was true. Furthermore, there were times the defendant would recoil with anger if anyone called him anything but False-Peace!

Therefore, based on the testimonies sworn against him,[404] the court ruled Mr. False-Peace was not charged with evil-doing for being a man of peace. He was charged with wickedly and satanically bringing, keeping, and holding the town of Mansoul in rebellion against its king through a false, lying, and damnable peace. Such peace was no companion of truth and holiness. Echoes of what Diabolus brought on Mansoul long before, anything False-Peace said was grounded in a lie. A deceitful and damnable lie.[405]

Mr. Know-All, having known the man for a long time, testified that False-Peace worked to sustain a sinful quietness among the people. "Come, come, let us fly from all trouble, on whatsoever ground it comes,"

---

[399] Sodom: Genesis 19:1-28

[400] Proverbs 1:31

[401] John 5:39; Acts 17:11; Ephesians 6:14

[402] Flatter: Psalms 5:9; 12:2-3; Proverbs 26:28; 29:5; Romans 16:18

[403] "Friends," in British vocabulary

[404] Deuteronomy 17:6

[405] John 8:44

he would say. "Let one have a quiet and peaceable life, even though there is no good foundation."

"No fewer than twenty times," Mr. Hate-Lies asserted, "the peace False-Peace advocated was a peace in a way of unrighteousness, which was better than troubling people with the truth." Hate-Lies added: "It was at the house of Mr. Simple[406] in Folly-yard,[407] next door to the sign of the Self-deceiver, that I would hear such things."[408]

Sparing the trouble of drawing on any further witnesses, the evidence being so damning, the Clerk directed the gaoler to take the accused from the courtroom.[409]

Next, also pleading not guilty, Mr. No-Truth (as all before court today, another intruder upon the town of Mansoul) was brought forward on the charges of bringing Mansoul almost to utter ruin by setting out to the spoiling of what remained of the law and image of Shaddai throughout the town.

Mr. Know-All was the first to come forward with evidence regarding the matter. "Yes," Know-All pointed out, "this man was present and actively involved in pulling down the image of Shaddai. I stood by and saw him do it! He then set up the horned image of the beast Diabolus in the same place. Also, at the bidding of Diabolus, he did rend and tear and shred anything that remained of the law of the King!"

Mr. Hate-Lies augmented the testimony with the word that No-Truth did not do any of this by stealth, or in a corner, but in the open for all to see; and he delighted in doing it![410]

On hearing this, the Clerk demanded how he could have such a face and plead not guilty, to which No-Truth asserted that speaking no truth up to this point had worked to his advantage. Consequently, the case was closed, and he was taken away by the gaoler!

Continuing throughout this long and tedious day, the gaoler brought Mr. Pitiless to the bar. Basically, this notorious intruder traitorously and wickedly cut off all bowels of compassion,[411] refusing to condole Man-

---

[406] Simple: Romans 16:17-19; 2 Timothy 3:6

[407] Folly-yard: Proverbs 13:16; 14:17-18, 29; 16:22; 17:12; 18:13

[408] John 8:44, 55

[409] Jeremiah 6:13-15

[410] Acts 26:26

[411] Bowels of Compassion (σπλάγχνα / splanchna) – in Biblical anatomy and physiology, the bowels are a reference to the lower part of the body, especially the womb and the loins, and extending substance as an evocative, forceful expression to the seat of impulsive actions – a kind of gut feeling – which as a word in the New Testament appears eleven times and refers to the heart, tender mercies, compassion and, in Paul's letter to Philemon (1:7, 12, 20), carries the idea of heart-felt emotional refreshment through consolation and

soul's misery when her people apostatized from their rightful King but worked to turn her mind away from any thoughts that might have led to repentance.

"I am not guilty of any lack of pity!" Mr. Pitiless exclaimed. "All I did was try to cheer people up because of the many sour-faced 'saints' Mansoul seems to have!"

"So you claim that your name is not Pitiless, but Cheer-up?" the Clerk confronted the puzzling matter.

Notwithstanding, it was Mr. Know-All that started to bring some clarity to the matter at hand. "These Diabolonians," he stated, "love to counterfeit their names. Mr. Covetousness covers himself with the name of Good-Husbandry. Mr. Pride, when needful, can call himself Mr. Neat, Mr. Handsome, or the like; and so on.

Then, Mr. Tell-True got deeper into the matter. Having known Mr. Pitiless all his life, he pointed out that Pitiless was like those people who bear no sensitivity for individuals struggling through their feelings of great loss or damnation. So, they slap a label of melancholy on such people and walk away when they should care to be helping them come to wholeness.

By the time Mr. Haughty was brought before the bar, he was being tried for traitorously and devilishly teaching the town to carry on loftily and stoutly against any summons by Shaddai's captains. In the same spirit, he led Mansoul to speak contemptuously of and vilify Shaddai, even to the extent of encouraging the people to take up arms against Shaddai and Emmanuel.[412]

"Gentlemen," Haughty protested, "I have always been a person of sheer courage and valor. Under the greatest clouds, I have not been one to sneak around nor have I been one to hang my head lowly like a bulrush. Nor did I like to see people veil their bonnets to anyone opposing them. It did not matter who was my foe, nor what was the cause, if I carried on bravely, if I fought like a champ, and if I became a victor, that was all that mattered."

"But, Mr. Haughty," the court moved, "you are not indicted for being a valiant person, nor for your courage and stoutness in times of distress. You are here because of your pretended valor to draw the town of Mansoul into acts of rebellion against the great King and his Son, Emmanuel. We must stick to the issue!"[413]

---

love (see Helmut Köster in *The Theological Dictionary of the New Testament*, vol. VII, edited by Gerhard Kittel and Gerhard Friedrich, translated by Geoffrey Bromiley (Grand Rapids, Michigan: Wm. B. Eerdmans, 1964), 548-559.

[412] Proverbs 21:24

[413] Proverbs 28:13

As the court had proceeded this far against the prisoners at the bar, they put them over to the jury for a verdict: "Gentlemen, you have been here and seen these men. You have heard the indictments, their pleas, and what the witnesses have testified. Now it remains for you to withdraw to some place where, without confusion, you may consider what in the way of truth and righteousness are the verdicts."

Sequestered, the jury members engaged in discussion. "Gentlemen," said Mr. Belief, the foreman: "I, for my part, believe the prisoners at the bar are deserving of death." "Very right," said True-Heart; "I am wholly of your opinion." "Oh, what a mercy it is," said Hate-Bad, "that such villains are apprehended!" "Ay! Ay!" said Love-God, "this is one of the most joyful days that ever I saw." Then said See-Truth, "I know if we judge them to death, our verdict shall stand before Shaddai himself." "Nor do I at all question it," said Heavenly-Mind; "when such beasts as these are cast out, what a goodly town we will have!" "Then," said Moderate, "it is not my manner to pass my judgment with rashness, but these crimes are so notorious, and the witnesses are so palpable, one must be willfully blind to say the prisoners ought not to die." "Blessed be God," said Thankful, "the traitors are in safe custody." "I join with you in this upon my knees," said Humble. "I am also glad," said Mr. Good-Work. Then, Zeal-for-God said, "Cut them off, for they have been the plague and have sought the intended destruction of Mansoul for a long time." Thus, upon reaching agreement, the jurors came back into the court.

After the jury members responded to the roll call, the Clerk asked who would be speaking for the group. "Our foreman," was the answer.

Then, with grave seriousness, the Clerk spoke: "You jury members being empaneled for our Lord the King to serve here in a manner of life and death, you have heard the charges and testimonies of each of the prisoners at the bar: what now do you say? Are they guilty or not guilty for the crimes for which they are indicted?"

"Guilty, my lord," the Foreman declared.

Thus, the Clerk instructed the gaoler to look to his prisoners. This done, the gaoler put them – i.e., Incredulity, Lustings, Forget-Good, Atheism, Hardness of Heart, False-Peace, No-Truth, Pitiless, and Haughty – into the inward prison for containment until the day of execution, which would come the next morning.[414]

---

[414] An interesting case in contrast is to take and compare this to John Bunyan's description of the trial of Christian and Faithful in the town of Vanity before Judge Hategood in *The Pilgrim's Progress*.

PRAYER STARTER: *O Lord, there are times we struggle to know the difference between what is good and what is not so good. Give us the peace we are not left to deal with this tangle of life alone. Come, Holy Spirit, come. Shed a light upon where we need it most. Wipe clear the lens through which we look that we might better see.* [From here on continue in your own prayerful words.] *In Jesus' name, we pray. Amen.*

Jail Break

1 Peter 4:12-13: Dearly beloued, thinke it not ftrange cócerning the fyrie trial, which is among you to proue you, as thogh fome ftrange thing were come vnto you: But reioyce, in afmuche as ye are partakers of Chrift's fufferings, that when his glorie fhal appeare, ye may be glad and reioyce (GEN, 1560).

Dearly beloved, think it not strange concerning the fiery trial, which is among you to prove you as though some strange thing were come unto you, But rejoice, inasmuch as ye are partakers of Christ's sufferings, that when his glory shall appear, ye may be glad and rejoice (GNV, 1599).

Although the Diabolonian prisoners were securely jailed, Incredulity, the most notorious of them all, made his escape. Managing to get out of the town, he lay lurking in such holes, dens, and other places as he was able to find shelter until he could slip back to Diabolus and, once again, wrest the opportunity to do Shaddai's town great mischief.

When Mr. Trueman, the gaoler, realized that he had lost his prisoner, he was in a heavy taking because Incredulity was capable of some of the worst damage when left on the run. So, Mr. Trueman hurried to the Lord Mayor, Mr. Recorder, and Lord Willbewill, to report the escape and get authorization to make a careful search throughout the town. Yet, it made little sense that Incredulity, at this point, would think it smart to hide somewhere about town. In fact, there were a few Mansoulians, including Mr. Did-see,[415] who caught a glimpse of Incredulity lurking outside the walls and ranging over the dry places.[416]

When Incredulity finally made connection with Diabolus on Hell-Gate Hill, he updated him on the developments in Mansoul since he had lost control of the town – for instance, matters such as the demolishing and desecrating of Diabolus's image, the defection of Willbewill to Emmanu-

---

[415] Did-see: Numbers 23:9; Job 28:26-28; Habakkuk 1:1
[416] Matthew 12:43; Luke 11:24

el, and the impending execution (probably already happened) of eight of his most trusted citizens.

Oh, how Diabolus did yell, snuff up the wind like a dragon, and make the sky darken with his roar – all in all swearing fiercely he would get his revenge!

Back in Mansoul, however, one can easily imagine the delicate work of dealing with the other Diabolonians around the town. They could be quite a sinister, unruly, and hard-to-handle bunch. Thus, the Mansoulian law officers had to cry out to the captains and men of war for help in holding the peace.[417]

It was at this time Emmanuel, the Prince, came down to hold audience with the people. Upon noticing their great faithfulness, Emmanuel found them to be lovers of his person, observers of his laws, and respectful of his honor. The Prince also informed them he would bring aboard another captain who would command a thousand for the good and benefit of the nowadays flourishing town.

Emmanuel called upon a person named Waiting[418] to go to the castle gate and inquire for a young gentleman named Mr. Experience[419] who waited upon Captain Credence. The people of the town knew him well, for he was born and bred there. He was one of good conduct and valor and prudence. He also was a comely person, well-spoken of, and successful in his undertakings. Consequently, the people were transported with joy regarding the appointment.

"I have thought," Emmanuel said to Mr. Experience who, upon arriving, bowed the knee before Emmanuel, "I have thought about conferring upon you a position of trust, responsibility, and honor.[420] You are to be one of my captains, a captain over a thousand in my beloved town of Mansoul."

To this Experience exclaimed: "Let the King live!" In keeping with a customary procedure, the Prince directed the King's Secretary to draw up a commission for Mr. Experience officially certifying him for the position. After being brought to Emmanuel for the placement of his seal,[421] the commission was delivered to Mr. Experience by the hand of Mr. Waiting.

---

[417] Romans 6:12-14; 8:13; Galatians 5:24

[418] Waiting: Romans 8:23; 1 Thessalonians 3:5

[419] Experience: Romans 5:4-6

[420] 2 Corinthians 9:12-13

[421] Princes, court officials, juries, and administrators used seals to mark and seal the authenticity and secrecy of important documents, charters, legal agreements, the assent of a jury, and administrative warrants (see John Cherry, "Sigillography," *Britannica*, for more extensive information and history of seals).

As soon as Captain Experience received his commission, he sounded his trumpet for volunteers and several young men responded. Indeed, the most notable and chief citizens of the town, in holding such great respect for him, sent their sons to serve under his command.

Then, Experience had Mr. Skillful[422] for his lieutenant and Mr. Memory[423] for his cornet.[424] His colors were the white colors for the town of Mansoul and his scutcheon was the dead lion and the dead bear.[425]

Upon Emmanuel's returning to the palace, the Lord Mayor, the Recorder, and the Lord Willbewill went to thank him for his love, tender care, and compassion. So, after a time of sweet communion, the townsmen left for their places. Then, at an appointed time, wherein they would renew their charter (enlarging and mending parts of it so that Mansoul's yoke could be made easier),[426] Emmanuel looked at the old one and laid it aside with the remark, "that which decays and waxes old is ready to vanish away," and then, he set out to bring about a new and better charter – a steadier and firmer one by far.[427] There was to be:

1. a free, full, and everlasting forgiveness;[428]

2. a holy law and testament;[429]

3. a portion of the same grace and goodness as is within my Father's heart and mine;[430]

4. a giving, granting, and bestowing freely this world and what is in it for the good and beneficial of life and death, and things present, and things to come;[431]

5. a free access to Emmanuel's palace at all seasons, to make the Mansoulians' wants and grievances known;[432]

6. a full power and authority to seek out, take and destroy all manner of Diabolonians straggling in or about the town; and

7. the authority not to suffer any stranger in the blessed town of Mansoul.[433]

---

[422] Skillful: 1 Corinthians 3:10
[423] Memory: Philippians 3:3-7
[424] A Baroque era trumpet was called a cornetto
[425] Judges 14:5-6, 8; 1 Samuel 17:34-36
[426] Matthew 11:28-30
[427] Hebrews 8:13
[428] Micah 7:19; Hebrews 8:12; 1 John 1:9
[429] 2 Corinthians 3:6; Hebrews 8:10
[430] 1 Corinthians 1:4-5; James 1:17; 2 Peter 1:4
[431] 1 Corinthians 3:21-22
[432] Matthew 7:7; Hebrews 4:16; 10:19-20
[433] John 10:5; Colossians 3:5-9

The gracious charter was taken to the marketplace, where the people gathered, and the Recorder, in the hearing of all, read it to the people. Then, it was taken to the castle gates and there fairly engraved upon the doors in letters of gold.[434]

What joy, comfort, and consolation the people of Mansoul did now possess for which the bells rung, the minstrels played, the people danced, the captains shouted, the colors waved in the wind, and the silver trumpets sounded.[435]

Meanwhile, Diabolonians were glad to shrink back and to hide their heads – at least, for the moment – for they looked like those who had long been dead.

As these celebratory moments had settled and life reached a new normalcy, the Prince sent for the elders to discuss a ministry that would make wholesome instruction available. For if people did not have such, how would they be able to know Shaddai's will for them?[436]

Such a ministry would teach them of law, judgment, statute, commandment,[437] things concerning the present and the future, and anything else wholesome.[438] One of these teachers would come from his Father's court and the other would come from Mansoul itself.

The one from Shaddai's court would be of no less quality and dignity than Shaddai and Emmanuel – the Lord Chief Secretary of the Father's house[439] – his being the one able to teach high and lofty things,[440] the one skilled in mysteries, and the knowledge of mysteries;[441] the one who could help bring lost things to remembrance,[442] the one being with Shaddai and Emmanuel in nature as well as in love and faithfulness to Mansoul's eternal concerns.[443]

"Such a teacher should have the pre-eminence in the people's affections and judgment,[444] said Emmanuel. "He can put life and vigor in all that he says.[445] This one can make seers of the people and tell what shall

---

[434] Jeremiah 31:33; 2 Corinthians 3:3; Hebrews 8:10

[435] John 15:11

[436] Jeremiah 10:23; 1 Corinthians 2:14

[437] Psalm 119:1-176

[438] 2 Timothy 2:15

[439] 1 Corinthians 2:11

[440] John 14:16-17, 26; 1 John 2:27

[441] Ephesians 3:5

[442] Luke 15:1-31

[443] John 1:1; 15:26-27; 16:12-14

[444] John 14:26

[445] Text and Song Interactional: Torwalt Bryan James and Torwalt Katie, songwriters, "Holy Spirit," by Francesca Battistelli, released 2014

be hereafter. By this person the people must frame all their petitions to the Father and me. Without his advice and counsel first, let nothing to enter the town and castle of Mansoul.[446]

"However, you Mansoulians, take heed not to grieve the minister.[447] If you shall hearken unto him and love him, you shall find him ten times better than the whole world. Yes, he will shed abroad the love of my Father in your hearts, and Mansoul will be the wisest and most blessed of all people."[448]

At this point, Emmanuel then called on Mr. Conscience, the old Recorder, to deliver the Master's will in all terrestrial and domestic matters.[449] He, too, would be a minister for the goodly town of Mansoul. However, his tutoring would limit itself to moral virtues and civil and natural duties – not presuming himself to be the one revealing the high and supernatural mysteries revealed by the Lord Chief Secretary.[450]

"What Mr. Conscience shall teach must be things appropriate to a scholar and a learner," Emmanuel said. "Go to him for information and knowledge. Although there be a spirit in man, this person's inspiration must give him understanding. Thus, this Mr. Recorder, being content with his station, must keep low and be humble."[451]

At this point, Emmanuel said, "Mr. Recorder, because you are old and have been through many abuses and made feeble, go to my fountain, my conduit, and there drink freely of the blood of my grape, for my conduit does always run wine. In doing such, you shall drive from your heart and stomach all foul, gross, and hurtful humors."[452]

Then, with the teachers in place, the Prince addressed Mansoul as a whole group: "I have added to all that is past this mercy, to appoint you preachers: the most noble Secretary to teach you in all high and sublime mysteries; and Mr. Conscience to teach you in all things human and domestic. However, Mr. Conscience is not debarred of telling to Mansoul

---

446 Romans 8:26; Ephesians 4:30; 6:18; 1 Thessalonians 1:5; Jude 20; Revelation 2:7, 11, 17, 29

[447] Ephesians 4:29-32; "Few scriptures drew more attention in the hearts and minds of Puritans in Bunyan's day than Ephesians 4:30: 'And grieve not the holy Spirit of God, whereby ye are sealed unto the day of redemption'" Daniel V. Runyon, "John Bunyan's Master Story: The Holy War as Battle Allegory in Religious and Biblical Context" (Published version of Ph.D. dissertation, Lampeter, Wales: Edwin Mellen Press, 2007), 184.

[448] Romans 5:5; 2 Corinthians 13:14

[449] Job 38:1-39:35

[450] 1 Corinthians 12:27-29; Ephesians 4:10-12; 2 Timothy 1:8-14

[451] 1 Kings 3:9; Job 32:8; Proverbs 19:8; 20:5; Jeremiah 3:15; 1 Corinthians 14:15; Ephesians 1:18; Philippians 4:6-8

[452] Luke 10:34; John 2:10; 1 Timothy 5:23

anything heard and received at the mouth of the Lord Chief Secretary; only he shall not attempt to presume to pretend to be a revealer of those high mysteries himself.

"One thing more," Emmanuel directed to his beloved Mr. Recorder, "You must not dwell upon anything that the most noble Secretary has as his commission to teach – for instance, your trust and expectation of the next world – but you must wholly and solely have recourse to the doctrine that is your first order.[453]

"I mentioned the next world because I purpose to give another world to Mansoul when this world with her is worn out."[454]

Then, turning abruptly to the inhabitants of Mansoul, Prince Emmanuel challenged them not to carry on ruggedly or untowardly to his captains as well as the ones entrusted to their leadership.[455]

"Even a little discountenance will cast down their faces and take away their courage. Do not carry it unkindly to my courageous in war, but love them, nourish them, succor them, and lay them close to your hearts. If any of them should at any time be sick, strengthen them and encourage them. They are your fence, your guard, your wall, your gates, your locks, and your bars. If they be weak, the town of Mansoul cannot be strong. If they are strong, Mansoul cannot be weak. Your safety lies in their health."[456]

Emmanuel went on to remind the people that, notwithstanding the reformation, there still were Diabolonians – sturdy and implacable Diabolonians even while he was with them – both inside and outside of the walls. "They still study, plot, contrive, invent and jointly attempt to bring Mansoul to desolation. Outside of your walls they have made themselves dens, and caves, and holes, and strongholds. Therefore, Mansoul, your work will be so much the more difficult. Be diligent; observe their holes; find their haunts; and make no peace with them. Wherever they haunt, lurk, or abide, and whatsoever peace they offer you, abhor it, then, all shall be well between you and me."[457]

---

[453] 1 Timothy 1:19; Hebrews 9:14

[454] Acts 1:8; Revelation 21:1-7; 22:1-17

[455] "Previously Mansoul was in physical bondage to the rule of Diabolus; the new threat is of a spiritual bondage. Living under an oppressive ruler was bad enough; becoming like him by embracing and internalizing his behaviors will lead to their eternal destruction" Daniel V. Runyon, "John Bunyan's Master Story: The Holy War as Battle Allegory in Religious and Biblical Context" (Published version of Ph.D. dissertation, Lampeter, Wales: Edwin Mellen Press, 2007), 188.

[456] Isaiah 35:3; 1 Thessalonians 5:14; Hebrews 12:12; Revelation 3:2

[457] Mark 7:21-22; Romans 7:18

"Should you come across any of them, know them not as natives of Mansoul. Among the chief of them, there are such damaging spirits[458] as Lord Fornication,[459] Lord Adultery,[460] Lord Murder,[461] Lord Anger,[462] Lord Lasciviousness,[463] Lord Deceit,[464] Lord Evil-Eye,[465] Mr. Drunkenness,[466] Mr. Reveling,[467] Mr. Idolatry,[468] Mr. Witchcraft,[469] Mr. Variance,[470] Mr. Emulation,[471] Mr. Wrath,[472] Mr. Strife,[473] Mr. Sedition,[474] and Mr. Heresy.[475] These are the chief of them that would try to overthrow Mansoul forever. It is important to find their physiognomy and characteristics!

"O, my Mansoul," said Emmanuel in a graphic way to put it, "if they can run and range about this town, they, like vipers, unless they are rooted out of the heart, will quickly eat your bowels out, poison your captains, cut the sinews of your soldiers, break the bars and bolts of your gates, and turn your most flourishing Mansoul into a desolate wilderness and ruinous heap.[476]

---

[458] Galatians 5:19-21 – works of the flesh

[459] Fornication: Matthew 15:19; Acts 15:29; 1 Corinthians 6:13, 18; Revelation 2:20-22; 14:8

[460] Adultery: Exodus 20:14; Deuteronomy 5:18; 2 Samuel 11:1-12:25; Proverbs 6:32; Matthew 5:27-32; John 8:1-11

[461] Murder: Numbers 35:30; Job 24:13-15; Matthew 15:19; 23:31; Romans 1:28-29; Revelation 22:14-16

[462] Anger: Proverbs 14:17; 15:1; 16:32; 27:4; Ephesians 4:26; Colossians 3:20-22

[463] Lasciviousness (KJV) / Wantonness, Uncleanness (Geneva): Mark 7:22; 2 Corinthians 12:21; 1 Peter 4:3; Jude 1:4

[464] Deceit: Psalms 12:2; 35:20; 38:12; 52:4; 55:23; Proverbs 12:5, 17, 20, 27; 20:17, 23; 21:6; 26:19, 24,26; 31:30

[465] Evil-Eye: 1 Kings 16:25; Proverbs 3:7; 16:30; 21:10; 23:6; Ezekiel 6:9; Luke 11:34

[466] Drunkenness: Ecclesiastes 10:17; Isaiah 5:11; Luke 21:34; Romans 13:13; Galatians 5:21-23

[467] Reveling: Galatians 5:21; 1 Peter 4:3 [in Geneva as gluttony]

[468] Idolatry: 1 Samuel 15:23; Acts 17:16; 1 Corinthians 10:14; Galatians 5:20; Colossians 3:5

[469] Witchcraft: Leviticus 19:26; Deuteronomy 18:10; 1 Samuel 5:23; 2 Kings 17:17; 21:6; Nahum 3:4; Acts 8:9; Galatians 5:20

[470] Variation: Matthew 10:35; Acts 15:39

[471] Emulation: Galatians 5:20

[472] Wrath: Acts 19:28; Romans 12:19; 2 Corinthians 12:20; Galatians 5:20; Ephesians 4:26, 31; 6:4; Colossians 3:8; 1 Timothy 2:8; James 1:19-20

[473] Strife: Proverbs 17:1; 22:10; 26:17, 20, 21; Luke 22:24; Philippians 1:15; 2 Timothy 2:23

[474] Sedition: Ezra 4:15; Luke 21:9; Acts 21:38; James 3:16

[475] Heresy: Acts 24:14

[476] Psalm 107:33-34, 39-40; Isaiah 37:21-26 [Prophet Isaiah, King Hezekiah and Assyrian invasion by Sennacherib]

"As I have identified the vagrants and runagates before your eyes and by name, I will tell you, some of them will creep in to beguile you, even if they would seem very rife and so hot for religion.

"Watch and be sober."[477]

PRAYER STARTER: *Come, Holy Spirit, and teach us. Teach us of sin, righteousness, and judgment. By each day guide our lives. Nurture our souls. Help us be a blessing to others. Be our continual enrichment. Fortify us against anything that would distract us from God's call and work for us.* [From here on continue with your own prayerful words.] *In Jesus' name, we pray. Amen.*

A Serious Relational Drift

Psalm 119:175-176: Let my foule liue, & it fhal praife thee, and thy iudgements fhal helpe me. I haue gone aftraye like a loft fhepe: feke thy feruant, for I do not forget thy commandments (GEN, 1560).

Let my soul live, and it shall praise thee, and thy judgments shall help me. I have gone astray like a lost sheep: seek thy servant, for I do not forget thy commandments (GNV, 1599).

After Prince Emmanuel had newly modeled the town and instructed the people in serious relational matters, he clothed them in glistening white robes[478] from his treasury. He gave the townsfolk a badge which when worn would make the world know to whom they belonged.[479] Against any false traitors who might try to creep in, it would distinguish them from the others who lived throughout the kingdom of Universe.[480]

How Mansoul did shine! It was fair as the sun, clear as the moon and terrible as an army with banners.[481] No other prince, potentate, or mighty one could give them the same!

While Emmanuel was engaging with the people, he gave them instructions stressing the importance of keeping in good relationship with one another. They were to wear what they were given daily and always keep it clean. By girding up their robes, they also were to keep from dragging

---

[477] 1 Thessalonians 5:6; 1 Peter 4:7; 5:8

[478] White as a Color: Isaiah 1:18; Daniel 7:9; Matthew 17:2-3; Revelation 3:4-5; 6:9-11; 7:9-10, 14-15; 19:8, 14

[479] Song of Solomon 2:16; Revelation 19:8

[480] John 10:16, 27; 17:20-26

[481] Song of Solomon 6:9

them in the dust. But, if sullied – which, not surprising, would please Diabolus greatly – they were to do quickly what was written in the law.[482]

Where now was a town, city, or corporation comparable to Mansoul! Redeemed from the power of Diabolus, the prince of the infernal cave! It was a town that King Shaddai loved. It was a town in which Emmanuel loved abiding. The benefits were not a few, nor were they little; they were great!

Emmanuel set his standard upon the battlements of the castle and frequently visited the people. He would host Mansoul for daily feasts.[483] He would bless the poor, lay hands upon the ill, and encourage the captains.

Throughout time, though, the townspeople started to take a lot for granted. Nonetheless, Emmanuel kept sending them meat that came from his court, and the bread and wine that had been prepared for his Father's table. But Mansoul kept drifting more and more off, her people looking like they did not care anymore. Still Emmanuel kept walking out to them, knocking at their doors and desiring entrance, while the once-bright glow of their responsiveness continued to fade![484]

The Prince commissioned a new officer for the town. He was a goodly person known as Mr. God's-Peace.[485] Not a native of the town, he came from Emmanuel's court and, thus, held position over Lord Willbewill, Mr. Recorder, Mr. Mind, and all the others. A great acquaintance of Captain Credence and Captain Good-Hope, Mr. God's-Peace[486] was made governor over the town and the castle and Captain Credence was appointed to help him. So long as all things went as this sweet-natured gentleman would have it, the town remained in a happy condition. There were no jars, chidings, interferences, and unfaithful doings. Meanwhile the people kept

---

[482] Leviticus 13, 14, 15, 17 [various verses]; Ecclesiastes 9:8; Isaiah 1:16; Ephesians 5:26-27; Revelation 3:4; 7:14-17

[483] 1 Corinthians 5:8

[484] Song of Solomon 5:2; Revelation 3:20

[485] Romans 15:13; Colossians 3:15; 1 Thessalonians 1:1

[486] In the New Testament, "The beatitude, 'Blessed are the peacemakers: for they shall be called the children of God' is an extremely striking saying, if one bears in mind that in the Roman Empire of that day the only persons elsewhere to be called Sons of God because they were peacemakers were the Roman emperors, the upholders of the *Pax Romana*. The very same Greek word for peacemaker, eirenépoios, is to be found upon the emperors' coins. Of this Jesus was presumably unaware, yet how amazing it is that a wandering Galilean rabbi, talking to a handful of fishermen, should have committed to them the role ascribed to emperors! Perhaps unwittingly he was saying that the peace of Rome had provided only an external framework which Galilean peasants must make real by setting within it the peace of God" (Roland H. Bainton, *Christian Attitudes Toward War and Peace* [Nashville: Abingdon Press, 1960], p.64).

to their own business and there was little other than harmony, quietness, joy, and health lasting all summer long.[487]

Over time, there happened to be one in Mansoul by the name of Mr. Carnal-Security[488] who, despite the recent mercies bestowed upon the town, brought a presumptuous attitude into the place.

To get a sense of how this all came about we must go back to the time Diabolus took possession of Mansoul and brought several Diabolonians aboard. Among them was a bricklike character, Mr. Self-Conceit,[489] who had many notable qualities. Accordingly, Diabolus teamed him with Lord Willbewill who had a daughter, Lady Fear-Nothing,[490] whom Self-Conceit eventually married. They had a son named Carnal-Security. Quite an egotistical chap, Carnal-Security shunned nothing, kept himself in the thick of things, and hung at the head or tail of anything noteworthy in and around the town.

When Shaddai and Emmanuel made war upon Mansoul, Mr. Carnal-Security was a great go-getter among the people, encouraging the rebellion. And yet, when he saw what was becoming of Diabolus who was being un-roosted while Shaddai's forces were taking over the town, Carnal-Security shifted sides.

Realizing Mansoul was becoming aligned with Emmanuel's captains, engines of war, soldiers, and provisions, he wheeled about slyly pretending to serve the Prince against his foes. Carnal-Security would venture into any company of townspeople. Shifting from street to street, house to house, and man to man, he, quite the chatty fellow, fueled people's pride. He affirmed how impregnable the town, how magnificent its captains, and how state-of-the-art their military slings, rams, fortifications, and strongholds were; and how greatly could he lay it on thick! He brought Mansoul to dance to his pipe without their comprehending the danger of becoming almost as carnally secure as he himself.

There was a time Emmanuel was still in town and observed such goings-on. Mr. Lord Mayor, Lord Willbewill, and Mr. Recorder had become so taken with Mr. Carnal-Security's chatter they had forgotten that the Prince had warned them against falling into the tricks hidden beneath such inflated talk.[491] As Emmanuel perceived what was happening to the people

---

[487] Romans 12:16

[488] Psalm 52:7; Proverbs 28:26

[489] Self-Conceit: 2 Timothy 3:2

[490] Fear-Nothing: Psalms 34:9; 55:19; Matthew 10:25-27

[491] "We decry the blindness and perverseness of men in that they will not receive the message of grace and salvation, or having received it they quickly let go of it, in spite of the fact that the Gospel bestows all good things spiritual . . . ¶I know how quickly a person

through this rascal and that they were losing a focus on his Father's love and care, it grieved him deeply: "Oh, that my people had hearkened unto me and walked in my ways. I would have sustained them with the finest of wheat and honey out of the rock."[492]

It was during this time Emmanuel started withdrawing from Mansoul because the people veered onto a path that kept turning away from him. The Mansoulian people lost their sense that something serious was going on. For instance, they fell into neglecting their love feasts. Puffed up in their seemingly self-sufficient ways, they stopped reaching out for any guidance and care.[493]

Perceiving Mansoul was drifting away through the craft of Carnal-Security, Emmanuel twice sent his Lord Chief Secretary to the town. The Lord Chief Secretary found them so preoccupied with dinner and fixed on other matters in Carnal-Security's parlor, that he grieved and went on his way – returning to Shaddai's court.[494]

Emmanuel's withdrawal from Mansoul was a progression. At first, he came about less and less than previously. Next, his speech was not so pleasant and conversational as formerly. Nor did he, as in times past, send to Mansoul those dainty bits which he was wont to extend from his table. Even when they came to visit him, as occasionally they did, he did not connect with them as easily as in the past.[495]

By carrying on in this way, Emmanuel was trying to make them be-think[496] themselves and return to him. But alas! they would not catch the drift and became increasingly desensitized to his ways. Consequently, he withdrew first from the palace, then from the gate, and so off and away from Mansoul.

---

can forfeit the joy of the Gospel. I know in what slippery places even those stand who seem to have a good footing in the matters of faith . . . I say the Gospel is frail because we are frail" Martin Luther, *Commentary on Galatians*, trans. by Theodore Graebner (Digireads. com Publishing, 2019), content on Galatians 1:6, 11-12; pp. 19, 25.

[492] Deuteronomy 32:13; Psalm 81:13, 16

[493] 1 Corinthians 4:14, 18-21

[494] "The physical, the spiritual and self-consciousness are all important to being human. However, the Bible defines human beings not in terms of a particular part of our bodies or minds. Instead, human beings are defined in terms of relationship, and in particular their relationship to God" David Wilkinson, *The Message of Creation: Encountering the Lord of the Universe*, in Bible Themes Series, ed. Derek Tidball (Downers Grove, Illinois: InterVarsity Press, 2002), 32.

[495] Text and Song Interactional: John Mark and Mark Hall, songwriters, "Slow Fade," by Casting Crowns, released 2007

[496] Bethink is an archaic transitive verb in formal English meaning to come to think, to think on reflection, to ponder something carefully.

Mr. God's-Peace even laid down his commission for the present and would no longer stay around the town.

By this time, the people had become so hardened in their ways, and so drunk with the doctrine of Mr. Carnal-Security, that the departure of their Prince Emmanuel made no serious impression upon them.[497]

There was a day, however, when Mr. Carnal-Security made a feast and seized upon the idea of inviting Mr. Godly-Fear, who was in town, to gull,[498] debauch, and abuse him at the banquet.[499] As everyone sat at table and was caught up in their merrymaking, Mr. Godly-Fear sat stilted like a stranger.

When Mr. Carnal-Security realized his dinner-guest was behaving like a wallflower, he chirped out to him in quite the demeaning way.

"Mr. Godly-Fear, are you not well? I have a cordial of Mr. Forget-Good's making. If you take a dram of it, it may make you bonny and blithe – indeed, more fit for our feasting companions!"

"Sir," responded Mr. Godly-Fear, "I thank you for anything courteous and civil, but I do not care to have your cordial. However, a word to the natives, it is strange to see you so jocund and merry, while the town of Mansoul is in such a woeful case."

Mr. Carnal-Security then said, "You lack sleep, good air, or something else, no doubt. If you please, lie down, and take a nap, and meanwhile let us be merry."

"Sir," the good man responded, "if you were not so destitute of an honest heart, you could not do as you have done."

"Why?" Carnal-Security replied.

"It is true," Godly-Fear continued on, "Mansoul was once strong and impregnable, but you and the townspeople have weakened it and now it lies vulnerable to its foes. It is not a time to flatter one another or be silent, because you, Mr. Carnal-Security, have wilily stripped Mansoul of her glory. If anyone questions that, I must simply ask, where is Prince Emmanuel? When last did anyone see or hear him? When was the last time you've tasted his dainty bits? Now, we are feasting with a Diabolonian monster, not our Prince!"[500]

"Fie! Fie! Mr. Godly-Fear, fie! – will you never shake off your fearfulness? Are you afraid of being sparrow-blasted?[501] Who has hurt you? I am

---

[497] Jeremiah 2:32

[498] Gull – to easily trick or cheat

[499] Psalm 11:1-2

[500] 2 Peter 2:12-15

[501] Sparrow-blasted: abused, stricken, zonked, slaphappy, a sense of [providing a] worthless word for the day. "An empty barrow rattles louder" (Russian proverb)

on your side. Only you are for doubting, and I am for being confident. A feast is made for mirth and merrymaking! Why do you break out into such glum language? We should be eating. We should be drinking. We should be enjoying ourselves!"[502]

"I may well be sad," said Mr. Godly-Fear, "for Emmanuel is gone from Mansoul and, sir, you have driven him away. My dear fellows, your gradual drawing away from Emmanuel provoked him to depart. Now, while you boast, your strength is gone. You are like one who has lost his locks once proudly waving about his shoulders.[503]

"You may, with this lord of your feast, shake yourselves off and do as at other times, but since Emmanuel has departed from you, you would be better off turning your feast into a sigh and your mirth into lamentation."[504]

At this point, the old subordinate preacher, Mr. Conscience by name, startled at what was being said, began to speak.

"Indeed, my brothers, I fear that what Mr. Godly-Fear tells is true. I, for my part, have not seen my Prince in a long season. I cannot even remember the day. In response to Mr. Godly-Fear's concern, I am afraid all is naught with Mansoul."[505]

"Yes, gone because of the elders," Mr. Godly-Fear reaffirmed!

By this time, the subordinate preacher looked as if he would fall over in a faint while the same concern struck the others hard, as well – except, of course, the man of the house, Carnal-Security, who did not like such dumpish talk, and so had stomped away into his withdrawing room.

The group then began discussing the hand Carnal-Security's prattle had played in having drawn them into this evil bent, not ignoring their own complicity, of course, but more important, what they should do to recover Emmanuel's love.

---

[502] Judges 19:6; 19:1-30 [violent story]; Song of Solomon 5:1-17 [includes an incident of abuse]

[503] Judges 16:19

[504] Judges 11:30-40; Jeremiah 31:13

[505] "Scripture indeed gives a vividly realistic picture of the horrible wreck and ruin caused by sin. The effects and ramifications of the entrance and development of evil into the moral universe assume stupendous proportions. The whole dark drama, at first glance, might appear to be a tragedy of unparalleled scope, unmitigated in its woe. But, on the contrary, the cataclysm of diabolical darkness calls forth an effulgence of divine light. The eruption of hellish hate evokes a flood of divine love. The doleful spectacle of rebellion and destruction becomes the occasion for the greatest and grandest event of the ages, the demonstration of God's unfathomable grace in the revelation of Himself in Christ . . . He is 'the Way,' leading out darkness; 'the Truth,' protecting from error; and 'the Life,' delivering from death (John 14:6). In Him there is full redemption; apart from Him, unalleviated woe" Merrill F. Unger, *Biblical Demonology* (Wheaton, Illinois: Scripture Press Publications, Inc., 1952), 28.

They then remembered something the Prince had said about dealing with false prophets, which brought them to presume that Carnal-Security was a Diabolonian false prophet and ignited their emotions to such a pitch as to burn his house down upon himself.[506]

With things swelling to such an intensity, they became more and more confirmed in what Mr. Godly-Fear said and kept bewailing their own vile misdoings, thus concluding that there was a progression of intent that led to the Prince's distancing from them.

What could they do? They hurried about in a frenzy looking for Emmanuel but could not find him.[507] So, they set out to speak with the Lord Chief Secretary, a seer, and sought to know if he knew where Emmanuel was, and how they might direct a petition to him. However, the Lord Chief Secretary would not admit them to a conference on the matter.[508]

The day was dark and gloomy, a day of clouds and thick darkness, as they were wallowing in the grief of pondering what all the company, prattle, and swaggering words of Carnal-Security had drawn them into.

PRAYER STARTER: *Gracious God, because of our inattentiveness, pre-occupations with other things, and just plain sin, it feels like you have drifted away from us. Or is it that we have drifted away from you? Rekindle a sensitive spirit within us. Reignite the spark that has become so faintly burning. Draw us back into a close communion with you. Fan the fire that nourishes us with the warmth of your guidance and loving care.* [From here on continue in your own prayerful words.] *In Jesus' name, we pray. Amen.*

Sunday Sermon

Amos 8:11: Beholde, the daies come, faith the Lord God, that I wil fend a famine in the land, not a famine of bread, nor a thirft for water, but of hearing the worde of the Lord (GEN, 1560).

Behold the days come, saith the Lord God, that I will send a famine in the Land, not a famine of bread, nor a thirst for water, but of hearing the word of the Lord (GNV, 1599).

---

[506] Deuteronomy 18:20
[507] Song of Solomon 5:6
[508] Isaiah 63:10; Ephesians 4:30; 1 Thessalonians 5:19

It was the Sabbath, and the people went to hear the subordinate preacher. Oh, how he did thunder and lighten on that day! His text came from the prophet Jonah: "They that observe lying vanities forsake their own mercy."[509] At the conclusion of the sermon, the people felt so dejected they could scarcely go home and engage productively in their work for the next week. To put it bluntly, the people were so sermon-smitten and sermon-sick that they scarcely knew what to do!

The preacher not only showed the Mansoulians their sin but anguished under a sense of his own. "That I, a preacher, should live so senselessly and sottishly[510] and be among the first to be found in transgression! I should have cried out against the wrong! Instead, I let Mansoul lie wallowing in wickedness, until it drove Emmanuel away!"

Then, the preacher also started in on the lords and gentry so severely he nearly distanced himself from them.

About this time, there fell a great sickness upon Mansoul that affected most of the people. Even the captains and men of war succumbed to the illness which lasted for such a long time that nothing much could be done should the town suffer from an enemy invasion.

Oh, how many pale faces, weak hands, feeble knees, and staggering people that could be seen walking its streets.[511]

Then, there were those garments Emmanuel had given the people. They fell into such a sorry case, some rent, some torn, and all in a nasty condition. Some also hung upon the people so loosely that the next bush would have snagged them off.

After a time spent in this sad condition, the subordinate preacher called for a day of fasting for the people to humble themselves for being so wicked. And he invited Captain Boanerges to preach.

Consenting to do it, the Captain chose the Gospel story of the barren fig tree, with the text, "Cut it down, why encumber the ground with it?"[512]

The need for the people's repentance or utter desolation was the point of it which made poor Mansoul to tremble even more. Throughout the town, there was little or nothing to be heard or seen but sorrow, mourning, and woe.

---

[509] Hosea 5:13; Jonah 2:8

[510] Sottish means drunken

[511] Isaiah 3:24; Micah 6:13-14; Hebrews 12:12-13; Revelation 3:2

[512] "The barren fig tree [of Luke 13:6-9] was a classic Puritan illustration of the depravity of the soul which could produce no fruits of grace" John Bunyan, *The Holy War* Annotated Companion to *The Pilgrim's Progress*, ed. Daniel V. Runyon, (Eugene, Oregon: Pickwick Publications, 2012), 54 footnote 103

After the preaching, the people got together to discuss what they should do. However, the subordinate preacher advised, "I would do nothing without consulting with Mr. Godly-Fear," who then advised the people to draw up a humble petition to be carried – in this matter, by the Lord Mayor – to their offended Prince Emmanuel in a desperate hope that he in his graciousness would turn and not keep angry forever.[513]

When the Mayor reached the court of Shaddai, where Emmanuel had gone, he found the gate shut, a strict watch kept, and himself forced to stand outside for a great while.[514] When he asked somebody to go tell the Prince that he was standing at the gate, the answer came back: "The people have turned their backs upon me. Now when they are in trouble, they cry out to me! Let the people go to Carnal-Security, who pretended to be so helpful in the past!"[515]

With a face drawn sad, perplexed, and sore, the Lord Mayor returned to Mansoul smitten, weeping, and bewailing the lamentable state of the town. As the Lord Mayor came within sight of the town, the elders and chief people went out to meet him, saluted him, and wanted to know how it had gone at court. He told his tale in such a doleful manner that they, too, all cried out, mourned and wept. They threw dust and ashes upon their heads and wrapped their loins in sackcloth. This was such a day of rebuke, and trouble, and anguish![516]

After a while, the people came together to consult with the reverend Mr. Godly-Fear, who told them that there was no better way than what they had done. They should not be discouraged even if met with silence, rebuke, or rejection. It was wise Shaddai's way to make people wait and exercise patience.[517] Therefore, Mansoul persisted with courage and sent petitionary letters again and again. The road was full of messengers coming and going and meeting one another along the way, some from the court, and some from Mansoul, all throughout that long, sharp, cold, and tedious winter.[518]

Although Emmanuel previously had wrested Mansoul from Diabolus, there remained many Diabolonians in several places throughout the corporation. Within holes, dens, and lurking places in, under, and about the town, there were – to mention a few – many of the old, notorious Diabolo-

---

[513] Psalm 85:4; Daniel 9:15-17; Hosea 14:5-6

[514] Lamentations 3:8, 44

[515] Judges 10:14-16; Jeremiah 2:27-28

[516] Job 42:6; Jeremiah 4:8; Ezekiel 27:30

[517] Amos 8:11

[518] Text and Song Interactional: Chris Stevens, Bryan Christopher Fowler and Kevin Michael McKeehan, songwriters, "Move (Keep Walkin')" by Toby Mac, released 2015

nians: Lord Fornication, Lord Adultery, Lord Murder, Lord Anger, Lord Lasciviousness, Lord Deceit, Lord Evil-eye, Lord Blasphemy, and that horrible villain, old, dangerous Lord Covetousness, and still others.

Even so, the Prince had granted Lord Willbewill and the Mansoulians a commission to seek, arrest, secure, and destroy any Diabolonians they could. However, the townspeople did not pursue the warrant and neglected their call. Thus, by degrees, the villains – Anger, Deceit, Blasphemy, Covetousness, and other forces – took courage to show their faces as the Mansoulians grew more and more blinded to the seriousness of their presence, thus opening their hearts and lives to various spiritual illnesses.

When a number of Diabolonian lords still living in the town of Mansoul perceived that the townspeople, through sinning, had offended their Prince who had withdrawn from them, they met together at the hold of Mr. Mischief to discuss how they might deliver Mansoul back into the hands of Diabolus.[519] With everyone's advice running at cross purposes, depending on each one's liking, Lord Lasciviousness raised the suggestion that some of the Diabolonians offer themselves as servants to the townspeople. In that way, they could woo the inhabitants eventually toward Diabolus's liking.

However, Lord Murder stood up and said this would not work because Mansoul currently was in a rage. It was because their friend, Mr. Carnal-Security, had once ensnared them into various offenses. In addition to this, the Mansoulians had a commission to take and slay any Diabolonians they might find. "Once dead," Lord Murder stressed the point, "we can do no harm; but while we live, we can. Thus, to be as wise as foxes!"

With a plan in some focus, the Diabolonians framed a letter in which they detailed their thoughts for Prince Diabolus, seeking his advice.

> We, true Diabolonians yet remaining in the rebellious town of Mansoul, cannot with contentment and quiet endure to behold how dispraised, disgraced, and reproached you are among the inhabitants. And yet, we are not without hope as this may become your habitation again, in that its people have drifted from its Prince and he has departed. Although they send, and send, and send petitions after him to return, they cannot get any good word from him.[520] Moreover, there has fallen a great sickness and fainting upon the townspeople – not only upon the poorer sort but on the lords, captains, and chief gentry, as well – while we Diabolonians remain ok.[521] Consequently, because of their great transgression in one regard and

---

[519] Ezekiel 11:2

[520] Psalm 18:41

[521] Converse to the Plagues in Exodus when the Egyptians were afflicted, and the Israelites weren't

because of their great sickness in another regard, we believe they lie ready for your grasp!

Mr. Profane carried the communication to Hell-Gate Hill, knocked at the brazen gates for entrance, and Cerberus, the porter,[522] delivered the communication from the Diabolonians living in Mansoul to Diabolus. As Beelzebub, Lucifer, Apollyon, and the rest of the rabble gathered to hear the communication, the command was given that, without let or stop, a dead-man's bell[523] – its sound spreading throughout all corners of the den – should be rung for joy. Yes, there was prodigious rejoicing that Mansoul was about to come to ruin!

After performing this enjoyably horrible (for them) ceremony, the evil associates set out to consult with one another about how they might respond to their friends in Mansoul. Some advised one thing. Some advised another thing. Because the business required haste, however, they thought best to leave the business to prince Diabolus for framing an adequate response, as follows:

"Beloved children and disciples, we, in our desolate den, have received, with great joy and contentment, your wondrous letter by the hand of your trusty Mr. Profane. That you might realize how acceptable your tidings were, we rang our bell in gladness. Oh, how wonderful we yet have friends in Mansoul, and such as seek our honor and revenge in its ruination. Also, it is good to hear the Mansoulian citizens are in such a degenerated condition they have offended their Prince and, yes, he is gone! Their anguishing sickness also pleases us, too, as does your health, might, and strength, as well! Whenever we get our clutches back upon Mansoul, you need not fear our being cast out again. We will come this time with a strength you can never imagine. We will lay a far greater hold upon the place than we ever did before.[524] We are glad, so horribly glad, that we can get that town again!

"O, our trusty Diabolonians, there is something else, though, in which you may be helpful. Pry into, spy out the weaknesses of the town and send a word by whatever means you think we can best regain it. Say if it should be by persuasion to vain and loose living, or by tempting them to doubt and despair, or by blowing the town up with the gunpowder of pride and self-conceit. Yes, vain and loose living, doubt and despair, pride and self-

---

[522] Cerberus: A monstrous watchdog with three heads (or fifty) guarding the entrance to Hades

[523] A dead-man's bell, dead bell, or deid bell (Scots), also a 'death', 'mort', 'lych', 'passing bell' or 'skellet bell', was a form of hand bell used in Scotland and northern England in conjunction with deaths and funerals up until the 19th century (Wikipedia).

[524] Matthew 12:43-45

conceit! Also say when you brave Diabolonians, true sons of the pit, are ready to make a most hideous assault from within, while we storm it from without. Blessings upon you!"

As Mr. Profane carried Diabolus's response back to the Diabolonians gathered in secret conference at the house of Mr. Mischief, there was great happiness for what they heard. Then, with bated breath they were eager to know how it fared with Lucifer, Beelzebub, and the rest of the evils. Altogether, how the bells rang for the joy for what those in this evil conclave came to feel upon this day! However, having gained the necessary directions, the Diabolonians in and about town underscored the importance of keeping their plans close. Basically, they shouldn't let Mansoul know what was being devised for bringing about her ruin and overthrow!

It was at this point Mr. Deceit stepped forward. It was his opinion that they should make Mansoul loose and vain by driving its people into doubt and despair as well as by endeavoring to blow them up by the gunpowder of self-conceit and pride.

"I think," advised Mr. Deceit, "if we tempt them to pride, that may do something.[525] If we tempt them to wantonness, that may help some more.[526] But, if we could drive them into doubt and desperation, aha! that would hammer the nail! We should then have them question the truth of their Prince's love, which would disillusion them and disgust him; and if all this will work as well as I think, they will quit sending petitions to him and it is farewell to Prince Emmanuel's help and supply."

As the group discussed how to make this happen, Mr. Deceit had still another plan. "Let some of our friends change their names, disguise themselves with a different apparel, and go into the market like far countrymen. Upon letting themselves out as servants and pretending to be beneficial – for the masters who would buy into this, of course – they might be able to so corrupt and defile the corporation that it will throw Prince Emmanuel into a rage. He would spew his Mansoulian people out of his mouth. Our prince Diabolus, then, should be able to prey upon them with ease.[527] And, yes, Mansoul – ha! ha! – would fall like a fig into the mouth of the eater."[528]

No sooner had the project been laid out than it was enthusiastically accepted. All the Diabolonians were stepping forward to engage in such a delicious enterprise. However, it was thought best that two or three (not all) would be better to accomplish this covert mission.

---

[525] Proverbs 13:10

[526] James 1:14

[527] 2 Corinthians 11:3

[528] Nahum 3:12

Lord Covetousness, who called himself Prudent-Thrifty was one. Lord Lasciviousness, who called himself Harmless-Mirth was another. And Lord Anger, who called himself Good-Zeal was the third.

What a smooth and clever change of names!

PRAYER STARTER: *Thank you, God, for Sundays, times for prayer, praise, and proclamation of your word! Indeed, thank you for any day you keep providing us guidance, enrichment, a reawakening, and an empowerment for our living. Goodness knows, we continually need it! The presence of evil lays deceptively close and all around us. Help us, Lord, as we draw from the means with which we are strengthened by your grace.* [From here on continue in your own prayerful words.] *In Jesus' name, we pray. Amen.*

Marketplace Deception

Mark 10:24b: Children, how hard is it for them that truft in riches, to entre into the kingdome of God! (GEN, 1560).

Children, how hard is it for them that trust in riches, to enter into the kingdom of God! (GNV, 1599)

On market-day, three lusty fellows – newly-named Prudent-Thrifty, Harmless-Mirth, and Good-Zeal – entered Mansoul clothed in russet. What a color contrast their dark brown orangish tinge attire would make amidst the white robes worn in and around the town![529]

It was such an opportune time for the rogues assuming the guise of far countrymen to slip in close to take advantage of the hustle and bustle of people's lives in and around Mansoul.

In effect, the three rogues offered a deal so hard to refuse – a low wage, faithful service, and a slick (or, should I say, slippery) sales presence for a town delighting in commerce![530]

With their diabolical plan off to a good start, Mr. Mind was drawn into hiring Prudent-Thrifty. Mr. Godly-Fear was drawn into hiring Good-Zeal. Since Mansoul was in the church season of Lent,[531] time passed before

---

[529] Matthew 7:15; Russet is a dark brown color with a reddish-orange tinge. As a tertiary color, russet is an equal mix of orange and purple pigments. The first recorded use of russet as a color name in English was in 1562 (Wikipedia).

[530] In a similar approach, C. S. Lewis, contrasting war and worldliness, describes "one of [Satan's] best weapons [as being] contented worldliness," in *The Screwtape Letters*, section 5 of 31 (C. S. Lewis Pte. Ltd, 1942; New York: HarperCollins, 2001), 24.

[531] Lent: The penitential and prayerful time, beginning with Ash Wednesday, for the six weeks in preparation for Holy Week culminating in Easter

Lord Willbewill was attracted to Harmless-Mirth as a waiting man and lackey.[532]

With the three villains – in heart: so filthy, arch, and sly – off to a good start at finding an edge for their mischief-making,[533] Mr. Prudent-Thrifty was able to slip a little beneath Mr. Mind's thinking cap. However, the scoundrel that went under the visor[534] of Good-Zeal – a.k.a., Lord Anger – did not fare well. His master, Godly-Fear, recognized the counterfeit as a rascal quite quickly, although the imposter managed to slip away before the master was able to grab ahold of him and hang him.[535]

Still, by the time the vagabonds accomplished as much as they could do inside the town, they turned their attention to the time that might be best for Diabolus to make his assault from outside the town.

A market day still seemed the way to go. Those in and around the market would be busy with the latest sales as the shoppers would be the least suspecting of being taken by surprise. On the other hand, if such did not go well, the Diabolonians could try slinking amidst the crowd and making a speedy escape.

Meanwhile the Diabolonian lords of looseness inhabiting Mansoul drafted another communication to Diabolus, which they had Mr. Profane carry for delivery.

> "O, great lord, the nourisher of our lives, Diabolus," the letter began, "how glad we are to hear of your willingness to collaborate with us! Just to see our enemies fly before us or die at our feet is a wonderful sight! Thus, while working against all appearances of the good,[536] we are hellishly contriving to the utmost of our ability to make a successful assault upon this Mansoul."

Detailing the proceedings of the last bit of time – e.g., what happened with Covetousness, Lasciviousness, and Anger (shrouded, of course, by their deceptively fictitious names) – the missive to Diabolus went on to entertain a discussion regarding the best day and best way to imperil Mansoul from within and without.

> "Of all the possibilities that would be most effective for gaining a hold, we have considered blowing them up with the gunpowder of pride and tempting them to lose themselves in vain living. Still, we believe driving them

---

[532] Lackey: a servant, especially a liveried footman or manservant

[533] Ephesians 5:6-7

[534] Visor – "An outward appearance or show under which something different is hid; a mask or disguise" OED.

[535] "Wow! a serious and immediate consequence, with no due process!" Dr. Janis Gibbs

[536] Romans 7:21; Galatians 5:17

into the gulf of desperation would do the best.

"Considering how we might accomplish this, we thought of making them as vile as we could and falling upon them with the utmost force at an appointed time. However, as we think of all nations that you have at your whistle, we think an army of doubters might be the most likely to lead the attack to overcome the town.

"As we've pointed out, the attempted works of Prudent-Thrifty, Harmless-Mirth, and Good-Zeal – you know their real names – started preparing the soil for a primary assault, despite the sad misfortune of Good-Zeal in the employ of that peevish old gentleman, Mr. Godly-Fear, who took pepper in the nose and turned our fitting companion out of his house, unfortunately generating an aggravating sinkhole to our work.

"However, that brings us to another part of the plan. I mean our suggested onslaught upon market day when people are so caught up in their business and are supposedly least suspecting of an assault. Hence, with Mansoul thrown into utter confusion, we can swallow them up before they can come to themselves![537]

"If, in your serpentine heads, you, our highly esteemed lords and subtle dragons, can suggest a better way, please let us know quickly. We are so ready to get going!"

Now, Mr. Profane who carried the document from the house of Mr. Mischief in Mansoul, happened upon Cerberus, the dog of Hell-Gate, who then, with expedience, delivered the writing to the monsters of the infernal cave.

Meanwhile, the epidemic kept raging throughout Mansoul among their captains as well as the inhabitants, notwithstanding the fact the Diabolonian enemies remained lively and strong. Quite the reverse of God's plagues upon Egypt! Nevertheless, the citizens of Mansoul kept firing petitions to Emmanuel and Shaddai and failing to obtain a response, let alone a smile. Thus, they wallowed in a slough of discouragement.[538]

At the time Cerberus and Mr. Profane met, they engaged in a brief conversation which kept underscoring how crucial the timing for an assault upon Mansoul would be.

Nothing like the present moment!

---

[537] James 3:16

[538] Text and Song Interactional: Ryan Dale Stevenson and Bryan Christopher Fowler, songwriters, "In the Eye of the Storm," sung by Ryan Stevenson as artist and Gabe Real as featured artist, released 2015.

**Pen and Ink Drawing Depicting Cerberus, the Dog of Hell-gate,
by Kaitlyn E. Priset, artist**

Likewise, there was the matter of those Diabolonians residing in continual fear, inside the town of Mansoul. Something must be done and quickly to alleviate their circumstances!

"Go on in, my brave Mr. Profane," Cerberus said. "My lords will welcome you as they would the best *coranto*[539] that this whole kingdom will afford. I have directed your letter to them already."

On entering Diabolus's den, Mr. Profane received a hearty welcome from the lords of the pit gathered there. In extending respect, Mr. Profane exclaimed, "Let my lord Diabolus conquer Mansoul and be the king forever!"

---

[539] Corantos were early informational broadsheets, precursors to newspapers. Beginning around the 14th century, a system developed where letters of news and philosophical discussion would be sent to a central collecting point to be bundled and sent around to the various correspondents.

Then, the hollow belly and yawning gorge of hell broke out into a loud and hideous groan – for that was the music of the den – thus, making the mountains about to totter.

Getting down to the affair of the letter from the Diabolonians of Mansoul, Lucifer was first to respond. "Making Mansoul more and more vile and filthy is certainly the best way to destroy a soul! Our old friend Balaam went this way years ago.[540] But let us be honest, for there is nothing that can mess our work up so effectively as this stuff called grace,[541] in which I hope the town of Mansoul has no share. However, I have a serious question regarding an attack on market day. If we do not time our business well, the whole matter may fail. The thought of capitalizing on a time when Mansoul will be the busiest is just the time that the guards would be doubled. Therefore, the mess-up could subject our Diabolonians in the town to unavoidable ruin."

At this point, Beelzebub acknowledged Lucifer's concerns altogether which provoked some charged discussion. An important matter, though, was in trying to understand how greatly the town of Mansoul comprehended her decayed state and to what extent were the designs they had afoot against her. Then, there were the matters of how it affected the watch set at the gates as well as whether it was doubled on market-days. And yet, if they were in a sleep, any day would do, although a market-day remained the best.

Needing some additional information, the evil conclave called Mr. Profane back into their conference room. Profane reiterated that the town of Mansoul had fallen into such decay of their faith and love[542] that Emmanuel seemed to keep ignoring their pleas for him to come back again.

It was at this point Diabolus broke into an expression of gladness that Mansoul had become so backward in any reformation. Additionally, he expressed fear regarding Mansoul's continual petitioning Emmanuel and, yet, given the looseness of their people's lives, it seemed there could not be much heart or good intentions behind any of their doings. Without heart, such supplications were of little worth.

Then, Beelzebub drove home the thought, "If this be so, as Mr. Profane has described it, it does not matter what day we attack. None of their prayers nor even their power will do them much good!"[543]

---

[540] Balaam: Numbers 22-24; 31:16; 2 Peter 2:1; Revelation 2:14
[541] Ephesians 1:6-7
[542] Revelation 2:4
[543] Isaiah 59:2

When Beelzebub ended his remarks, Apollyon added his thoughts: "We should not hurry. Just go fair and softly. Let the people of Mansoul go on polluting and defiling and drawing themselves into sin. There is nothing like sin to devour people. The effects? They will leave off watching over their souls, petitioning Emmanuel for help, and anything else tending to safety and security. Ultimately, the people in Mansoul will forget Emmanuel and won't even care if he is around. Should they get into a fix and panic, Emmanuel won't come, especially if the current pattern of their behavior continues. For example, our trusty friend, Mr. Carnal-Security did drive him out of town with his tricks. Then too, Lord Covetousness and Lord Lasciviousness – oh, I mean Prudent-Thrifty and Harmless-Mirth! – are keeping Emmanuel at a distance by what they are doing. Let me tell you, two or three Diabolonians entertained within Mansoul will accomplish more than a legion of forces we could send. Let us keep with the same cunning and craft we have perfected right from the beginning. Perhaps we may not need to engage in a war at all. Or, if a war is necessary, the more sinful Mansoul is, the more unable she is to resist. Anyhow, let us just keep on with the same means that drew the people into sin in the first place and Prince Emmanuel may be driven off forever. He will go away with his rams, slings, captains, and soldiers and leave Mansoul naked and bare!"[544]

As soon as Apollyon concluded, Diabolus started blowing out his own malice. "My lords and powers of the cave, my true and trusty friends, I have given enough ear to your long and tedious oratory. My furious gorge and my empty paunch are so greatly lusting for a repossession of my famous town of Mansoul that I can no longer wait to see the outcomes of our lingering projects. I must, without any further delay, fill my insatiable void with the soul and body of Mansoul. Quit diddling away my time. Lend me your heads, hearts, and help!"

Upon seeing how enflamed Diabolus was to devour Mansoul, these lords and princes of the pit stepped away from making any further suggestions and shifted their discussion to the technical aspects of military procedure. For instance, what kind of and how many soldiers would Diabolus need? It was also noted that there were none more fitting for such an expedition then an army of between twenty and thirty thousand sturdy doubters. And since Diabolus was so fired up and, quite naturally, a compelling army recruiter, Diabolus should be the one to go ahead and beat his drum for soldiers from the land of Doubting, a land which lay next to

---

[544] Psalm 71:10-11

Hell-Gate Hill. Furthermore, these lords of the pit themselves would assist by heading up and managing Diabolus's forces.

So, having framed a response, they called for Mr. Profane to come back, get what they had written, and carry it back to the Diabolonians residing in and around Mansoul.

It would be a fierce battle!

PRAYER STARTER: *Lord, increasingly we realize the difficulties people face when plagued by treachery and trickery. Keep us spiritually alert. Help us whenever we face challenges seeking to undo us. At times, we feel so weak. Empower us with the strength of your guidance.* [From here on continue with your own prayerful words.] *In Jesus' name, we pray. Amen.*

Battle Plans from Hell

Ephesians 6:12-13: For we wreſtle not againſt fleſh and blood, but againſt principalities againſt powers, and againſt the worldlie gouernours, the princes of the darkenes of ths worlde, agaiſt ſpiritual wickedneſſes, which are in the hie places. For this cauſe take vnto you the whole armour of God, that ye may be able to reſiſt in the euil daye, & hauing finiſhed all things, ſtand faſt (GEN, 1560).

For we wrestle not against flesh and blood, but against principalities, against powers, and against world governors, the princes of the darkness of this world, against spiritual wickedness, which are in the high places. For this cause take you the whole armor of God, that ye may be able to resist in the evil day, and having finished all things, stand fast (GNV, 1599).

From the dark and horrible dungeon of hell, Diabolus and the whole entourage of princes sent a communication to the Diabolonians in and about Mansoul waiting impatiently for an answer to their design against Mansoul. It went like this:

"O native ones, in whom we boast daily and in whose actions all the year-long we greatly delight, we received your letter delivered by our trusty and greatly beloved Mr. Profane. We were so pleased with what you articulated that this yawning hollow-bellied place in which we were meeting let out a most hideous and resounding shout of great joy. It was so great the mountains around Hell-Gate Hill were nearly shaken to pieces by the sound.

"At our full assembly and conclave of princes and principalities, your project was tossed from one side of the cave to the other. We could not but admire the subtlety and skill apparent in your plan. A more effective scheme could not have been devised by the very wits of hell. There were a few alternatives which fell to the ground. In the end, though, there was no rival to yours for taking over the rebellious town of Mansoul, Diabolus being your primary cheerleader! Thus, we can do no less than highly approve and admire your plan of action.

"You might be interested in knowing Diabolus is raising, for your relief in the ruination of Mansoul, more than twenty thousand doubters to come against the enemy. They are stout, sturdy, and experienced men of old, accustomed to war and able, hearts pounding, to endure the drum.[545] Diabolus is engaging in this work with all the possible speed he can.

"One thing more, though. We desire that you in Mansoul keep using your power, cunning, and skill, with all the delusive persuasions you can, to draw the town into more sin and wickedness, especially the sin that when finished brings forth death.[546]

"We have concluded that the more decadent Mansoul is, the weaker and more unable to provide any resistance and, consequently, the better for us to make our assault and swallow her up.[547]

"Here is hoping further that the mighty Shaddai might cast them out of his protection, send his captains and soldiers home with their slings and rams, and leave the town stark naked. Then, with Mansoul laid open, the fruit will fall, yes, as a fig into the mouth of the eater.

"As to the timing, we yet have not fully come to a decision. At the present time, some think as you do, that it could be a market day or a market day at night. Whatever it becomes, be ready. Whenever you hear the roaring drum without, be as busy to make a horrible confusion within. In this way, Mansoul will be distressed before and behind and won't know which way to turn.

"My Lord Lucifer, my Lord Beelzebub, my Lord Apollyon, my Lord Legion, and my Lord Diabolus, from our dreadful confines in the most fearful pit, we salute you, as also those many legions here with us – we wish you may be as hellishly prosperous as we desire ourselves to be."[548]

---

[545] "On the field of battle, the spoken word does not carry far enough: hence the institution of gongs and drums. Nor can ordinary objects be seen clearly enough: hence the institution of banners and flags" Sun Tzu, "Maneuvering," #23, in *The Art of War*, 6th century BC (UK: Arcturus Holdings Limited, 2018), 66.

[546] Hebrews 3:13

[547] Matthew 13:19

[548] 1 Peter 5:8

As he came up the stairs from the depth of the cave, having completed his mission to the horrible pit and ready to return to Mansoul, Mr. Profane once again met Cerberus.

"How did matters go below?" Cerberus asked.

"As well as expected," Mr. Profane responded. "The letter I carried here was highly approved by the lords and I am heading back to tell our Diabolonians in Mansoul the great news."

"Does Diabolus intent to go against Mansoul himself?" Cerberus inquired.

"Does he!" Profane answered. "Yes, and he will take twenty thousand men of war, all sturdy, picked men from the land of Doubting."

"Wonderful!" exclaimed Cerberus. "What is more, I would love to be put at the head of a thousand."

"Your wish may come to pass," Profane said to Cerberus. "You look like one who has the fortitude for it!"

"Ay," Cerberus swelled. "Get going fast back to Mansoul with all the harms that this place can afford. When you come to Mr. Mischief's house tell those gathered that Cerberus wishes to serve against the famous town!"[549]

"I will," Profane agreed. "I know the lords there will be glad to hear it!"

Then, with great haste, Mr. Profane hurried back to the house of Mr. Mischief in Mansoul with the report from the high and mighty principalities and powers from whom the Diabolonians were eagerly awaiting to hear.

The present state of Mansoul was miserable. She had offended Prince Emmanuel. He was gone. By her foolishness she had opened herself up to the powers of hell threatening utter destruction. It is true Mansoul was somewhat sensible of her sin, but the Diabolonians had gotten so deeply inside of her. Although she was crying out to Emmanuel, her cries did not bring him back. As far as she knew, he would not return.[550] Moreover, no Mansoulian knew the enemy's power, industry, or most recent plans.

---

[549] Psalm 94:21

[550] "To doubt the good will of God is an inborn suspicion of God with all of us. Besides, the devil, our adversary, goeth about seeking to devour us by roaring: 'God is angry at you and is going to destroy you forever.' In all these difficulties we have only one support, the Gospel of Christ. To hold on to it, that is the trick . . . The Law scolds us, sin screams at us, death thunders at us, the devil roars at us. In the midst of the clamor the Spirit of Christ cries in our hearts: 'Abba, Father.' And this little cry of the Spirit transcends the hullabaloo of the Law, sin, death, and the devil, and finds a hearing with God" Martin Luther, *Commentary on Galatians*, trans. by Theodore Graebner (Digireads.com Publishing, 2019), content on Galatians 4:6; p. 108.

The Mansoulian people kept sending petition after petition to Prince Emmanuel, but no response came back. All their hopes hung in silence. Notwithstanding, Mansoul attempted no reformation. Whatever its people in desperation paraded as spiritual, Diabolus banked on the fact that if Mansoul kept harboring iniquity in its people's hearts, the King would not listen to their prayers.[551] Much like a rolling weed whipped before the whirlwind, the Mansoulian people kept growing weaker and weaker and weaker. Although they kept crying out to Shaddai for help, the Diabolonians kept growing in strength and confidence as the townspeople of Mansoul kept diminishing.[552] And sadly, the men, women, and children kept dying by the plague sweeping through their numbers.

There was a man, Mr. Prywell, who had a love for Mansoul and held respect for Shaddai. While walking around town he had a knack for coming upon friendly gossip and other bits of information. To put it briefly, if somehow, someone caught what was going on in and around Mansoul, it was Prywell. One evening, while passing a particular house in Vilehill, once known to be a house where Diabolonians lived, he heard someone muttering something that perked up his ears. Unnoticed, he softly drew closer to the house and learned of a plot being hatched against Mansoul. Already Prywell was astute enough to realize that mischief could befall either from Diabolonians within or without. It was at this point he learned Diabolus was on the move with an army twenty thousand strong, intending to possess Mansoul. The plan, and it was a vile one, was to put all Mansoulian people to the sword, kill and destroy the King's captains, and drive Emmanuel's soldiers out of town.

At this point, Prywell went without delay to the house of the Mayor, who in turn sent for the subordinate preacher and broke the news to him who caused the lecture bell to be rung. The people quickly came together. He gave them a short exhortation upon watchfulness.[553] Then, citing Prywell's news as to the source of the great concern, the Mayor announced that a horrible plot was contrived against Mansoul, even to the point of a massacre.

What brought strength to the information was that Mr. Prywell was the one who caught wind of the plot. Everyone knew Prywell was a lover of Mansoul, a sober and judicious man, a man who was not a tattler, nor an instigator of false report, but one the people could trust to get right to the bottom of things and present the news very carefully.

---

[551] Psalm 66:18
[552] Proverbs 5:21-23
[553] Matthew 26:41; 1 Peter 5:8

Thus, the town of Mansoul was swept up into a frenzy of enormous concern. Thoughts of their inattention to and defection from Shaddai turned raw like a freshly felt wound. They had forsaken their former mercies and grown weaker and weaker.[554] And now they realized it! Many a good man was dead and the Diabolonians of late had been growing stronger and stronger.

The subordinate preacher also conveyed Prywell's news that several letters had passed back and forth between the Diabolonians and the furies pertaining to the intended annihilation of Mansoul. Upon hearing this, the people could not help but raise their voices and weep. They then passed word to the captains, high commanders, and men of war, entreating them to use whatever means they could to be strong,[555] take courage and make ready by day or by night to do battle with Diabolus.

Consequently, the captains shook themselves like Samson and came together to contrive how to defeat those bold and hellish contrivances that were upon the wheel by the means of Diabolus and his friends against the sickly, weak, and impoverished town of Mansoul; and they agreed upon the following:

1. The gates should be kept shut, made fast with bars and locks, and any people coming in or going out should be carefully examined by the captains of the guards.[556]

2. A strict search should be made for all Diabolonians throughout the whole town.[557]

3. Wheresoever or with whomsoever any Diabolonians were found, they should make penance in an open and public place.[558]

4. A public fast and a day of humiliation should be kept throughout the corporation; and anyone not engaged in such should be considered Diabolonian.[559]

5. It was further resolved that, quickly and with gracious warmth, Mansoul would renew their humiliation for sin and petition Shaddai for help.[560]

---

[554] Psalm 32:5
[555] Psalm 31:24
[556] 1 Corinthians 16:13
[557] Lamentations 3:40; Hebrews 12:15-16
[558] Jeremiah 2:34; 5:26; Ezekiel 16:52
[559] Psalm 35:13
[560] Isaiah 37:4

6. Furthermore, thanks should be extended to Mr. Prywell for his ever-diligent efforts seeking the good.[561]

Shortly afterwards, Mr. Prywell went out into the country toward Hell-Gate Hill where the Doubters were and, having done this reconnaissance work, he perceived Diabolus was almost ready to head to Mansoul. So, he hurried back to Mansoul and, calling the captains and elders together, told them what he had learned. Almost ready to march, Diabolus had made Incredulity in charge of the army, which consisted of more than twenty thousand Doubters. He also reported Diabolus resolved to bring the princes of the infernal pit to assist in command over the warriors. It was certainly true several of the black den would ride reformades with Diabolus to reduce Mansoul to the obedience of their prince.

What is more, while sneaking around the Doubters, Prywell picked up on why Incredulity was made general of the whole army. It was because there was none truer than he to the tyrant. He more easily and more dexterously could beleaguer the town. And he had an implacable spite against the Mansoul for affronts he previously had experienced there – pure revenge![562]

Jarred awake by the news, Mansoul bore down with plans to protect and strengthen the town. Diligent and impartial search was made for any Diabolonians. Two Diabolonians were discovered in the homes of Mr. Mind and Lord Willbewill. In Mr. Mind's house, Lord Covetousness, disguising himself as Prudent-Thrifty, was found. In Lord Willbewill's house, one Lasciviousness, who had changed his name to Harmless-Mirth, was found. The two culprits were arrested and taken to Mr. Trueman, the gaoler, who handled them so severely and bound them so tightly that they eventually fell into a deep consumption and died.

Subsequently, their masters, Mind and Willbewill, via an earlier civic agreement, came forward to face a public confession and strict amendment of their lives, as a warning to the rest of Mansoul.[563]

After this serious wake-up call, the captains and elders of Mansoul expanded their search for Diabolonians wherever they could find them.[564] Although they could catch the scent of them and track them right up to the mouth of their holes, vaults, caves, dens, and elsewhere, they could hardly do any justice with them. Diabolonian ways were ever so crooked. Their

---

[561] 1 Corinthians 4:2
[562] Hebrews 12:1-8
[563] John 3:19
[564] John 3:20

holds were so strong. They were ever so quick to evade detection and slip away.[565]

Nonetheless, Diabolonians realized Mansoul put a tighter rein on things where previously matters had taken an easier trend. There was a time Diabolonians could boldly walk out in the open during the day. But now, because of tighter surveillance and continual stakeouts, the Diabolonians were forced to keep themselves in seclusion.

Gone were the days when a Mansoulian would have a Diabolonian companion. Now they were marked deadly enemies. Such were the changes that Prywell's intelligence ventures and search patterns brought about throughout the land.

PRAYER STARTER: *There are times, Lord, tensions and troubles become so overwhelming. We've lost a sense of where to turn, even how to turn. Life feels so confusing. Please, God, do not let our hopes become obscure or be blotted out. Too long we have turned a deaf ear. We know it. Now, help us recover a discerning spirit.* [From here on continue with your own prayerful words.] *In Jesus' name, we pray. Amen.*

The Battle Early On

2 Samuel 22:32-33: For who is God befides the Lord? And who is mighty, faue our God? God is my ftrength in battel, and maketh my way vpright (GEN, 1560).

For who is God besides the Lord? And who is mighty save our God? God is my strength in battle, and maketh my way upright (GNV, 1599).

Diabolus finished organizing his army to bring ruin to Mansoul. Diabolus, no less, was the lord paramount, and Incredulity was the commanding general. Those promoted to be captains and field officers were those who liked Diabolus's furious cravings for destruction and revenge the best. The command postings, the military roster of unit captains, regimental colors, standard bearers, and other identities made an intimidating lineup:

---

[565] 1 Corinthians 4:5

Captains	Over the	Colors	Standard-Bearer	Scutcheon
Captain Rage	Election Doubters	Red	Mr. Destructive	Red Dragon
Fury	Vocation Doubters	Pale	Mr. Darkness	Fiery Flying Serpent
Damnation	Grace Doubters	Red	Mr. No-Life	Black Den
Insatiable	Faith Doubters	Red	Mr. Devourer	Yawning Jaws
Brimstone	Perseverance Doubters	Pale	Mr. Burning	Blue & Stinking Flame
Torment	Resurrection Doubters	Pale	Mr. Gnaw	Black Worm
No-Ease	Salvation Doubters	Red	Mr. Restless	Ghastly Picture of Death
Sepulchre	Glory Doubters	Pale	Mr. Corruption	Skull & Dead Men's Bones
Past Hope	Felicity Doubters	Red	Mr. Despair	Hot Iron & Hard Heart

Thus, Captains Rage,[566] Fury,[567] Damnation,[568] Insatiable,[569] Brimstone,[570] Torment,[571] No-Ease,[572] Sepulchre,[573] and Past Hope[574] – quite a terrifying roster of warriors – were those who commanded various fighting units of Doubters![575]

---

[566] Rage: Psalms 2:1-3; 7:6; 102:8; Proverbs 14:16; Revelation 12:3-4

[567] Fury: Numbers 21:6; Deuteronomy 32:27-28; Psalm 64:1; Ephesians 4:4

[568] Damnation: Matthew 23:14; Mark 3:29; 2 Peter 2:4

[569] Insatiable: Proverbs 27:20; Ezekiel 16:28

[570] Brimstone: Genesis 19:24; Job 18:15; Isaiah 34:9; Luke 17:29; Revelation 9:17-18

[571] Torment: Judges 10:9; Job 19:2; Luke 16:23-25, 28; Hebrews 11:37

[572] No-Ease: Psalm 37:39; Acts 24:23; Revelation 14:11

[573] Sepulchre: Jeremiah 5:16; Luke 24:1; Colossians 1:27

[574] Past-Hope: Job 17:15; Psalm 119:116; Acts 26:6; Romans 8:24-25; Ephesians 2:12; 1 Thessalonians 4:13

[575] Doubters: Numbers 14:29-31; 1 Kings 20:22-26; Job 5:2; Matthew 21:21; 2 Corinthians 1:8; 4:8; 1 Timothy 2:8

The Standard Bearers accompanying them: Destructive,[576] Darkness,[577] No-Life,[578] Devourer,[579] Burning,[580] Gnaw,[581] Restless,[582] Corruption,[583] and Despair.[584]

To superintend the officers Diabolus brought aboard seven superior captains. They were Lord Beelzebub, Lord Lucifer, Lord Legion, Lord Apollyon, Lord Python,[585] Lord Cerberus, and Lord Belial.[586] Incredulity ranked above the seven. He was second to only Diabolus. Completing the attack force were a few reformades – some captains of hundreds or more – eager to set out from Hell-Gate Hill.

Tipped off by Prywell that Diabolus's army was coming in fast, the Mansoulians doubled their guards, set a strong watch at the gates, and mounted the slings in strategic places from which to cast enormous stones. Consequently, the Diabolonians in and around Mansoul could not be as effective for Diabolus as had been anticipated because the town was awake![587]

But alas! the poor Mansoulian people were so sorely frightened at the first appearance of their foes – even as early as their hearing the drum

---

[576] Destructive: Isaiah 59:7

[577] Darkness: Job 3:4-9; 10:21-22; 19:8; 30:26; Ecclesiastes 11:8; Isaiah 8:22; 9:2; 60:2; Matthew 4:16; 6:23; John 1:5; 3:19; Romans 1:21; Ephesians 6:12; 1 John 1:5-6; Jude 13

[578] No-Life: John 3:36; 1 Peter 3:10; 1 John 3:15; Revelation 13:1-9

[579] Devourer: Malachi 3:11

[580] Burning: Exodus 21:25; Proverbs 16:27; 26:21, 23; Isaiah 9:5; Amos 4:11; Revelation 18:9, 18

[581] Gnaw: Revelation 16:10

[582] Restless: Job 7:4-5; Psalms 32:3-4; 107:4-5; Daniel 2:1; Matthew 6:31-32; 11:28-30

[583] Corruption: Psalms 5:9; 16:10; Acts 2:27, 31; 1 Corinthians 15:42; 2 Peter 2:19

[584] Despair: 2 Corinthians 4:8

[585] Python: Leviticus 20:27; Deuteronomy 18:11; 1 Samuel 28:1-25; 1 Chronicles 10:13; Acts 16:16-18 – J. N. Darby translation. Walter Martin, citing Adam Clarke, in part, helps bring clarity to the nature of the Python spirit Paul encountered in Philippi: "The spirit of divination associated with this girl, *puthon* in the Greek, is directly linked in translation to an area in Greece known as Delphi, where the Oracle or Pythia answered wealthy pilgrims' questions about their futures (fortune-telling). 'Having a spirit of Python, or of Apollo, Pytho was, according to fable, a huge serpent, that had an oracle at Mount Parnassus, famous for predicting future events; Apollo slew this serpent, and hence, he was called Pythius, and became celebrated as the foreteller of future events; and all those, who either could or pretended to predict future events, were influenced by the spirit of Apollo Pythius.' This slave girl possessed a spirit of divination associated with the Delphic spirit, and through her powers she brought much gain to the people who utilized her services" (Walter Martin, Jill Martin Rische and Kurt Van Gorden, *The Kingdom of the Occult* [Nashville, Tennessee: Thomas Nelson, 2008], 57-58).

[586] Belial: 2 Corinthians 6:15

[587] Ephesians 5:14-15

which was within an earshot seven miles away – their hearts sank in great despair.[588]

As Diabolus came up against the town, assuming his friends in Mansoul were ready to do as planned, he came at Ear-gate with a most furious assault. However, hampered by the absence of their inside help, he unwittingly led his army right into a spray of slingstones, thus driving his forces back into an entrenchment on the field out of reach of the missiles.[589] Even so, Diabolus managed to cast up four mounts against the town to provoke a terror like what a lion would do to maneuver its prey. The first mount he named Mount Diabolus – after himself, of course – situated on the north side of town. The other mounts he named Mount Alecto, Mount Megara, and Mount Tisiphone, after the dreadful furies of hell.[590] And Diabolus's scutcheon was a fierce depiction. It was a masterpiece of demonic art portraying the town Mansoul burning up in a raging fire.

Next, Diabolus instructed his drummer to approach the walls of the town each night and beat a parley. No noise ever heard upon earth seemed more terrible than the haunting sound of the war drum.[591] With this tactic, Diabolus hoped to drain the strength of the townspeople by wearing away their resolve.

The tactic was effective; the people of Mansoul reacted as they might if some terrifying creature had threatened to devour them. "Behold darkness and sorrow, and the light was darkened in the heaven thereof."[592]

Having got the people's attention amidst a backdrop of such harrowing fear, the drummer delivered the word: "My master bids me to tell you that, if you submit, you will enjoy the food of the earth; however, if you, stiff-necked people that you are, continue in stubbornness, he resolves to take you by force."

---

[588] 1 Peter 5:8

[589] James 4:7

[590] See earlier note on Alecto, Megara and Tisiphone on page 47

[591] Military forces have used drums to deliver information, mark drill time, pass orders, and sound off for attack in many cultural backgrounds. In certain settings, the drum was more effective than the spoken word when communicating to large numbers of trained soldiers. As to psychological impact, the drum could imbue spirit or instill fear depending upon which side of the battlefield from which drumbeat is coming. Although the use of military drums had a long history in Asia, in the Middle East and in Africa, their use in Europe did not start until the Crusades. Later, in the seventeenth century, Bunyan imagined Diabolus's war drum, a terrifying sound possibly heard from as far as seven miles away, bringing Mansoul to quake over the enemy's approach. Moreover, military drums in Bunyan calling for a parley meant calling for a conference between enemies. In the present times, "beating the drum" is a metaphor for war.

[592] Isaiah 5:30

However, sensing the drum did not accomplish what he had expected, Diabolus once again sent his drummer out on the next night, but without his drum, to let the townsmen know he had a mind to parley. But the so-called parleying turned into what sounded as bully-like as it had the night before. In response – or should I say, in no response – the townspeople, remembering what a few of Diabolus's words had cost them previously, did not want to fall into the same mistake again.

On another night, who should be the messenger but the terrible Captain Sepulchre. "You inhabitants of Mansoul," Captain Sepulchre stormed, "I summon you in the name of Prince Diabolus! Set open your gates. Admit the great lord. If you still rebel when we take you by force, we will swallow you up as the grave. My lord is your undoubted prince. The brutal assault Emmanuel gave my lord when he dealt with him so dishonorably before shall not prevail. Consider, O Mansoul, whether you will submit peaceably or not. If you yield quietly, our old friendship shall be renewed. If you persist in rebellion, expect nothing but raging fire and sword!"[593]

As the suffering town of Mansoul felt the impact of such haunting words, it threw them into more desperation. Nonetheless, they granted Captain Sepulchre no response.[594] Instead, they approached their Lord Chief Secretary, their chief preacher, for some counsel. Although knowing him ill at ease at the time, they begged for his consideration upon two or three things. First, they hoped he would not keep himself so aloof from them but look caringly upon their miserable condition.[595] Second, they needed some advice, but all he offered was the directive to look to the Prince's law to see what was there.[596] Third, they pleaded he would help frame a petition to Shaddai and Emmanuel his Son. For they had already sent many of their own and received no response. In the end, all the chief preacher said was that they had so offended Emmanuel they must partake of their own stratagems.

The Lord Chief Secretary's response felt like a millstone dropped upon them. It crushed them so greatly that they hardly knew what to do. In no way did they dare to comply with Diabolus's demands. They were in a tight spot.[597]

---

[593] Text and Song Interactional: Micah Kuiper, Krissy Nordhoff and Jordan St. Cyr songwriters, "Fires" sung by Jordan St. Cyr, released 2021

[594] Psalm 123:4

[595] 1 Thessalonians 5:19-21

[596] James 1:25

[597] 2 Corinthians 7:10

The straits were that Mansoul felt caught betwixt her foes being ready to swallow her up and her friends withholding any compassionate and constructive help.

On the other hand, the Lord Manor, whose name was Lord Understanding, began to pick away at the Lord Chief Secretary's words by pulling some comfort out of what previously had seemed so bitter. For instance, this suffering for their sins and enduring a few more sorrows could lead them into trusting Emmanuel more significantly for help and being saved from their enemies.[598] Then, the Lord Understanding extended a searchlight further into the thoughts, as he was more than a prophet. Thus, he encouraged the townspeople to pry into what it all seemed, interact within the range of meanings, and expound them to their best advantage. All in all, it sounded a sense of hope, not despair. That hope encouraged the captains, preparing them to make a brave assault upon the enemy.[599]

With hope rekindled, they all took to their own places – the Captains to theirs, the Lord Mayor to his, the subordinate preacher to his, and Lord Willbewill to his. Then, on the next day, at the rising of the sun and Diabolus venturing closer to the wall, the Mansoulians responded with their slings, which fell upon the enemy like a swarm of hornets.[600] As there was nothing so discomforting to Mansoul as the roaring of Diabolus's drums, there was nothing so terrible to Diabolus as the Mansoulians' skillful deployment of Emmanuel's slings. In this way, they drove Diabolus into retreat. So, the Lord Mayor of Mansoul caused the bells to ring.[601]

When prince Diabolus realized his captains, soldiers, high lords, and others – indeed, the whole military forces – were beaten down by the stones that came from the golden slings, Diabolus shifted tactics to catch them by fawning. "I will flatter them into my net!"

So, after approaching the wall, Diabolus laid the sweetness on really thick! No beating the drums! No intimidating Captain Sepulchre! Instead, Diabolus came as the sweet-mouthed, peaceable prince.[602] No seeking revenge for injuries previously done! Rather he came as one posing to seek their advantage, welfare, and good pleasure.

---

[598] Among Alexander Whyte's last words in his character study lectures on Bunyan's *The Holy War*, there is the statement: "I have loved thee with an everlasting love, and it is to everlasting life that I am leading thee. And thou must let Me lead thee through fire and through water if I am to lead thee to heaven at last" Alexander Whyte, *Bunyan Characters – Third Series* [Public Domain] (Astounding-Stories.com, 2015), 97.

[599] Text and Song Interactional: Danny Gokey, Colby Wedgeworth and Ethan Gregory Hulse, songwriters, "Haven't Seen It Yet," by Danny Gokey, released 2019

[600] Joshua 24:12.

[601] Zechariah 9:15; James 4:7

[602] Proverbs 10:18

"You, my good friends of times ago, the desire of my heart, how many nights have I watched and how many weary steps have I taken that I might do you some good! I don't want to make war with you.[603] How must you forget those years when you enjoyed me as your prince? You had no wants back then. There were so many worldly delights I could get for you. You never had so many hard, dark, and troubled times as you do now. Oh, just look at yourselves since you bolted away from me. Oh, how weighted down you are! If you'd just embrace me again, I'd grant you your old charter – yes, I'd even enlarge it – with such an abundance of privileges. And look, I will not even charge you for those incivilities with which you offended me. Nor shall any of my dear friends who lie lurking in dens, and holes, and caves in Mansoul be hurtful to you anymore. They would even become your servants and minister unto you out of their substance. Previously you enjoyed their company. Why should it be different now? Come, come, let us renew our old friendships again.[604]

"Bear with me, my friends. Look at the liberty to which I am subjecting myself to speak freely with you. Consider the love I have that presses me to reach out to you. Oh, I am so zealous for us to be friends again. Don't put me to any further trouble. Subject yourselves to no more frights and fears. Listen! I'll have you back whether it is in peace or in war! Do not flatter yourselves with the seeming power and force of your own captains. You think Emmanuel will come to your help? Such strength will do nothing for you!

"Look with what stout and valiant army I am coming to you and how all its chief princes of the den are at the head of it. My captains are swifter than eagles. They are stronger than lions. They are greedier for prey than evening wolves. What is Og of Bashan![605] Or, Goliath of Gath![606] What are a hundred more to one of the least of my captains! How can you, Mansoul, think you can escape my hand and force?"[607]

Having stomached enough of Diabolus's flattering, fawning, and deceitful words, the Lord Mayor replied: "O Diabolus, prince of darkness, we are done falling for your destructive lies and flatteries. Should we give in to you once again and break away from the life-giving commandments of Shaddai? If so, how, in the end, would we be salvaged from the place you will be cast? O you who are so empty and void of truth, we would

---

[603] Psalm 36:3
[604] Matthew 4:8; Luke 4:6-7; James 4:4, 1 Peter 5:8; Revelation 12:10
[605] Numbers 21:33-34; Deuteronomy 3 and Joshua 13; Psalm 135:10-12
[606] 1 Samuel 17
[607] Sounds like an Abuser (so sweet and then the punch)

rather die by your hand than fall in with your flattering, mendacious and lying deceits!"[608]

When the tyrant realized that there was little to be gained parleying with the Lord Mayor, he fell into a hellish rage, resolving that he with his army of doubters would assault the town of Mansoul at another time.

Thus repulsed, Diabolus called for his drummer to strike up the battle beat, much to place terror into the hearts of Mansoul again, but also, to turn his soldiers into formation for fighting. In positioning the forces, Diabolus placed Captain Cruel and Captain Torment against Feel-gate; if needful, he would send Captain No-Ease in as a relief force. He placed Captain Brimstone and Captain Sepulchre at Nose-gate. The sulphureous smell of brimstone was painfully overpowering! Diabolus placed grim-faced Captain Past-Hope at Eye-gate – enough to sink the Mansoulians' spirits into the pit! Then, he positioned voracious Captain Insatiable to look to the carriages and take into custody any people or things fallen as prey.

On the other hand, the inhabitants of Mansoul kept a sally port at Mouth-gate. It was a place by which the townsfolk had the advantage of sneaking communications in and out to Emmanuel. It was also a spot from which the captains had an advantage of firing slingstones at the tyrant's army. It was for this reason, in part, that Diabolus sought to block up Mouth-gate there with as much dirt as possible.

As Diabolus was preparing his assault upon Mansoul, the captains and soldiers in the Mansoulian corporation were busy mounting slings, setting up banners, sounding trumpets, and maneuvering themselves for the best advantages against the enemy. The Lord Willbewill took charge of watching against any rebels from within.

Ever since he had done penance for his fault, Willbewill had shown as much honesty and bravery as any of the best. Indeed, Willbewill's transformation was wonderful!

---

[608] Mendacious - given to or characterized by deception or falsehood or divergence from absolute truth

Pen and Ink Drawing Depicting a Sally Port
As at Warwick Castle, England
by Kaitlyn E. Priset, artist

Now, this act of Lord Willbewill made a considerable impact upon both sides. It greatly abashed Captain Past-Hope. It discouraged the army of Diabolus. It put fear into the hearts of the Diabolonian runagates in Mansoul. It instilled strength and courage in Emmanuel's captains. The Mansoulian people were better resolved to fight. Furthermore, Diabolus's hopes with what the Diabolonians within the town could do were seriously foiled.

The children of Prudent-Thrifty and Mrs. Hold-fast-Bad, namely, Gripe and Rake-All, who dwelt with Mr. Mind (their grandfather), were quite stricken, perceiving Willbewill apprehended the Diabolonian boys, Jolly and Griggish, and so they tried one night to make their escape – for they were Diabolonians, as well. However, Mr. Mind caught wind of their attempt, put them in chains, and carried them to the place where Lord Willbewill hanged the other two hooligans previously.

Upon this, the townspeople stepped into place trying to search for and apprehend other Diabolonians around the town. However, so many of them lay so squat and close that it was difficult to detect and apprehend them.

As already pointed out, Diabolus and his army were somewhat abashed and discouraged at the sight of what Lord Willbewill did when he hanged two young Diabolonians. War brings about severe measures. That discouragement, however, turned itself into furious madness and rage.

In another regard, the townspeople and captains within the walls of the town had their hopes and expectations heightened. They started to believe the day could be theirs. The subordinate preacher even drew a text from the Old Testament, "Gad, a troop shall overcome him: but he shall overcome at the last," and from that preached an enthralling sermon.[609]

PRAYER STARTER: *Gracious God, there are times that deception, fear, pretended love, and violence tear away at what is dear to life. We can't pretend such doesn't exist; nor can we whisk it all away. Help us, though, not to keep wallowing there. Guide us on with a determination to keep under the presence and power of your counsel and loving care.* [From here on continue in your own prayerful words.] *In Jesus' name, we pray. Amen.*

Diabolus, a Conqueror – almost

Psalm 140:6-8: Therefore I faid vnto the Lord, Thou art my God: heare, ô Lord, the voice of my praiers. O Lord God the ftrength of my faluacion, thou haft couered mine head in the daie of battel. Let not y wicked haue his defire, ô Lord: performe not his wicked thought, left thei be proude. Selah (GEN, 1560).

Therefore I said unto the Lord, Thou art my God: hear, O Lord, the voice of my prayers O Lord God the strength of my salvation, thou hast covered my head in the day of battle. Let not the wicked have his desire, O Lord;

---

[609] Genesis 49:19

perform not his wicked thought, lest they be proud. Selah (GNV, 1599).

Beginning military maneuvers, Diabolus ordered his drummer to beat the drum, while the captains in Mansoul responded with the sound of their silver trumpets. Those in Diabolus's camp came down against the town, while the captains in the castle at Mouth-gate entered the fray with their slingers. Meanwhile, all that was heard in the camp of Diabolus was rage and blasphemy; while in Mansoul were good words, prayers, and the singing of psalms; again, to which the enemy replied with horrible objections and the haunting tone of the drum; to which, in turn, the town responded with the slapping of slings and melodious noise of trumpets – quite a cascade of contrasts.[610] In a pattern such as this, the fighting continued for days, broken now and then by a brief pause in which townspeople refreshed themselves as the captains made ready for still another assault.

The captains of Emmanuel were clad in silver armor and the soldiers were clad in what was proof. The soldiers of Diabolus wore armor made of iron to withstand Emmanuel's engine-shot. There were some in town hurt and others greatly wounded. The worst of it, chirurgeons[611] were scarce in Mansoul and Emmanuel was still absent, as well. By dressing the wounds with tree leaves, many people were scarcely kept alive. With the wounds putrefying there was a grievous smell.

Among the townsmen, Lord Reason suffered a head wound. The Lord Mayor suffered an eye injury. Mr. Mind received a wound about the stomach. The subordinate preacher received a shot not far from the heart. The fortunate news was that none of these wounds were mortal.[612] However, such was not the case with so many of the common soldiers – soldiers not only wounded, but slain.

The casualties in Diabolus's camp raised serious concern, too. Captain Rage and Captain Cruel were wounded. Captain Damnation driven into retreat entrenched himself a good distance from the town. Diabolus's standard-bearer, Captain Much-Hurt,[613] was beaten down and had his brains beaten out with a sling-stone. Many of the doubters were slain outright, although the group was not totally decimated.

---

[610] Ephesians 5:18-19

[611] Chirurgeon - An archaic noun for surgeon, first known to be used in the 13th century, which comes from the Middle English *cirurgian*, from Anglo-French *cirurgien*, from *cirurgie* surgery (*Merriam-Webster Dictionary*)

[612] Psalm 38:1-22; Revelation 22:2

[613] Much-Hurt: Acts 27:10

The victory which turned to Mansoul that day put a great valor into the townspeople and captains, but covered Diabolus's camp with a cloud – all to the effect of making Diabolus's army more furious!

On the next day, though, Mansoul rested, commanded the bells should be rung and the trumpets joyfully sounded, while its captains cheered throughout the town.[614]

In local administration, Lord Willbewill was far from idle. He did notable service against the Diabolonians posing as domestics in the town. He lit on Mr. Anything, the one who brought the three fellows who defected from Shaddai to list themselves in Diabolus's service. Lord Willbewill also caught a notable whose name was Loose-Foot[615] who had served as a scout for the vagabonds in Mansoul and carried intelligence reports out of town to Diabolus's camp. Willbewill sent both fellows, Anything and Loose-foot, off to Mr. True-man, the gaoler, to be put in irons and in due course executed – at a time, of course, that would be best for the corporation and discouragement for the enemies.

Although he could not stir around as much due to the wound he had recently suffered, the Lord Mayor ordered all the natives of Mansoul to look to their watch, stand on their guard, and prove themselves strong against any enemy onslaughts.[616] Mr. Conscience, the preacher, did his best to keep all his vital information alive in people's hearts. Meanwhile, the captains and stout ones agreed on an opportune time to sally out at night and play havoc on Diabolus – although at night they remained more vulnerable to the enemy – but this was the folly and current self-confidence of Mansoul.[617]

At an appointed time, the Prince's captains cast lots to see who should lead the van on the nighttime expedition of – let's be honest – forlorn hope. The lot fell to Captain Credence, Captain Experience, and Captain Good-Hope.

While executing the battle plan, the soldiers fell upon the main body of the enemy. With Diabolus and his army especially skilled in night work the battle was fierce. The blows fell hard upon every side. The hell drum beat furiously while the Prince's trumpets – such a contrast –sounded sweetly. Meanwhile, Diabolus's Captain Insatiable reached the battlefield in time to look for the enemy's carriages and seize the prey.

---

[614] 1 John 5:4
[615] Deuteronomy 25:5-10; Isaiah 20:1-5
[616] Nahum 2:1; 1 Corinthians 16:13
[617] 1 Thessalonians 5:5

The Prince's captains fought hard and, more than expected, played havoc upon the enemy so that they, in pursuit, drove Diabolus into retreat. Despite this, Captain Credence stumbled and fell, got seriously hurt, and cried out in pain, not to rise until Captain Experience turned back to help. The sad turn of events, though, played on everyone's fears and threw the army into great disarray. Diabolus, the observing and crafty one that he was, did an about-face and drove back on the Prince's army with such a fury as only hell could supply. Consequently, Diabolus fell hard upon the three captains, cutting, wounding, and piercing the troops dreadfully.

The Prince's army observed how their captains were turned to the worst and thought it best to return through the sally port and lay aside their present attempts. But Diabolus was so inflated regarding his night's work, he swelled with thoughts of an easy and complete conquest within a few days or so. In a similar spirit, the Diabolonians hiding within Mansoul swelled with confidence, as well. And yet, the Lord Mayor fired the response out to Diabolus that what he would get he must get by force as long as Emmanuel was alive![618]

Then, the Lord Willbewill lashed out at the demon prince: "Diabolus, you master of the den and enemy to all that is good, we may be the poor inhabitants of Mansoul, but we are well acquainted with your manner of rule. We were like a bird who did not see the fowler's snare and fell into your dastardly control. Since we have been turned from darkness to light, though, we have turned from the power of Satan to the power of God. By means of your subtlety we have suffered loss and come to much perplexity, and yet we will not lay down our arms to such a horrid tyrant as you. We remain hopeful for in time our deliverance will come.[619] Until then, we'll keep fighting as best we can."[620]

This brave speech of the Lord Willbewill and that of the Lord Mayor did not set well with Diabolus. It rekindled the fury of his rage. But it was a soothing ointment for the Mansoulian townspeople. It, too, was a

---

[618] Psalm 27:12; John 6:39; 1 Peter 3:15

[619] Psalm 40:16-18

[620] "Christians should never fear Satan, but wisdom dictates a healthy respect for an ancient, deadly enemy. When you are dealing with Satan, do not treat him lightly; remember and respect what the Scripture says of him. 'But even the archangel Michael, when he was disputing with the devil about the body of Moses, did not dare to bring a slanderous accusation against him, but said, 'The Lord rebuke you!' (Jude 9). Christians should particularly remember the daily power of the Lord's Prayer, which includes this sentence: 'And do not lead us into temptation but deliver us from the evil one' (Matt. 6:13). Jesus Christ would not have commanded us to pray that prayer unless we needed that kind of divine protection every day" (Walter Martin, Jill Martin Rische and Kurt Van Gorden, *The Kingdom of the Occult* [Nashville, Tennessee: Thomas Nelson, 2008], 427).

soothing plaster applied to the brave Captain Credence's wound. Indeed, as these captains of the town with their men of war came home routed, such a brave response was the right word in a very tender season.[621]

While the captains and soldiers kept fighting in the field, the Lord Will-bewill was busy at home. Wherever he found any Diabolonians, they felt the weight of his heavy hand and the edge of his penetrating sword. For instance, he maimed the Lord Cavil,[622] the Lord Brisk, the Lord Pragmatic, and the Lord Murmur[623] as well as several others of the meaner sort.

What Willbewill realized was that due to their recent inflated confidence, Diabolonians within and about Mansoul would think this was a good time to stir and make an uproar in the town. So, they quickly got themselves into a body as if it were just the moment for the whirlwind and the tempest to tear throughout.

On the other hand, this, as well, was the time Willbewill, undaunted, took opportunity to fall in among them in such haste that the Diabolonians returned quickly back to their holds – thus, to a certain extent clipping the wings of Diabolus who had worsted Mansoul in the nighttime battle.

Diabolus resolved to go at another bout with Mansoul. He beat the people once. He should beat them again! He commanded his forces to be ready at such a nighttime hour and bend all their force against Feel-gate to break into the town. The battle cry that he gave his officers and soldiers was: Hell-fire![624]

"In breaking through," he said, "either with some or all, no one must forget the word 'Hellfire!' The drummer must beat the drum without ceasing. The standard-bearers must raise the colors high. The soldiers must press forward with courage and manfully play against the town! Let nothing be sounded in this town but 'Hellfire! Hellfire! Hellfire!'"

By nighttime, Diabolus made his assault upon Feel-gate, for such a gate, centering upon nothing but feelings, was weak and most easily made to yield. Having got this far, Diabolus placed captains Torment and No-Ease at the gate. But the Prince's captains came down upon them and made their entrance more difficult. To speak the truth, the captains did as well as they could, while three of the best and most valiant were wounded and made incapable in holding off the enemy. Thus, Diabolus and his army overpowered the defenses. Accordingly, the Prince's captains betook themselves to the castle. It was partly for their own security, and partly

---

[621] Proverbs 25:25; Isaiah 28:12a; Acts 3:19b

[622] Luke 19:8 – see Geneva Bible

[623] Exodus 16:1-2, 7-9, 12; 17:3; Numbers (many references); Isaiah 8:19; 29:24; 59:3; Luke 5:30; 15:2; 19:7; 1 Corinthians 10:10; Philippians 2:14; Jude 1:16

[624] Deuteronomy 32:22; Matthew 5:22; James 3:6; Revelation 20:14

for the security of the town, and to preserve the prerogative royal for Emmanuel. In consequence, Diabolus succeeded initially to this extent with his plans!

With Emmanuel's captains having fled into the castle and the enemy now facing too little resistance, the forces of Diabolus went on to possess the rest of the town, cheering "Hellfire! Hellfire! Hellfire!" Nothing could be heard but the doleful clamor, "Hellfire!" and the roaring of the drum.

Meanwhile the clouds hung so dark over Mansoul that nothing, but ruin seemed to attend its hopes and expectations. Having gained possession of the town, Diabolus quartered his soldiers in the houses throughout. Even the subordinate preacher's house was as full of outlandish doubters as ever it could be. There was not a corner, cottage, barn, or hog-stye not filled with the vermin. The Diabolonians turned people out of their homes, and would lie in their beds, and sit at their tables. Ah, how this poor Mansoul came to reap the fruit, sin, and venom that once lay in the flattering words of Mr. Carnal-Security![625]

The havoc the Diabolonians played throughout the place was horrific. They viciously forced, ravished and, like beasts, abused so many of the young and old in Mansoul that many of its people swooned, miscarried, and died. Mansoul seemed to be nothing but a den of dragons, an emblem of hell, and a place of total darkness. Like the barren wilderness, it wore a face as if infested with nettles, briars, thorns, weeds, and stinking things.[626]

In effect, these Diabolonian doubters turned the Mansoulians out of their beds, wounded, mauled, and, yes, almost brained many of them.[627] They so laid harm to Mr. Conscience that his wounds festered, and he found no ease by day or by night, but lay as if continually on a rack, these Diabolonians' having stopped short of having slain him outright.[628] Then, they so abused Mr. Lord Mayor that they almost put his eyes out. And had not Lord Willbewill got into the castle, they would have chopped him to pieces, for they, vicious as they were, regarded him – a turncoat! – to be the worst among those in Mansoul against Diabolus.

Nobody who walked the streets in Mansoul appeared religious anymore. Every corner of the town swarmed with outlandish doubters who filled the houses with their hideous noises, vain songs, lying stories, and blasphemous language against Shaddai and his Son, Emmanuel.[629] Even so, those Diabolonians who once lurked in the walls, dens, and holes in

---

[625] Job 4:8; Proverbs 22:8; Hosea 8:7; 1 Corinthians 9:11
[626] Judges 9:8-15
[627] Psalm 137:9; Isaiah 13:16, 18; Nahum 3:9; Zechariah 14:2-3
[628] Job 1:12; 2:6
[629] Galatians 6:7-9

hiding could now show themselves plainly, and even walk with open face in company with doubters who surged in Mansoul. Once again, how the tables had turned! The Diabolonians had more boldness to walk the streets, haunt the houses, and show themselves abroad than any of the woebegone honest inhabitants.

Yet, a strange thing – Diabolus and his powerful forces were not at peace in Mansoul, for they were unable to enjoy the hospitality and enter-tainment previously accorded Emmanuel's captains and forces.

If once there were a chance of any courtesy, it was now withheld, hid-den, resented, or not freely given.

With the Diabolonians having encroached upon the Mansoulian homes to this extent, the Mansoulians suffered as captives in their own places. Basically, they discountenanced their invaders as much as they were able and risked showing what dislike that they could.[630]

The captains from within the castle held the invaders off for a while with their slings, to the chafing and fretting of the enemies' minds, even though Diabolus had made numerous attempts to break through the castle gates.

However, with bold Mr. Godly-Fear, the keeper of the gates, and a per-son of courage, conduct, and valor, it was in vain for Diabolus to think he could succeed, as long as Mr. Godly-Fear's life lasted.

For two and a half[631] years, though, this was the sorry condition of the town of Mansoul. For two and a half years, the body of the town was the seat of war! Its good people were driven into holes. The glory of Mansoul was laid in the dust. What rest, what peace, what sunshine could Mansoul have?

The town had become the enemy's tent, trench, and fort posed threaten-ingly against the castle until they could take it and spoil it and demolish it – so terrible![632]

---

[630] Romans 7:14-24

[631] Daniel 12:7; Revelation 12:13-15

[632] C. S. Lewis's insight in *The Screwtape Letters*, on the seeming absence of a sense of God makes a fitting wrap for and preface to the Mansoulians' plea for help at this point. Screwtape (representing Satan) is warning an understudy demon: "Do not be deceived, Wormwood. Our cause is never more in danger than when a human, no longer desiring, but still intending, to do our Enemy's will, looks round upon a universe from which every trace of Him seems to have vanished, and asks why he has been forsaken, and still obeys" (C. S. Lewis, *The Screwtape Letters*, section 8 of 31 [C. S. Lewis Pte. Ltd, 1942; New York: HarperCollins, 2001], 40).

PRAYER STARTER: *Oh, God, we struggle to find the right words. Our thoughts are in jagged pieces. Brokenness, futility, and terror. All we thought we had, has been ripped away. Come! Rescue! We yearn for your power. Oh, come, help, although help seems so forlorn.* [From here on continue with your own prayerful words.] *In Jesus' name, we pray. Amen.*

The Petition

Philippians 4:6: Be nothing careful, but in all things let your requefts be fhewed vnto God in praier, and fupplicacion with giuing of thankes (GEN, 1560).

Be nothing careful, but in all things let your requests be showed unto God in prayer and supplication with giving thanks (GNV, 1599).

After the town of Mansoul had fallen into its grave and lamentable condition, the elders and chiefs of Mansoul felt the need to draw up another petition and send it to Emmanuel, pleading for help. At this point, Mr. Godly-Fear pointed out that his Lord Prince never did nor ever would receive such a petition unless the Lord Chief Secretary put his hand to it. Also, the Lord Chief Secretary would not be a signatory of any such communication unless he had a hand in composing it.[633]

Paying heed to Mr. Godly-Fear's guidance, the group went to the Lord Chief Secretary, with their humble acknowledgements: "O Lord, you know how backslidden and degenerated we have been. You know of Diabolus who has come fiercely against us and the barbarous usages our men, women, and children have suffered at his hands. We hardly need to elaborate on how homebred Diabolonians walk the streets of Mansoul with more boldness than our own people dare to walk. We urgently need your heart and skill to make a humble and penitent plea to Prince Emmanuel."

After listening attentively, the Lord Chief Secretary responded: "I'll draw up a petition for you and set my hand to it, but you must be present at the doing of it. You must put your desires into it. The hand and pen shall be mine. The ink and paper must be yours. Else how can you say it is your petition? No petition goes in my name to the Prince and so to his Father unless the people who are concerned join with heart and soul."

After the petition had been drafted, the next discussion regarded who would carry it to Emmanuel. Again, the Lord Chief Secretary played the key role in this matter and suggested Captain Credence should be the one. Though not having fully recovered from a serious wound received in bat-

---

[633] John 14:15-17, 25-26; 16:7b-15; Romans 8:26-27

tle, the captain gladly accepted the task. "I will do this business for you with as much speed as I can."

The petition humbly cited their prior transgressions and rebellion, their current miserable condition being captive to Diabolus and, though not deserving it, their pleading for God's grace, mercy, and forgiveness.

> "We are compassed on every side, Lord; our own backslidings reprove us; the Diabolonians within our town frighten us; and the army of the angel of the bottomless pit distresses us.[634] We have no inkling of where to go but to you. Your grace is our only hope for salvation.

> "Our enemies are arrogant, lively, strong and threatening to part us among themselves for booty. They have fallen upon us, Lord, with many thousand doubters against whom we have no idea what to do. They are all grim-looking, unmerciful ones. They defy us and they defy you! Our captains, even those in whom we used to put the most confidence, are discouraged, sick, wounded, and grievously worsted and beaten out of the field by the power and force of the tyrant.

> "Our wisdom is gone. Our power is gone. We have nothing that we may call our own but our shame and confusion. Take pity on us, Lord. Take pity on your miserable town of Mansoul."[635]

Upon its completion, the Lord Chief Secretary handed the petition to Captain Credence, who carried it out of Mouth-gate – the sally port for the town – and then on to Emmanuel.

It was not clear how the petition's existence as well as the identity of its bearer leaked out to Diabolus. However, he fell into a fuming rage, but was a bit shaken, as well. After casting a biting word out at the town of Mansoul, Diabolus commanded the drum to beat again, of course to intensify the terror already felt by the Mansoulian people.

"Be it known," Diabolus announced to his own followers, "that there is treachery hatched against us in this rebellious town of Mansoul. These miserable Mansoulian people have dared to reach out to Emmanuel once again for help. Therefore, I command you to bring more distress on this wretched place. Vex it with your wiles, ravish their women, deflower their virgins, slay their children, brain their ancients, fire their town, and do what other mischief you can think of. Let them painfully realize this as reward for what they have dastardly done!"

Not surprisingly, this was what you would expect Diabolus to say. All said, though, they remained words expressed in a rage. Then, something

---

[634] Psalm 57:1
[635] Psalm 38:21-22

unknown stepped in betwixt and between and the words ran no further than that!

Not to be foiled any further, though, Diabolus stomped up to the castle gates demanding upon pain of death – their deaths – that they open the gate to him and his men. Mr. Godly-Fear, who had charge of the gate, refused to be bullied and declared, even if Mansoul were to suffer for a while, she would be made perfect, strengthened, and eventually settled.[636]

Diabolus then ordered Mansoul to deliver the petition that had been carried to Emmanuel against him and Captain Credence, the one who carried it, and then Diabolus would go away from the town.

At this point, one of the Diabolonians, Mr. Fooling, stepped into the fray of words. "My lord is offering you a fair deal. Say, it is better for you if one man should perish than for the whole town!"[637]

"O, you are a devouring tyrant!" the Lord Mayor responded. "We shall harken to none of your words! We will push back upon you as long as we have a captain, a man, a sling and a stone to throw remaining in the town!"

Increasingly incensed, Diabolus fired a spray of words: "Do you hope, do you wait, do you look for deliverance? Although you've cried out to Emmanuel, your wickedness hangs close to your skirts. Do you think your prayers are so innocent? You will fail because it is not only I, but your Emmanuel who is against you. What a bogus, forlorn, and pathetic hope you hold onto!"

"Yes, we have sinned," the Lord Mayor said. "But that is no help to you.[638] Great is God's faithfulness[639] and those who come to him are in no wise cast out."[640] He has also said that all manner of sin and blasphemy shall be forgiven the sons of men.[641] We will not despair.[642] We will look for, wait for, and hope for deliverance still."[643]

By this time, Captain Credence returned with a packet from the court of Emmanuel. So, the Lord Mayor, having received word of this, withdrew from the noisy tyrant, leaving him to yell against the gates of the castle. On reaching the captain, the Lord Mayor promptly asked what the news would be. As the water stood in his eyes, Captain Credence reported,

---

[636] Romans 5:2-4; 2 Corinthians 1:5-7; 12:9-10

[637] Proverbs 26:1-3; John 11:49-50

[638] 1 John 1:9

[639] Lamentations 3:23

[640] Luke 12:37

[641] "But the blasphemy against the holy Ghost shall not be forgiven" Matthew 12:31 GNV

[642] 2 Corinthians 4:8

[643] Proverbs 13:12

"Cheer up, my lord, for all will be well in time." And with that spoken he laid down the packet, which would be taken as a good sign by anyone who observed it.[644]

Now, the season of grace having come, the Lord Mayor summoned all the captains and elders to come together for a special unveiling of what had arrived from Emmanuel by the hand of Captain Credence.

As they all quickly gathered and eagerly asked the captain about his journey, he responded to them as he did to the Lord Mayor.

"All will be well at last!"[645]

On opening the packet, Captain Credence drew out several notes Emmanuel had directed to various notables among the Mansoulian leaders.

To the Lord Mayor, Emmanuel extended an affirmation for his being so true and trusty in his office, thus, bearing great concern for the people and maintaining strong resistance against Diabolus.

To the Lord Willbewill, Emmanuel extended praise for how valiant and courageous he had been, keeping so strict a hand, eye, and reins over the Diabolonians still lurking around the town.

To the subordinate preacher, Mr. Conscience, Emmanuel extended a gracious note for how faithfully he executed the trust committed to him, exhorting, rebuking, and forewarning Mansoul according to the laws of the town,[646] also calling for fasting, and the sackcloth and ashes while Mansoul was under revolt – not forgetting he had called Captain Boanerges for help when he knew the town needed it.

To Mr. Godly-Fear, Emmanuel noted the tears he shed over the decay of goodness that Mr. Carnal-Security brought upon the town of Mansoul. And how Mr. Godly-Fear stood so stoutly at the gates of the castle against all threats and attempts of the tyrant; and even further, encouraged the townspeople to draft a petition to their Prince.[647]

---

[644] "God is the God of the humble, the miserable, the afflicted. It is His nature to exalt the humble, to comfort the sorrowing, to heal the broken-hearted, to justify the sinners, and to save the condemned. The fatuous idea that a person can be holy by himself denies God the pleasure of saving sinners. God must first take the sledgehammer of the Law in His fists and smash the beast of self-righteousness and its brood of self-confidence, self-wisdom, self-righteousness, and self-help. When the conscience has been thoroughly frightened by the Law it welcomes the Gospel of grace with its message of a Savior who came into the world, not to break the bruised reed, nor to quench the smoking flax, but to preach glad tidings to the poor, to heal the broken-hearted, and to grant forgiveness of sins to all the captives" Martin Luther, *Commentary on Galatians*, trans. by Theodore Graebner (Digireads. com Publishing, 2019), content on Galatians 3:19; p. 90.

[645] Psalm 97:10

[646] 2 Timothy 4:2

[647] Luke 6:23

In the end, Captain Credence unpacked the note Prince Emmanuel prepared *for the whole town*. In essence, the Prince had taken note of their petitions and in time they would see the fruit of their doings. The Prince affirmed how their hearts and minds at last stayed fixed upon him although Diabolus so aggressively wreaked havoc with their lives. Emmanuel also noticed that neither flatteries on the one hand nor hardships on the other could draw them into Diabolus's cruel designs. Then, Emmanuel stated that he was leaving the town to the Lord Chief Secretary and the conduct of Captain Credence.[648] Thus, the people must remain responsive to their governing and that, in due time, they would receive their reward![649]

After completing his mission, Captain Credence retired to the Lord Chief Secretary's lodgings so they could converse further with each other. Indeed, both had so much more to discuss than what they had been able to relate to the whole town. The Lord Chief Secretary had great love for Captain Credence and there were times a choice morsel would have been extended him from the Lord Chief Secretary's table.

After an evening spent in extensive discussion, the captain retired to rest. Not long after that, though, the Lord sent for the captain again to convey he had commissioned him as lieutenant over all the forces. So, from that day forward, all the military would fall under Captain Credence's leadership as he would be managing the great war for Prince Emmanuel against the forces and power of Diabolus.

The townspeople began to realize what interest Captain Credence held with the court and with the Lord Chief Secretary. No one else, for instance, could carry out a mission so quickly and bring back good news so aptly from Emmanuel as he did. Consequently, there arose a lament that they did not use him more in their distresses. So, they sent a request to the Lord Chief Secretary by the subordinate preacher, that all that they were and had might be placed under the government, care, custody, and conduct of Captain Credence.[650]

As the subordinate preacher carried out the errand and retrieved the news that, yes, the captain would lead the King's army against the King's enemies, he was pleased to return to the townsfolk with such news.

However, such information was carried out with secrecy because Emmanuel's foes still had great strength in the town.[651]

---

[648] John 16:7-15
[649] 2 John 8
[650] Romans 13:3-4
[651] Deuteronomy 29:29

PRAYER STARTER: *Our hearts cry out to you, O God. And, yes, you do respond. We have suffered for our sins. Forgive us, Lord. As we place ourselves under your command, bring us to peace once again. Forces to undo us still clamor about. And yet, you, God reassure that in due time, your help does come. We praise you, God, and await the revelation of your redemptive presence!* [From here on continue in your own prayerful words.] *In Jesus' name, we pray. Amen.*

What Comes by Surprise

Ephesians 3:20: Vnto him therefore that is able to do exceeding abundantly aboue all that we afke or thinke, according to the power y worketh in vs (GEN, 1560).

Unto him therefore that is able to do exceeding abundantly above all that we ask of think, according to the power that worketh in us (GNV, 1599)

Realizing he had been boldly confronted by the Lord Mayor and given another wallop by Mr. Godly-Fear, Diabolus fell into a rage and called for a council of war. All the princes of the pit came together, with old Incredulity at the head, no less, and they were joined by all the captains of the army. The outcome of that council was to discern how they might take the castle, because they really could not be masters of the town of Mansoul if they had no control of the castle.

As had happened previously, the demons went back and forth, stuck at cross purposes. Then, Apollyon, the council president, stood up to speak. "My brothers, I have a proposal. Let us withdraw from the town. Our presence around town does us no good and the castle remains in enemy hands. If their captains are around and that bold fellow, Godly-Fear, keeper of the gates, is there too, we have a meager chance of success. But, if we withdrew to the plains, they might slacken their defenses and we could come at them by surprise with a hard blow. Or, even if we drew their captains out into the field – we hold the advantage in field work – we might be able to ambush them and rush in to take possession of the castle."

Not taken by Apollyon's suggestions, Beelzebub stood up with his remarks. "Draw them out of the castle? Inevitably some will remain poised to make a counter defense. I think that a previous plan Apollyon raised makes a better one. Draw them into sin! It is not our being in the town, nor in the field, nor our fighting, nor our killing, that can make us masters. As long as one is in the town able to lift a finger against us, Emmanuel will take his part. Nonetheless, there is no better way to bring them into bondage except inventing a way to draw them into sin. Get them to sin!

"Had we left our doubters at home, we would have done as well as we have done now, that is, unless we could have made the doubters political leaders, for doubters at a distance are but like objections re-felled with arguments. The most effective approach for getting into the castle, I say, is to get the town into sin!"[652]

At this point, Lucifer stood up, applauding Beelzebub's counsel. "Yes, the way to bring this to pass is by withdrawing our forces from the town. Let us terrify them no more. No summons, no threats, no noise of the drum, nor any other means of awakening. Let us lie in the field at a distance, acting as though we'll pay them no regard. Frights awaken them and make them more prone to fight. Mansoul is a market-town.

"Let us have some of our Diabolonians pretend to be far countrymen peddling their wares at a very good price. These salespeople must be true to us and quite witty. There are two I know who would be excellent. No matter the unusually long-winded names – they are Mr. Penny-wise-pound-foolish and Mr. Get-i'the-hundred-and-lose-i'the-shire.[653] Let me tell you that they are among the best sales personnel. There are another two to assist them: Mr. Sweet-world[654] and Mr. Present-good[655] – civil and cunning traders, but true friends and helpers! Let Mansoul grow full and rich.[656] Let Mansoul get taken up with the better-is-more-and-more. Remember how we prevailed in Laodicea[657] and how unwary people can be caught in such

---

[652] 2 Peter 2:18-21

[653] A county or a shire was described and enumerated by the poll-sheriff of that day as containing so many enfranchised hundreds, and the total number of hundreds made up the political unity of the shire. To this day we still hear from time to time of the 'Chiltern Hundreds,' which is a division of Buckinghamshire that belongs, along with its political franchise, to the Crown, and which is utilized for Crown purposes at certain political emergencies. This proverb, then, to get i' the hundred and lose i' the shire, is now quite plain to us. You might canvass so as to get a hundred, several hundreds, many hundreds on your side, and yet you might lose when it came to counting up the whole shire. You might possess yourself of a hundred or two and yet be poor compared with him who possessed the whole shire. Thus the proverb has been preserved out of the old political life of England and has been moralized and spiritualized to us in *The Holy War* (Alexander Whyte, *Bunyan Characters – Third Series* [Public Domain] (Astounding-Stories.com, 2015), 46.

[654] Sweet-world: Job 20:12-14; Ecclesiastes 2:1

[655] Present-good: Romans 7:18

[656] David Wilkinson regarding Commerce or Relationship: "Relationship is at the heart of the Universe. This is important, especially in a materialistic and consumer-dominated society. If we want to find purpose in life, we find it not in possessions nor in wealth, but in relationship with this God" David Wilkinson, *The Message of Creation: Encountering the Lord of the Universe*, in Bible Themes Series, ed. Derek Tidball (Downers Grove, Illinois: InterVarsity Press, 2002), 39.

[657] Revelation 3:14-22

snares. No fright tactic here! Let us just lull them to sleep! They will then slip off into neglecting their town watch, castle watch, and gate guard![658]

"Surfeiting Mansoul with such abundance while we lay hiding behind our screen might get them to turn their castle into a warehouse and less and less a place for any army stuff and men of war! Then, if we made a sudden assault, it would be quite difficult for their captains to find shelter. Don't you know the old sayings: 'The deceitfulness of riches chokes the word'[659] and 'When the heart is over-charged with surfeiting and drunkenness' and 'the cares of this life'[660] and 'all that is mischievous comes upon them unawares'?[661]

"You, know very well," Lucifer continued, "it is not easy for people to be filled with our things and not welcome some Diabolonians as retainers into their houses. Where are any Mansoulians full of this world who don't have such servants and waiting-men as Mr. Profuse,[662] Mr. Prodigality,[663] Mr. Voluptuous,[664] Mr. Pragmatical,[665] Mr. Ostentation,[666] or others from our gang? Such as these can take the castle, blow it up, or make it unfit as a garrison for Emmanuel. They may accomplish it sooner than an army of twenty thousand.

"So, I end where I began. We should quietly withdraw, not offering any more force at least at this time; and let us set out on a new way of doing what we want, and I wager they may destroy themselves!"

The advice was applauded by everyone. The very masterpiece of hell! Choke Mansoul with the fullness of this world![667]

Just as this council was breaking up, Captain Credence received a word from Emmanuel. Come the third day, Emmanuel would meet him in the

---

[658] Among C. S. Lewis's insights on how the Evil One uses the ages of life – in this example, the middle years – to erode a sense of God's continual call upon people's lives: "Prosperity knits a man to the World. He feels that he is 'finding his place in it', while really it is finding its place in him. His increasing reputation, his widening circle of acquaintances, his sense of importance, the growing pressure of absorbing and agreeable work, build up in him a sense of being really at home in earth, which is just what we [the Evil Ones] want" (C. S. Lewis, *The Screwtape Letters*, section 28 of 31 [C.S. Lewis Pte. Ltd, 1942; New York: HarperCollins, 2001], 155).

[659] Matthew 13:22
[660] Matthew 6:25-34
[661] Luke 21:34
[662] Profuse: Proverbs 27:6
[663] Prodigality: Luke 15:11-31
[664] Voluptuous: Luke 8:14 (Note difference between Geneva Version and King James Version)
[665] Pragmatical: Judges 21:25; Proverbs 14:12; 16:25
[666] Ostentation: Proverbs 25:14; 27:2; Matthew 6:1
[667] 1 John 2:15

plains about Mansoul.[668] Although puzzled by what that might mean, he took it to the Lord Chief Secretary who, upon reading it, conveyed that the Diabolonians had just had a consultation and were contriving a way in which to bring utter ruination of the town. According to intelligence reports, the bent of their thoughts was that they would betake themselves back to the field and, by seeming to ease up on Mansoul, attempt to take the town and castle in such a way Mansoul would self-destruct. To undermine their surprise, Captain Credence, realizing Emmanuel's impending approach, was to bring a mighty force against the Diabolonians.

Captain Credence reported the matter pertaining to Emmanuel to the other captains who, upon hearing it, were extremely gladdened by the news. Then, Captain Credence commanded the King's trumpeters go atop to the battlements of the castle to stir up the best music the heart could invent, especially so Diabolus and the whole town could hear.

The whole awakening jolted Diabolus into a startling. "What is the meaning of this?" he snapped. "They are not sounding Boot-and-saddle, Horse-and-away,[669] or even a charge. How can these madmen go on so merry and glad?"

At this point, someone then responded it was the joy their Prince Emmanuel was coming to deliver Mansoul!

With this preying upon their minds, the Diabolonian leaders wondered what they should now do. As already suggested, their military strategy was to quit the town. They were banking on the assumption they had a fighting edge on the open plain. Moreover, should the Prince close in fast upon them in the town, it would be like their being trapped in a pit. Thus, they withdrew and settled at a distance before Eye-gate out of reach of those annoying slings!

The day arrived for the captains to close in upon the Diabolonians. The expectation that they would see the Prince in the field of battle was like applying oil to a flaming fire. For such a long time, they felt stuck at a distance, but now, they were strengthened by this glorious hope.[670]

Captain Credence, at the head of the army, drew the forces out of the hold by way of the sally port. The word rallying the captains, under-officers, and soldiers was: "The sword of the Prince Emmanuel, and the shield of Captain Credence," which in Mansoulian meant: "The word of God and faith."[671]

---

[668] Genesis 22:4; Exodus 19:11; Hosea 6:20; Matthew 16:21; John 2:19-21
[669] A Cavalier image echoed in a poem by Robert Browning 240 years later
[670] 1 Samuel 4:6-7; Psalm 33:20-22
[671] Romans 10:17; 1 Thessalonians 1:8; Hebrews 13:8

To advance the troops the Mansoulian military set forth roundly to the front, and the flank, and the rear of Diabolus's camp.

While advancing on the enemy, the forces left Captain Experience in the town recovering from battle wounds. However, realizing what was starting to happen he called for his crutches and pressed out of sick bay to join with the fight. When the enemy saw this they were daunted even more.

"What spirit has possessed these Mansoulians," they cried, "that they fight us upon their crutches?"

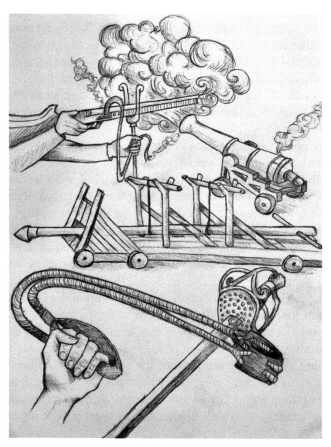

Pen and Ink Drawing Depicting 17th-century Military Weapons
(Arquebuse, Cannon, Battering Ram, Sling, and Sword)
by Kaitlyn E. Priset, artist

When Diabolus saw that the captains had come out upon them and were so valiantly surrounding his men, he concluded for the present that nothing could be accomplished except by blows and the dint of the "two-edged sword."[672]

On the front, Diabolus met Captain Credence and Lord Willbewill in battle. Willbewill's blows fell on the election doubters, the lifeguard for Diabolus, like the blows of a giant. When Captain Credence saw this happening, he circled back into the fray from the other side and like a pincher[673] the two units fiercely engaged in the fighting – thus, sending this arm of Diabolus's military into great disarray. On another flank, Captain Good-Hope engaged with the vocation doubters, sturdy soldiers as they were, and, with the aid Captain Experience sent, pushed the doubters into retreat. Then, the Lord Chief Secretary commanded slings from the castle to be played upon the enemy.

The slings were a most intimidating weaponry capable of being fired within a hair's breadth of accuracy. Notwithstanding, the enemy rallied, and the Prince's army started to fade. Remembering they would see the face of the Prince by-and-by, the warriors rekindled courage and strength once again.[674] "The sword of Prince Emmanuel, and the shield of Captain Credence!" they kept crying out! However, Prince Emmanuel yet had not shown up, and the Mansoulians' success in battle was therefore in doubt.

"Gentlemen soldiers," Captain Credence cried out to strengthen his wearied soldiers' confidence,[675] "I cannot help rejoicing to see such a stout and valiant army in the field, and such faithful lovers of Mansoul. You have shown yourselves as a people of truth and courage against those intimidating Diabolonian forces. Despite all their boasting they do not have much in which to be proud. Now, pluck up your courage and show yourselves fighters once again. Shortly – in a little while – you will see the Prince arriving in the field."[676]

---

[672] Hebrews 4:12

[673] The *pincer* movement, or double envelopment, is a *military* maneuver in which forces simultaneously attack both flanks (sides) of an enemy formation https://en.wikipedia.org

[674] Psalm 17:15

[675] Deuteronomy 31:6

[676] According to Sun Tzu, "There are five dangerous faults which may affect a general: (1) Recklessness, which leads to destruction; (2) cowardice, which leads to capture; (3) a hasty temper; which can be provoked by insults; (4) a delicacy of honour which is sensitive to shame; (5) over-solicitude for his men, which exposes him to worry and trouble" (Sun Tzu, "Variations in Tactics ," # 12, in *The Art of War*, 6th century BC [UK: Arcturus Holdings Limited, 2018], 76). Interesting contrast considering the differences between Diabolus against Emmanuel's captains.

No sooner had Captain Credence made this speech, Mr. Speedy[677] arrived with a post from Prince Emmanuel that he was right at hand.[678] When the field officers and soldiers heard the news, it was like beholding a resurrection, which brought the Mansoulians to cry out with more spirit than they had before: "The sword of Prince Emmanuel, and the shield of Captain Credence!"[679]

It also startled the Diabolonians, who resisted as best they could. As the Diabolonians lost courage, with many doubters having fallen to the ground, Captain Credence was lifting his eyes to behold Emmanuel coming with colors flying, trumpets sounding, and men of war so fleet of foot hastening with celerity[680] to the Mansoulian captains thus engaged. Then did Credence turn with his men toward town and gave to Diabolus, so it seemed, the field.

With Emmanuel coming onto Diabolus from the one side and Credence from the other side, it was but a short time Emmanuel and Captain Credence met, trampling over the slain as they advanced.

When the Mansoulian captains saw Emmanuel had swept onto the field, falling on the Diabolonians with such force, what did Diabolus, his lords of the pit, old Incredulity, and the Diabolonian captains do but turn, hasten to make their escape, and forsake the soldiers, leaving them all to fall by the hand of Emmanuel and Captain Credence.

In the end, there was not one common doubter left. It was a sad and ugly sight. The poor dead soldiers lay strewn across the battlefield like dung spread across the ground.[681]

The battle being over, the camp came to order and headed into the town. As Emmanuel drew toward Mansoul, the gates as well as the castle were flung wide open to receive and welcome him with a thousand welcomes. Smiling upon them, he said, "Peace be to you." And the people acclaimed:

"Lift up your heads, O ye[682] gates; and be ye lift up, ye everlasting doors; and the King of glory shall come in." Then, they cheered, "Who is the King of glory? The Lord, strong and mighty; the Lord mighty in battle.

---

[677] Speedy: Psalm 38:22; Zephaniah 1:18

[678] Text and Song Interactional: Micah Kuiper and Toby Mac, producers, "Help Is on the Way (Maybe Midnight)," sung by Toby Mac, released 2021.

[679] Judges 7:18; Ephesians 6:16-17

[680] Celerity – Archaic noun in old writings meaning "swiftness of movement"

[681] Jeremiah 9:22-24

[682] Ye is an old-fashioned, poetic, or religious word for you when you are talking to more than one person. Ye is sometimes used in imitation of an old written form of the word 'the (Collins English Dictionary).

Lift up your heads, O ye gates; even lift them up, ye everlasting doors."[683]

During this grand processional, the most skilled musicians added regality to the day with vibrant songs, trumpets, and timbrels.[684]

Accompanying Emmanuel to the castle were the captains. Captain Credence and Captain Good-Hope went before. Captain Charity came behind. Captain Patience followed. The rest of the captains, some on the right, some on the left, attended to the Prince, as well. All the while, their brilliant colors were displayed, the trumpets sounding, and the soldiers shouting!

It was a dazzling sight. The Prince's armor was of beaten gold. The pillars of his chariot were of silver; its bottom, gold; and its covering, purple. Upon reaching the town, he found streets strewn with lilies and flowers and homes made ready with various adornments. As the Prince would be passing by, the people's voices soared in acclamations of joy, "Blessed be the Prince that comes in the name of his Father Shaddai."[685]

While all was happening, the Lord Mayor, the Lord Willbewill, the subordinate preacher, Mr. Knowledge, and Mr. Mind, with other gentry, stood in honor guard at the castle gates. They all bowed before him, kissed the dust of his feet, and thanked, blessed, and praised his Highness for having pity upon and extending mercy to them. Swept along by such honor and pageantry, Emmanuel entered the castle, his royal palace made ready by the Lord Chief Secretary and Captain Credence. Lastly, the citizens came before him in mourning, weeping, and lamentation because of their wickedness which had forced him from the town. They bowed to the ground seven times,[686] wept aloud, asked forgiveness, and prayed that, as of old, he would confirm his love to Mansoul.

"Do not weep," the Prince replied, "go your way, eat the fat, drink the sweet, and send portions to them for whom nothing is prepared. The joy of the Lord is your strength.[687] I have returned to Mansoul with mercy. My name shall be set up, exalted, and magnified by it." Then, he took the

---

[683] Psalm 24:7, 9

[684] Psalm 68:25-26

[685] Mark 11:8-9

[686] "In the Old Testament, the act of bowing was the customary act of self-abasement performed by an individual before a person in a superior position . . . It is possible that the act of bowing seven times before a person in a superior position was to acknowledge that person as having the characteristics or the attributes of a god" (Claude Mariottini, Professor of Old Testament, Northern Baptist Seminary). Among the many references in the Amarna Letters, see 137, 147, 244. For a sampling of Biblical references, see Genesis 18:2; 23:7; 27:29; 33:3, 6-7.

[687] Nehemiah 8:10

inhabitants, kissed them, and laid them in his bosom. He gave to each of the elders and town officers a chain of gold and a signet. He sent earrings, jewels, bracelets, and other valuables to their spouses. He bestowed many precious things upon the children. Having done this, Emmanuel told the people of Mansoul to wash their garments in the fountain that was set open for Judah and Jerusalem and make their garments white, put on their ornaments, and come to the castle and stand before Emmanuel.[688]

Once again, there was music and dancing throughout all Mansoul because the Prince had granted his presence with the light of his countenance. The bells rang and the sun shone comfortably upon them.

And yet, there was a residual concern: to seek out remaining Diabolonians who still hung around the town, for some were fortunate enough to have escaped the recent battle. Nonetheless, Lord Willbewill was a greater terror now than previously in that his heart was more fully bent to seek, contrive, and pursue them to the end.

In terms of still another matter, Emmanuel ordered the townspeople to go out into the battlefield and be engaged in the necessary business of burying the dead lest the fumes and ill savors arising from the dead would infect the air and annoy the town. Thence, the Lord Mayor brought the workforce together as needed. Mr. Godly-Fear and Mr. Upright[689] were to be overseers.

The workers were to scour the land for the skulls, bones, bodies, and bone pieces of the slain. Among those soldiers buried in the plains about Mansoul there were – all deserted by their commanding officers – the election doubters, vocation doubters, grace doubters, perseverance doubters, resurrection doubters, salvation doubters, and glory doubters.[690] The weaponry also to be buried were the arrows, darts, mauls, firebrands, and the like – the cruel instruments of death – along with the soldiers.

In one regard, this would hopefully provide a proper burial. In another regard, this would drive the remembrance of any Diabolonian doubters

---

[688] Ecclesiastes 9:8; Zechariah 13:1; Revelation 7:14-15

[689] Upright: Deuteronomy 18:13; Job 1:8; 2:3; Psalms 19:13; 119:1, 7, 80; Proverbs 2:21; 28:6; Zechariah 8:16

[690] "From creation to glorification this God is working his purposes out. We may not understand how he foreknows and how he predestines while at the same time giving freedom, but we do know that our hope is located in him rather that the circumstances around us. Hope for the future must be based on the action of God the Creator" David Wilkinson, *The Message of Creation: Encountering the Lord of the Universe*, in Bible Themes Series, ed. Derek Tidball (Downers Grove, Illinois: InterVarsity Press, 2002), 242.

who died more into the background and cleanse the plains.[691] Finally, Mr. God's-Peace took up his commission to act again as in former days.[692]

[For poignant thoughts that contrast Bunyan's depiction of war with a present-day retired pastor, military veteran and chaplain's views for advocating conflict resolution and making way for peace, see Appendix Three containing remarks contributed by Reverend Dr. J. Paul Womack, 231-233, while pointing toward some contemporary theologians.]

PRAYER STARTER: *Oh, God, it so very sad that offences do come. The fact that there is any lust for place and power and any grave conflicts that precipitate war – all bringing about its spoils – is such an unfortunate reality and painful sight. Any life lost is a grave misfortune. Oh, come, Emmanuel, and heal the land. And help us to be instruments of that wholeness, goodness, and peace.* [From here on continue with your own prayerful words.] *In Jesus' name, we pray. Amen.*

The Battle Belongs to the Lord[693]

2 Corinthians 10:4-5: (For the weapons of our warrefare are not carnal, but mightie through God, to caſt downe holdes) Caſting downe the imaginations, and euerie high thing that is exalted againſt the knowledge of God, and bringing into captiuitie euerie thoght to the obedience of Chriſt (GEN, 1560),

(For the weapons of our warfare are not carnal, but mighty through God, to cast down holds.) Casting down the imaginations, and every high thing that is exalted against the knowledge of God, and bringing into captivity every thought to the obedience of Christ (GNV, 1599).

With all the goings on in and around Mansoul, Diabolus got back to Hell-Gate Hill with Incredulity, his old friend, and descended into the den commiserating their unfortunate losses – a commiseration which swelled into a hot passion regarding how to pay out some damaging revenge.

---

[691] Ezekiel 39:14

[692] Mr. God's-Peace, who was not a native of Mansoul, came from Emmanuel's court to serve as governor of the town and the castle. A great acquaintance of Captain Credence and Captain Good-Hope, God's-Peace also held position over Lord Willbewill, Mr. Recorder, Mr. Mind, and the others. Captain Credence was appointed to help him. So long as all things went as God's-Peace, notably a sweet-natured gentleman, would have it, the town remained in a happy condition.

[693] Text and Song Interactional: This chapter title is drawn from the title of a song by Jamie Owens-Collins, "The Battle Belongs to the Lord," based on 1 Samuel 17:47, released in 1989, and sung by Petra.

Upon calling a council, their yawning paunches could hardly wait to hear what Lord Lucifer and Lord Apollyon might advise.

The long or the short of it was they resolved to make another attempt, and in this case, more vicious than the last. It would be by an attack force made partially of doubters and partially of blood-men.

From the land of Darkness and from the province of Loath-good, Diabolus recruited an army twenty-five thousand strong: ten thousand of them doubters and fifteen thousand of them blood-men. They were placed under the authority of several captains and old Incredulity, of course, commanding general of the whole army.

The role the doubters would play would lie in undermining every truth and confidence that could be associated with Emmanuel. Their native country was the land of Doubting, a far-away land that lay off to the north, between the land of Darkness and the "valley of the shadow of death." Natives from this land of Doubting supplied Diabolus with beguiling warmongers greatly intent on ruining the soul of the town.

On the other hand, blood-men were those whose name was derived from the malevolence of their nature. They were fierce warriors[694] from a land that lay beneath the dog-star.[695] Their country was the province of Loath-good. The remote parts of it were far from the land of Doubting. Yet, they did butt and bound close to one another upon Hell-Gate Hill.

Blood-men and Doubters in league with each other would work jointly to sabotage the faith and fidelity of Mansoul.

Regarding the doubters, five of the seven who led the regiments with the last Diabolonian army were also captains for this military campaign: Captain Beelzebub, Captain Lucifer, Captain Apollyon, Captain Legion, and Captain Cerberus.

Among the cadre of other captains before, some were made lieutenants, and some were made ensigns.

To be clear, Diabolus did not count on the doubters as his primary warriors. Yes, they had strengths that had been tried in previous warfare; still the Mansoulians had just put them to the worst. His intent on bringing them aboard this new campaign was to increase the size of the army and, if needful, be helpful in a pinch.

However, Diabolus's primary trust fell to the blood-men, rugged and terrifying villains, in whose venom, backbone, and skill he had tremendous confidence. As for the commanders over blood-men he installed some notable captains.

---

[694] Job 24:13-14

[695] Sirius in *Canis Major* thought to wield a menacing influence

Captains	Over the Band of	Over the Band of	Color	Scutcheon
Cain	The Zealous	The Angry	Red	Murdering Club
Nimrod	The Tyrannical	The Encroaching	Red	Great Blood-hound
Ishmael	The Mocking	The Scorning	Red	One Mocking at Abraham's Isaac
Esau	Those who begrudged the blessing of another	Those for executing their private revenge upon others	Red	One Privately Lurking to Murder Jacob
Saul	The Groundlessly Jealous	The Devilishly Furious	Red	Three Bloody Darts Cast at Harmless David
Absalom	Those who'll kill a father or a friend for the glory of this world	Those who'll hold one fair in hand with words, till they shall pierce him with their swords	Red	Son Pursuing the Father's Blood
Judas	Those who'll sell a man's life for money	Those'll betray their friend with a kiss	Red	Thirty Pieces of Silver and the Halter
Pope	All Spirits are Joined in One under Him	No Information	Red	The Stake, the Flame, and the Good Man in it

Thus, Cain,[696] Nimrod,[697] Ishmael,[698] Esau,[699] Saul,[700] Absalom,[701] Judas,[702]

---

[696] Cain: Genesis 4:1-24; Proverbs 29:22; Hebrews 11:4; 1 John 3:12; Jude 1:11

[697] Nimrod: Genesis 10:8-9; 1 Chronicles 1:10; Isaiah 10:1; Micah 5:6

[698] Ishmael: Genesis 16:1-16; 17:18-27; 21:9-21; 37:25-28; Proverbs 17:5; Jeremiah 41:1-18

[699] Esau: Genesis 25:25-28:9; 32:1-33:16; Deuteronomy 2:4-29; Joshua 24:4; Obadiah 1:1-21; Malachi 1:2-3; Romans 9:13; Hebrews 11:20; 12:16

[700] Saul: 1 Samuel 9:1-2 Samuel 2:7; 1 Chronicles 10:1-13; Psalms 4; 7; 11; 17; 26; 35; 52; 54; 55; 57; 58; 59; 63; 109; 116; 118; 120; 141; 142; Acts 7:58; 8:1, 3; 9:1-31; 12:25 and following to the end of Acts

[701] Absalom: 2 Samuel 13:1-18:33; Psalms 3; 61

[702] Judas: Matthew 10:4; 26:14-16, 20-25, 36, 45-50; 27:3-10; Mark 14:10-12, 17-21,

and Pope[703] – quite a rogue's gallery – were those who commanded various fighting units of blood-men!

Those accompanying them: Angry,[704] Encroaching,[705] Scorning,[706] Private Revenge,[707] Devilishly Furious,[708] Fair Words and Piercing Sword,[709] and Betraying with a Kiss[710] – were associated with the various bands.

Certainly, the doubters had been faithful and did much to strengthen Diabolus's kingdom, but the time had come for Diabolus to turn with greater confidence toward the blood-men. Of great, intimidating qualities, they seldom returned from battle empty-handed. Like mastiffs,[711] they would fasten upon the enemy, whether father, mother, brother, sister, prince, governor, and even the Prince of princes. And so, this army of twenty-five thousand strong was led up against Mansoul by their general, the infamous Lord Incredulity.

Diabolus's troops were a harrowing, intimidating force ready to strike fear in the people's hearts yearning for a hope-against-all-hope end!

Nonetheless, there was this scout-master-general, Mr. Prywell (you met him previously) who'd go out and spy for Mansoul. He caught onto Diabolus's scheme and, accordingly, brought word of Incredulity's com-

---

32, 42-46; Luke 22:3-6, 47-48; John 6:70-71; 12:1-8; 13:2, 18-30; 18:1-12; Acts 1:16-20

[703] Pope: Severe imagery pertaining to conflicted relationship between the Church of England at its founding and the Roman Catholic Church lingering to this time in this reference to the Pope; Revelation 13:7-8; Daniel 11:33.

[704] Angry: Proverbs 15:18; 22:24; 29:22; Ecclesiastes 7:11; Matthew 5:22; Ephesians 4:26

[705] Encroaching: Deuteronomy 2:37; 1 Thessalonians 4:6

[706] Scorning: Job 12:4; Psalm 79:4; Proverbs 1:22; 3:34; 9:8, 12; 22:10; 29:8

[707] Private Revenge: Luke 9:55; Romans 12:9; 2 Corinthians 10:6

[708] Devilishly Furious: Proverbs 22:24

[709] Fair Words and Piercing Sword: Proverbs 16:23-25

[710] Betraying with a Kiss: Matthew 26:46-50; Mark 14:42-46; Luke 22:47-48

[711] According to editors of Encyclopaedia Britannica, the Mastiff had been "used as a guard and fighting dog in England for more than two thousand years." According to the American Kennel Club, "the colossal Mastiff [recognized as a breed in 1885] belongs to a canine clan as ancient as civilization itself. A massive, heavy-boned dog of courage and prodigious strength, the Mastiff is docile and dignified but also a formidable protector of those they hold dear . . . A male stands at least 30 inches at the shoulder and can outweigh many a full-grown man. The rectangular body is deep and thickly muscled, covered by a short double coat of fawn, apricot, or brindle stripes. The head is broad and massive, and a wrinkled forehead accentuates an alert, kindly expression. Mastiffs are patient, lovable companions and guardians who take best to gentle training. Eternally loyal Mastiffs are protective of family, and a natural wariness of strangers makes early training and socialization essential." [Interestingly, John Bunyan features the blood-men as mastiffs who, while in the employ of Diabolus, their handler, were imposing, terrifying fighters; but there were some – once upon being confronted by Emmanuel – who recognized the ignorance or evil of their ways, and God's transformational power.]

ing with a powerful army of blood-men and doubters. So the people of Mansoul shut the gates tight, poured their hearts out in prayer, and put themselves into a posture of defense.[712]

As Diabolus reached the now beleaguered town of Mansoul, he placed the doubters round about Feel-gate – an entry point where the how-it-feels-kind of people were vulnerable to doubts – and he placed the blood-men before Eye-gate and Ear-gate. Then, old Incredulity directed a summons to Mansoul in a word as searing as a red-hot iron: "Surrender! If not, we'll burn Mansoul to the ground."

Even so, a body surrendering would not quench the thirst of the blood-men. They would crave absolute destruction! Diabolus would play the blood-men as the last and sure card against the town of Mansoul.[713]

Upon receiving the message, the townsmen engaged in a flurry of thoughts. All agreed in less than half an hour to speed the summons to the Prince with the words inscribed at the bottom: "Lord, save Mansoul from the blood-men!"[714]

After looking at it, including the line scrawled at the bottom, the Prince directed Captain Credence with Captain Patience to go and take care of that side of Mansoul to be besieged by the blood-men.[715] Then, he directed Captain Good-hope, Captain Charity, and Lord Willbewill to take charge of the other side against the doubters. "I," the Prince added, "will set my standard upon the battlements of the castle." He then sent Captain Experience to the marketplace to exercise his men each day before the people of Mansoul.

The siege was long and the enemies, especially the blood-men, were fierce and some of the townsmen met with many a shrewd brush, especially Captain Self-Denial who also had been positioned to take care of Ear-gate and Eye-gate against the blood-men.

Captain Self-Denial was a young and very stout soldier. During Emmanuel's second return to Mansoul, he made Self-Denial captain over a thousand. A hardy man of courage and willing to venture out for the good, Captain Self-Denial would now and then sally out upon the blood-men, take them by surprise, and enter brisk skirmishes with them. But not to assume any of this was easy, Captain Self-Denial met with several brushes and carried the marks on his face and other parts of his body.

---

[712] Text and Song Interactional: Bart Millard, Benjamin Glover, Robby Shaffer, Nathan Cochran, Barry Graul and Michael Scheuchzer, songwriters, "Almost Home," sung by MercyMe, released 2021

[713] Isaiah 59:7; Jeremiah 22:17

[714] Psalm 59:2

[715] Hebrews 6:12, 15

After a time spent for the trial of the faith, hope, and love, Emmanuel called his captains and men of war together, divided them into two companies and commanded them at a time appointed one morning, very early, to sally out upon the enemy – half to fall upon the doubters and half to fall upon the blood-men. The doubters were to be slain but the blood-men, not. They were to be taken alive.

At the appointed time, Captains Good-Hope, Charity, Innocent, and Experience centered their attack on the doubters, while Captains Credence, Patience, Self-Denial, and the rest went against the blood-men.

When the forces against the doubters drew up before them on the plain, the doubters, not wanting to face another defeat, fled from the Prince's army although a number were slain. Some of those who escaped fled for home. Others scattered by fives, nines, and seventeens wherever they could go.

They were vagrant wanderers straggling about the countryside, abusing, and enslaving the people they met who cowered before them. Sometimes they would even side up in companies before the town of Mansoul but scrambled away if Captain Credence, Captain Good-Hope, or Captain Experience appeared on the scene.

The troops who went out to face the blood-men did as ordered. They did not slay any of them. Instead, they compassed them about, which surprised the blood-men. Passing it all off, though, the blood-men presumed these troops of Emmanuel – and where was He, by the way? – were playing some wild and foolish fancies! Still, the Prince's captains kept pressing forward, thus surrounding the blood-men. And then, it was too late! The blood-men were trapped.[716] Although blood-men were mischievous and cruel brutes when prevailing upon others, they were crippled by fear when meeting their match. Consequently, the captains took them captive to Emmanuel.

On interrogating them, the Prince drew from the blood-men that they originated in three of several counties throughout a single land. The group from Blind-man-shire did what they did in ignorance[717] while the group from Blind-zeal-shire were impelled by superstition.[718] The third group

---

[716] "There is nothing more difficult. The difficulty of tactical manoeuvring consists in turning the devious into the direct, and misfortune into gain" (Sun Tzu, "Manoeuvring," #3, in *The Art of War*, 6th century BC [UK: Arcturus Holdings Limited, 2018], 64).

[717] Blind-man-shire and ignorance: Leviticus 4:13-14; 5:18; Joshua 20:3; Habakkuk 3:2; Acts 17:30; 1 Peter 1:14

[718] Blind-zeal-shire and superstition: Acts 25:1-12; Ephesians 4:17-19

which came from the town of Malice[719] in the county of Envy[720] did what they did through spite and implacableness.[721]

When the blood-men from Blind-man-shire realized where they were and with whom they fought, they trembled pleading for mercy and Emmanuel touched their lips with his golden scepter.[722] Those who came out of Blind-zeal-shire insisted on their rights to be doing whatever they did because they must fight against the people and places whose laws and customs were different than theirs. However, some blood-men from Blind-zeal-shire who could recognize their evil ways asked for mercy and mercy was given![723]

And yet, the group who came out of the town of Malice in the county of Envy neither wept, nor disputed, nor repented, but stood gnawing their tongues for anguish and madness, wanting to have their way with Mansoul.[724]

These blood-men from various shires who did not care for pardon for their sin and willful behaviors against Mansoul were bound to eventually stand before the Lord and King of the country and kingdom of Universe at the great and general assize[725] to answer for the evil they had done throughout their lives.[726]

Now, there were some from the land of Doubting, who, having wandered the countryside for a while and perceiving that they had succeeded in their escape, thrust themselves back toward the town of Mansoul knowing they would still find some Diabolonians there.

Benefitting with good directions, these doubters found hospitality in the house of old Evil-Questioning, a very notorious enemy of Mansoul, who made them feel welcome, pitied their misfortune, and nourished them with the best he had in his house.

After a little acquaintance, the old man asked the doubters if they were all from one town or another. One said he was an election doubter; an-

---

[719] Town of Malice in Envy county and spite and implacableness: Psalms 28:3; 34:21; 94:23; Proverbs 14:32; 26:26

[720] Envy: Job 5:2; Proverbs 14:30; 27:4; Matthew 27:17-19; Acts 7:9; Galatians 5:26; 1 Timothy 6:3-5; James 3:14

[721] Matthew 5:44; John 8:40-43; 1 Timothy 1:13-15; Revelation 9:20-21

[722] Esther 5:2; 8:4

[723] Text and Song Interactional: Michael Neale and Krissy Nordhoff, songwriters, "Your Great Name," sung by Natalie Grant, released 2010

[724] Revelation 16:8-11

[725] An assize was a court which formerly sat at intervals in each county of England and Wales to administer the civil and criminal law, until 1972 when civil matters were transferred to the High Court and criminal matters to the Crown Court.

[726] Revelation 20:11-15

other, a vocation doubter; another, a salvation doubter; and a fourth, a grace doubter.

Then the old gentleman, pleased with their responses, said: "Be of whatever shire you are, you have the very length of my foot, are one with my heart, and are welcome here."[727]

So, they thanked him profusely being glad they found a seemingly "safe" harbor in Mansoul.

At this point, old Evil-Questioning said to them: "How many of your company might there be that came with you to the siege of Mansoul?"

"In all, there were only ten thousand doubters, for the rest of the army consisted of fifteen thousand blood-men. These blood-men border upon our country; but poor men! as we hear, they all were captured by Emmanuel's forces."

"Ten thousand doubters!" remarked the old gentleman, "that is a round company. How came it to pass, since you were so mighty a number, that you fainted, and did not dare to fight?"

"Our general," said they, "was the first man that did run for it."

"Pray," chafed the landlord, "who was that cowardly general?"

"He once was the Lord Mayor of Mansoul, but we pray, do not call him a cowardly general. Whether anyone from the east or west has done more service for our Prince Diabolus than this Lord Incredulity, it would be a hard question to answer. Besides, if they had caught him, they would have hanged him. And we promise you, hanging is a bad business."

The old gentleman said, "I would that all the ten thousand doubters were now well armed in Mansoul, and myself at the head of them. I would see what I could do."

"Ay," said they (not just as thoughts, but words spoken aloud), "that would be well, if we could see that, but wishes, alas! what are they?"

"Well," said old Evil-Questioning, "be careful about what you say out loud. You must be quat[728] and close, and take care of yourselves while you are here, or I assure you, snap, you will be taken."

"Why?" quote the doubters.

"Why!" repeated the old gentleman, "because both the Prince and Lord Chief Secretary, and their captains and soldiers, are all here in town. The town is infested with them!

---

[727] A contrast to John Wesley's rendering of Jehu's greeting, "as mixed a character as he was," to Jehonadad: "Is thine heart right, as my heart is with thy heart . . . give me thine hand," from 2 Kings 10:15 in Wesley's "Catholic Spirit" (Sermon 39), edited by Albert C. Outler, Volume 2, *The Works of John Wesley* series (Nashville: Abingdon Press, 1985), I.1.

[728] Quat - satisfied

"Besides, there is one whose name is Willbewill, a most cruel enemy of ours, who the Prince has made keeper of the gates and has commanded, with all diligence to look for, search out and destroy all manner of Diabolonians. If he lights upon you, down you go, even though your heads were made of gold!"

PRAYER STARTER: *O God, who works deeply in our hearts and lives, there is so much within us that needs your sorting, sifting and renovating work. Work within us to bring about your redemptive plan. Redeem us by the graciousness of your love. Prepare us for the better living of our days.* [From here on continue with your own prayerful words.] *In Jesus' name, we pray. Amen.*

Another Day in Court

1 Peter 1:7: That the trial of your faith, being muche more precious then golde that perifheth (thogh it be tried with fyre) might be foúde vnto your praife, & honour and glorie at the appearing of Iefus Chríft (GEN, 1560).

That the trial of your faith, being much more precious than gold that perisheth (though it be tried with fire) might be found unto your praise, and honor and glory at the appearing of Jesus Christ (GNV, 1599).

One of Lord Willbewill's faithful soldiers, Mr. Diligence,[729] in whom Willbewill had great confidence, stood listening outside old Evil-Questioning's house and beneath the eaves and caught in its fullness everything being said and, consequently, went straight to report to his master. Upon getting the drift, Willbewill remarked to Diligence he knew this old Diabolonian Evil-Questioning well, for they were great friends back in the time of his own apostasy, but as for the present, he had no awareness where the old man lived. "But I do," exclaimed the soldier. Together they traced their way to the house, broke open the door, rushed in upon all five together, arrested them, and took them to Trueman, the gaoler,

By the next morning, the Lord Mayor became acquainted with what Willbewill had done overnight and was happy regarding news of the arrest, not only because some doubters were apprehended, but because old Evil-Questioning, a notorious troublemaker of long standing, was taken at last. They then set a day for a trial of the five prisoners.

Though they were caught and notably guilty, Lord Willbewill thought it more honorable to the Prince, more comfortable to Mansoul, and a de-

---

[729] Diligence: Proverbs 4:23; Romans 12:8; 2 Peter 1:4-6; Jude 1:3-4, 12-13

terrent to the enemy, if a fair trial be the structure with which to deal with these prisoners.

When the day arrived, Mr. Trueman brought the prisoners in chains to the town hall, where judgment was traditionally handed down. The jury was empaneled; the witnesses sworn; and the prisoners tried. The jury members were the same as those who had tried Mr. No-Truth, Pitiless, Haughty and others before.

First, old Evil-Questioning was set to the bar because he was the receiver, entertainer, and comforter of these doubters who allegedly were outlandish people. Mr. Evil-Questioning was instructed to listen carefully to the charges presented and welcomed if he had anything to say in his own defense.

"Mr. Evil-Questioning, you are indicted by the name of Evil-Questioning, an intruder in the town of Mansoul, and you are a Diabolonian by nature, a hater of the Prince Emmanuel, and one studied in the ruination of this town. You are indicted for countenancing the King's enemies in violation of the laws made for the health and wholeness of the people. 1. You have questioned the truth of our doctrine.[730] 2. You have openly wished there were a thousand doubters in and about Mansoul. 3. You have granted declared enemies a sanctuary in your home. What do you say to this? Are you guilty or not guilty?"

"My Lord," responded the accused, "I do not know the meaning of this indictment. I am not the man with whom you are concerned. The man accused is called by the name of Evil-Questioning. I deny that that's my name. My name is Honest-Inquiry. Though the names sound similar, there is a wide difference between the two. I hope that a person, in even the worst of times and that, too, among the worst of men, may make an honest inquiry into things, without running the danger of a death sentence."

"My Lord and honorable bench and magistrates," said Lord Willbewill stepping forward as a sworn witness, "you have heard the prisoner at the bar has denied his name and thinks he can shift from the charge. I know him to be the man concerned. His proper name is Evil-Questioning. I have known him for more than thirty years. He and I (I'm ashamed to speak of it) were great acquaintances when Diabolus governed Mansoul. I testify he is a Diabolonian by nature, an enemy to our Prince, and a hater of our blessed town. During the rebellion, he had been at my house many times – twenty or more nights altogether – and we used to talk back then as he and his doubters have talked right now. It is true I have not seen him many a day since. I suppose that the coming of Emmanuel to Mansoul has made

---

[730] Hebrews 13:8b-9a

him shift his lodgings and this indictment has driven him to change his name. But this is the man!"

Pen and Ink Drawing Depicting
Mr. Diligence's Discovery during a Night-watch
by Kaitlyn E. Priset, artist

After this, Mr. Diligence testified. "My lord," he said, "I was upon my watch on such a night at the head of Bad Street. I chanced to hear a muttering within this gentleman's house. Then, I wondered what was going on? So, I stepped up close, but very softly, to the side of the house to listen, thinking, and, indeed, it fell out, that I might light upon some Diabolonian conventicle.[731] So, as I got up close to the wall, it was but a while before I perceived there were outlandish men in the house. I did well understand their speech, for I have been a traveler myself. Now, hearing such language in such a tottering cottage as this old gentleman dwelt in, I clapped my ear to a hole in the window, and there heard their talk. This old Mr. Questioning asked these doubters what they were, whence they came, and what was their business in these parts; and they responded to all his questions. He also asked what their number was, and they told him ten thousand men. He asked them why they made no more manly assault upon Mansoul and they told him. So, he called their general a coward, for marching off when he should have fought for his prince. Then, this old Evil-Questioning wished, and I heard him say it, if all those ten thousand doubters were now in Mansoul and he at the head of them, he would see what he could do! Also, he bid his guests to take heed and lie quat, for they would be taken to die, although they had heads of gold."[732]

Then said the court: "Mr. Evil-Questioning, here is now another witness against you, and his testimony is full: 1. He swears you received these men into your house, and you did nourish them there, though you knew they were Diabolonians, and the King's enemies. 2. He swears you did wish ten thousand of them were in Mansoul. 3. He swears you did give them advice to be quat and close, lest they were taken by the King's servants. All of this manifested you are a Diabolonian."

"The men who came into my house were strangers and, yes, I took them in," Mr. Evil-Questioning responded. "Is it a crime in Mansoul for one to entertain strangers? That I also nourished them is true. Why should my charity be blamed? As to wishing I had ten thousand of them in Mansoul, I never said it that way. For all you know, I might have wished them to be taken and that might have meant well for Mansoul. Yes, I also bid them to take heed they fall not into the captains' hands; but that might be because I am unwilling for anybody to be slain and not because I would help the King's enemies to escape."

---

[731] In Bunyan's day a conventicle could be as few as five people.
[732] Psalm 64:5-6

The Lord Mayor replied: "Although it is a virtue to entertain strangers,[733] it is treason to entertain the King's enemies. And then, by your twisting of words, you work to evade and defer the execution of judgment. However, could there be no more proven against you than that you are a Diabolonian? You cannot escape the penalty of the law. But, as a receiver, nourisher, and countenancer for having harbored these outlandish Diabolonians – the concern keeps on growing!"

At this point, Evil-Questioning, chafed by the whole proceedings, blurted out: "I see how the game will go. I must die for my name, and for my charity." So, he said no more.

Next, the court called the outlandish doubters to come forward. The first to be arraigned was the election doubter.[734] His indictment was read, the substance of it being that he was an enemy of Emmanuel, a hater of the town of Mansoul, and an opposer of its wholesome doctrine. When the judge asked how he pled, the election doubter said that that was the religion in which he had grown up. If he must die as a martyr for that, he did not care.[735]

The judge replied: "To question election is to overthrow a great doctrine of the gospel, namely, the omniscience, power, and will of God, to take away the liberty of God with his creature, to lay a stumbling block to the faith of the town of Mansoul, and to make salvation to depend upon human works and not upon God's grace."[736]

The second one to be called was the vocation doubter. The substance of his indictment was the same as the other, except he was particularly charged with denying the calling of Mansoul. When asked for a statement, he replied that he never believed there was any distinct and powerful call of God. Nonetheless, there was a general voice of the word and people

---

[733] Hebrews 13:2

[734] Don H. Compier in Philip Sheldrake's *Dictionary of Christian Spirituality* introduces the concept of election as follows: "Christian doctrines of election attempt to express key spiritual insights and experiences in theological language. Election (God's choice of us) affirms that God has always loved us first, unconditionally and freely. The immense and wholly gracious gift of the divine affection comprises the basis of our relationship with God, always shaping the possibility of spiritual response. The doctrine of predestination represents one way to emphasize these realities by stressing that election of specific individuals has been God's plan from the very beginning. Unfortunately, the history of Christian theology suggests that this manner of speaking about divine love can spark controversies that may detract attention from the strength of the originating spiritual impulse."

[735] "The kernel of the theocratic ideal was the doctrine of election, with more and more tangible tests of the elect, who could be identified, in reasonable charity by faith, upright deportment, and participation in the sacraments" (Roland H. Bainton, *Christian Attitudes Toward War and Peace* [Nashville: Abingdon Press, 1960], p. 145).

[736] Romans 9:11-12; 11:5, 33-36

were exhorted to forbear evil and, in so doing, there was a promise of happiness annexed.[737]

Subsequently, the judge ruled: "You are a Diabolonian. You have denied a great part of one of the most experimental truths of the Prince; for he has called and Mansoul has heard a distinct and powerful call, by which Mansoul has been quickened, awakened, and held with a heavenly grace, and desires communion with her Prince by serving him, doing his will, and looking for happiness in his good pleasure."

The court then called the grace doubter to come forth and being indicted, he was from the land of doubting – his father being the offspring of a Pharisee – and though he lived in good fashion among his neighbors, and though there was so much the Lord and King could teach him about God's blessings, he, as also with the salvation doubter, still held tight to his belief that Mansoul would never be freely saved by God's grace.

"Why, the law of the Prince is plain," the judge declared: "1. Negatively, 'not of works'; 2. Positively, 'you are saved by grace.'[738] However, your religion settles in and upon the works of the flesh; for the works of the law are the works of the flesh.[739] Besides, in saying this, as you have done, you have robbed God of God's glory, and given it to a sinful man; you have robbed Christ of the necessity and sufficiency of His undertaking and relinquished these to the works of the flesh. You have despised the work of the Holy Spirit and have magnified the will of the legalistic mind. Thus, for your Diabolonian principles, you must die."

The court, having proceeded this far with the prisoners, sent out the jury, who forthwith came back with a verdict of guilty.

At this point, the Recorder stood and addressed the prisoners: "You have been indicted," he declared, "and proven guilty of high crimes against Emmanuel our Prince, and against the welfare of the famous town of Mansoul, crimes that bring about death.

The place and means of execution – ironically, the cross – was the same place Diabolus drew up his last army against Mansoul, save only that old Evil-Questioning was hanged at the top of Bad Street, just over against his own door.

---

[737] Ephesians 4:3-5; 2 Timothy 1:9
[738] Romans 3:24, 27; Ephesians 2:8-10
[739] Galatians 2:16

PRAYER STARTER: *O God, as the heart of our faith is your grace and goodness, help this be such that marks the blessing that we radiate to others around us. In each day of our lives, let it be clearly experienced by those with whom we touch hearts. Help us, gracious God, to be vessels of your love to others.* [From here on continue in your own prayerful words.] *In Jesus' name, we pray. Amen.*

Until Eternity Dawns

1 John 2:17: And the worlde paffeth awaye, and the lufte thereof: but he that fulfilleth the wil of God, abideth euer (GEN, 1560).

And this world passeth away, and the lust thereof: but he that fulfilleth the will of God, abideth ever (GNV, 1599).

Mansoul had rid itself of many enemies and troublers. A strict commandment was given that Lord Willbewill and Diligence search for and apprehend any other Diabolonians remaining in the town.

Among those arrested were Mr. Fooling,[740] Mr. Let-Good-Slip,[741] Mr. Slavish-Fear,[742] Mr. No-Love,[743] Mr. Mistrust,[744] Mr. Flesh,[745] and Mr. Sloth.[746] It was also commanded that the Mansoulians apprehend the late Mr. Evil-Questioning's children and demolish his house. Those children were: Mr. Doubt, the eldest,[747] Legal-Life,[748] Unbelief,[749] Wrong-Thoughts-of-Christ,[750] Clip-Promise,[751] Carnal-Sense,[752] Live-by-Feeling,[753] and Self-Love.[754] Quite a slew of offspring![755] Their mother was No-Hope,[756] a kins-

---

[740] Fooling: Proverbs 26:1-12

[741] Let-Good-Slip: Psalms 38:15-16; 73:2-3, 18; 121:2-4; Jeremiah 23:11-13

[742] Slavish-Fear: Psalm 73:3, 26-28

[743] No-Love: 2 Thessalonians 2:9-11; 2 Timothy 3:3

[744] Mistrust: Matthew 6:28-30

[745] Flesh: Galatians 3:3; 5:13, 16-17, 19, 24; 6:8, 12-13

[746] Sloth: Proverbs 10:26; 15:19; 18:9; 19:15, 24; 20:4; 21:25; 22:13; 24:30-34; 26:13-15; Ecclesiastes 10:18; Matthew 25:26; Romans 12:11; Hebrews 6:12

[747] Doubt: Matthew 21:21; Romans 4:20; 1 Timothy 2:8

[748] Legal-Life: Matthew 12:2, 10; Luke 6:2

[749] Unbelief: Matthew 13:58; 17:20; Mark 6:1-6; 9:24; Romans 11:18-25

[750] Wrong-Thoughts-of-Christ: Psalm 118:22-23; Matthew 7:21-23; 10:16, 37; 21:42; 2 Corinthians 11:4

[751] Clip-Promise: Opposite of Promises Kept

[752] Carnal-Sense: Job 10:4; Romans 7:14; 1 Corinthians 3:3-4

[753] Live-by-Feeling: Ephesians 4:18-20; Hebrews 4:15

[754] Self-Love: 2 Timothy 3:1-17

[755] Parents unto the Children: Exodus 20:5-6

[756] No-Hope: Romans 5:5; 8:20, 24-25; 15:13; Ephesians 2:12; 1 Thessalonians 4:13

woman of old Incredulity, her uncle, for when her father, old Dark,[757] died, the uncle brought her up.

The executions were conducted without delay. Lord Willbewill took Fooling into the streets and hanged him in Want-wit-Alley,[758] over against his own house. This Fooling was the one who offered to hand Captain Credence over to Diabolus if the demon withdrew his forces from the town. Willbewill also took Let-Good-Slip who was busy in the market and he dealt with him according to the law.

Now, there was a poor man in Mansoul, namely Mr. Meditation,[759] an honest man, who was of no great account in the days of apostasy but then had risen to some significance in these latter times. Consequently, by the time of Emmanuel's coming, it was noted that Mr. Let-Good-Slip had accumulated a great deal of wealth which, at the Prince's direction, was sequestered and directed for the common good to Mr. Meditation and afterwards, his son, Mr. Think-Well,[760] whose wife, by the way, was Mrs. Piety,[761] the daughter of Mr. Recorder.

Lord Willbewill then apprehended Mr. Clip-Promise, a businessman notorious for greatly abusing the King's coin, and therefore made him a public example. Arraigned and judged by Willbewill, Clip-Promise was the first to be placed in the pillory, then whipped by all the children and servants in the town, and finally hanged.

I am sure that hearing about the severity of such punishments in Mansoul sounds awful, but those honest traders there were extremely unsympathetic for the abuse one clipper of promises could accomplish in a slight bit of time throughout the whole town.

Willbewill also arrested Carnal-Sense and put him into a hold, but the man broke prison and made his getaway. How he accomplished it remains a mystery. The bold villain did not even vacate the town but continued lurking in and around Diabolonian dens during the days and haunting honest citizens' houses like a ghost at nights. Nevertheless, there was a proclamation displayed in the marketplace offering a daily admittance to the Prince's table as well as being made keeper of the treasure of Mansoul to anybody who'd discern Carnal-Sense's whereabouts, apprehend him, and rid the town of such a nuisance. Many tried to pick up on the offer and even caught sight of him but he was such a slippery character, so nobody

---

[757] Dark: Matthew 6:23; Luke 1:79; 11:34-36; 23:44-45; John 1:5; 3:19; 8:12; 12:35, 46
[758] Want-wit-Alley: 2 Corinthians 5:19 (King James Version)
[759] Meditation: Psalms 19:14; 119:97
[760] Think-Well: 2 Corinthians 9:1-16
[761] Piety: Psalms 40:1-17; 51:16-17; Proverbs 21:3, 27

could catch him and put the whole matter to an end. Unfortunately, Carnal-Sense remained in and around Mansoul.

However, Willbewill was able to apprehend Mr. Wrong-Thoughts-of-Christ and imprison him. After a long season of ailing health, this Diabolonian died of consumption.[762]

On the other hand, Self-Love was taken into custody. But there were so many who drew close to him that his judgment was deferred. Disgusted with such waffling leniency, though, Mr. Self-Denial protested, "If we wink at such villainy in Mansoul, I will lay down my commission." Consequently, Mr. Self-Denial was accorded the chance to take Self-Love from the crowd and place him among some Mansoulian soldiers, who brained him.

Even so, some individuals in Mansoul started muttering about this. Still, nobody dared to speak out. Emmanuel was in town. There was a pall of respect for that. Consequently, as Captain Self-Denial's brave act came to the Prince's ears, he sent for him and made him a lord in Mansoul.

Lord Willbewill, too, obtained great commendations from Prince Emmanuel for all that he had done.

By this moment, Lord Self-Denial took courage and, with Lord Willbewill, kept pursuing the Diabolonians. They arrested Live-by-Feeling and Legal-Life and held them in prison until they died. Mr. Unbelief, though, was a nimble Jack whom they could never lay hold of, although they tried many times.

So many of the Diabolonian escapees or untouchables – whatever you want to call them – kept under close cover in their dens and holes. Whenever anyone of them was caught in the open, the whole town would get up in arms!

Even the children got caught up in a detective mode and would raise a ruckus whenever they thought they had caught sight of such a thief.[763]

Mansoul came to quite a degree of peace and quiet, with Prince Emmanuel abiding in her borders and her captains and soldiers doing what they were intended to do. Mansoul even kept busy with her manufacturing and engaged in trade with a faraway country.

With the community having come this far in health and wholeness, Emmanuel appointed a day to meet with the people in the marketplace and provide an additional word concerning their safety and comfort. Upon that day, he arrived in Mansoul in his chariot with his captains on the right and

---

[762] A using up of resources, a wasting disease
[763] Matthew 21:15-16

the left. Then with the crowd extending mutual expressions of love and brought to silence, the Prince began to speak.[764]

"You, my Mansoul, beloved of my heart, I bestowed upon you many and great privileges. I have chosen you, not because of your worthiness, but for my own sake.[765] I have redeemed you, not only from a dread of the law, but from the hand of Diabolus. I have done this because I have loved you and set my heart upon you![766]

"So that things that might hinder your way to paradise might be taken out of your way, I have bought you to myself. I have bought you with a price not of corruptible things such as silver and gold, but a price of blood, my own blood, which I have freely spilled upon the ground to make you mine.[767]

"So, I've reconciled you, O Mansoul, to my Father, and entrusted to you the mansions[768] with my Father in the royal city where there are things eye has not seen, nor entered the heart of anyone to conceive.[769]

"Besides, you see what I have done by having taken you out of the hands of your enemies with whom you had revolted from my Father, and by whom you were content to be possessed and destroyed. I first came to you by my law, then I came to you by my gospel to awaken you and to show you my glory.[770]

"No matter how often you rebelled against my Father and me, I have not abandoned you. I have come to you. I have borne your manners. I have waited on you and, after all, I have accepted you. Even when you were out of my grace and favor, I would not let you be lost as you most willingly would have been.[771] I have compassed you about. I have afflicted you on every side. It was that I might weary you of your ways. When I got complete dominion over you, I turned it to your advantage.

"Look what a company of my Father's host I have lodged within your borders. There are captains and rulers, soldiers and men of war, engines, and excellent devices to subdue and bring down your foes. O Mansoul,

---

[764] John Bunyan's *The Holy War* is not an allegory detailing the life, death, and resurrection of Jesus. However, it exudes the depth and breadth of the Gospel with Christological ingredients presumed throughout the whole.

[765] Deuteronomy 7:6

[766] Jeremiah 29:11; John 15:9

[767] 1 Peter 1:18-19

[768] John 14:2-3

[769] 1 Corinthians 2:9

[770] Text and Song Interactional: Andrew Bergthold, Edmond Martin Cash, Franni Cash, Martin Cash, Scott Mctyeire Cash, songwriters, "Light of the World (Sing Hallelujah)," by We the Kingdom, Released 2021.

[771] 2 Peter 3:9

you know what I mean. My design through each of them has been to defend, purge, strengthen, and sweeten you for myself – yes, recreating you for my Father's presence, blessing, and glory.[772]

"You see, my Mansoul, how I have passed by your backslidings and healed you. I was angry with you, but I turned my anger away from you. It was because I have still loved you. It was not any of your goodness that brought me back to you. The way and means of your recovery were mine.[773] I invented the means of your return.[774]

"It was I who made a hedge and a wall, when you began to turn to things in which I did not delight. It was I who made your sweet bitter, your day night, your smooth way thorny, and confounded all that sought your destruction. It was I who set Mr. Godly-Fear to work in Mansoul. It was I who stirred up your conscience and understanding, your will and your affections, after your great and woeful decay. It was I who put life into you, O Mansoul, to seek me, that you might find me, and in your finding, find your own health, happiness, and salvation.[775]

"My Mansoul, I have returned to you in peace, and your transgressions against me are as if they had not been. Nor shall it be with you as in former days, but I will do better for you than at your beginning.

"In yet a little while, O my Mansoul,[776] I will take down this famous town of Mansoul, stick and stone. Don't be troubled at what I say.[777] I will carry the stones thereof, and the timber thereof, and the walls thereof, and the dust thereof, and its inhabitants thereof, into my own country. I will set it up there in such strength, newness, and glory, as it never seemed at first. There will I make it a spectacle of wonder and a monument of mercy.[778]

"There you natives of Mansoul shall see all beyond what you had and held since the first. And there, O Mansoul, you shall have communion with me, my Father, and your Lord Chief Secretary, as never before, even if you should live in this Universe that now is for the space of a thousand years.

---

[772] 2 Corinthians 5:16-18

[773] Text and Song Interactional: Osinachi Okoro, songwriter, "Waymaker" by Michael W. Smith and featuring Vanessa Campagna and Madelyn Berry, released 2019

[774] Deuteronomy 32:39; Isaiah 53:5; Jeremiah 17:14; 33:6; Matthew 9:35; 1 Peter 2:24

[775] Psalm 107

[776] The words "in a little while" leads us toward an Ending with an anticlimax, "a conclusion emphasizing continued conflict rather than ultimate victory, [...] the story ends a little short of heaven" Daniel V. Runyon, "John Bunyan's Master Story: The Holy War as Battle Allegory in Religious and Biblical Context," (Published version of Ph.D. dissertation. Lampeter, Wales: Edwin Mellen Press, 2007), 43, 9.

[777] John 14:1-3, 27

[778] Revelation 21:24, 26 (see various translations)

"In that place I envision for you, O my Mansoul, you shall not be afraid of any murderers or Diabolonians, and their threats anymore. No more plots, no contrivances, no designs against you! You shall not hear of any evil-doings or even the noise of the Diabolonian drum. Nothing Diabolonian shall be there to make you afraid. No longer shall you have need of captains, engines, soldiers, and men of war.[779]

"You shall not meet with any sorrow, or grief, or Diabolonian creeping into your skirts, burrowing into your walls, or being seen within your borders for all eternity.[780]

"Life shall last longer there than you are able to even desire here. It will always be sweet and new, with no impediment attending it forever.[781]

"In that place, O Mansoul, you shall meet with many who, like you, have been partakers of your sorrows – even such as I have set apart, redeemed, and chosen, as you, for my Father's court and city royal. All they will be glad in you and you, when seeing them, shall be glad in them.[782]

"There are things, O Mansoul, of my Father's and my providing that never were since the beginning of the world. They are laid up for you with my Father and sealed among his treasures until you can come to enjoy them. I told you before I would remove my Mansoul and set it up elsewhere. Where I set it, there are those who love and rejoice in you now, but so much more when they see you exalted to honor![783]

"My Father will send them to fetch you. Their bosoms are chariots in which you shall ride upon the wings of the wind. They will come to convey, conduct, and bring you to that. When your eyes see more, you will be at your desired haven.[784]

---

[779] 2 Peter 3:8-9; Revelation 21 and 22

[780] Revelation 21: 8, 27; 22:15

[781] Psalm 30:5

[782] Text and Song Interactional: Mia Fieldes, Bernie Herms and Natalie Grant, songwriters, "Enough" by Natalie Grant, released 2015

[783] In Romans 8:19-20, creation "waits in eager expectation for the revelation of that glory. The *eager expectation* is indicative of stretching the head forward or craning the neck . . .Creation waits in eager expectation . . . because it has been subjected to *frustration*. This word is found thirty-seven times in the Septuagint translation of Ecclesiastes and has the sense of emptiness, futility, purposelessness, and transitoriness . . . Creation, as it now is, is both necessary to new creation and a pointer to new creation. The 'out of jointedness of creation' is testimony that it was not always intended to be like this and that it will not always be like this in the purposes of God" David Wilkinson, *The Message of Creation: Encountering the Lord of the Universe*, in Bible Themes Series, ed. Derek Tidball (Downers Grove, Illinois: InterVarsity Press, 2002), 235, 238, 240.

[784] Psalm 68:15-19

"O my Mansoul, as I have shown you what shall be hereafter, I will tell you what your present duty and practice must be, until I come and fetch you to myself, according to how it appears in the Scriptures of truth.[785]

"First, keep clean the liveries which I gave you before my last withdrawing from you. Do it, I say, for this will be your wisdom and honor and greatly for my glory. These liveries are fine linen which you must keep clean.[786] When such is so, the world will count you as mine and I am delighted in your ways. Your goings to and fro will be like a flash of lightning, that those who are present, with eyes bedazzled, must take notice. So, deck yourself with these linens according to my bidding and make my law straight steps for your feet.

"As I have already told you, I have an open fountain in which to wash your garments. Look to it and do not go about in defiled garments, for it is to my dishonor and disgrace and it is your discomfort as well when you walk in filthy garments. Let what I gave you not be defiled or spotted by the flesh. Keep your garments clean, and let your head lack no ointment.[787]

"My Mansoul, there have been considerable times I delivered you from the designs, plots, attempts, and conspiracies of Diabolus. For all of this I ask nothing, except that you do not render me evil for good.

"Bear my love in mind, and the continuation of my kindness. Let it provoke you to walk according to the benefit bestowed upon you.[788]

"O my Mansoul, I have lived, I have died, I live, and will die no more. I live, that you may not die. Because I live, you shall live also. I reconciled you to my Father by the blood of my cross.[789] Being reconciled you shall live through me. I will pray for you. I will fight for you. I will do you good![790]

"There is nothing that can hurt you but sin. Nothing can grieve me but sin. My Mansoul, take heed of sin![791]

"And do you know why I at first and still do suffer Diabolonians to dwell in your walls, O Mansoul?[792]

---

[785] Luke 24:27, 32; John 5:39; Romans 15:4; 2 Timothy 3:15

[786] Esther 8:15; Proverbs 31:22; Revelation 18:16; 19:8-10

[787] Zechariah 3:3-4; 13:1; Revelation 3:4; 7:14

[788] Genesis 44:4; Job 30:26; Psalms 37:27; 38:20; Isaiah 5:20; Matthew 7:17-18; 12:35; 1 Thessalonians 5:15

[789] Mark 8:34; Philippians 2:8; 1 Peter 2:24

[790] Text and Song Interactional: John Mark Hall and Matthew West, songwriters, "Scars in Heaven" by Casting Crowns, released 2021; Jason Roy, David Blake Neesmith and Riley Lee Friesen, songwriters, "Fear No More," sung by Building 425, released 2019

[791] Romans 6:15

[792] "It is interesting that modern scholars seem to need to get closure on this issue while Bunyan is able to live with dichotomies that resist resolution. That 'darker subtext'

"That is a good and poignant question!

"I have a serious answer!

"It is to keep you awake, to try your love, to make you watchful, and to cause you to prize my noble captains, their soldiers, and my mercy.[793]

"It is also, so that you may not forget the deplorable condition you used to be in. I mean when all, not some, Diabolonians dwelled, not just in your walls, but in your castle, and in your stronghold, and close to your hearts.[794]

"O, my Mansoul, if I should slay all Diabolonians within, there would be many without who would yet bring you into bondage. They would find you sleeping and, in a moment, swallow you up.[795]

"I left them not to do you hurt (the which they will if you hearken to them and serve them) but to do you good,[796] which they could if you would watch and fight against them.

"Know that, however they may tempt you, my design is not that they should drive you further away. My intent is that they should drive you nearer to my Father.[797]

---

is probably Bunyan's practical recognition that, whatever the theological explanations for the tenacious grip of evil, unbelief continues to be a chronic problem in human experience, therefore it must also persist in Mansoul." Daniel V. Runyon "John Bunyan's Master Story: The Holy War as Battle Allegory in Religious and Biblical Context." [Published version of Ph.D. dissertation] (Lampeter, Wales: Edwin Mellen Press, 2007), 234.

[793] "On our earthly pilgrimage we pant after peace, yet are involved in constant strife – with the pagan, with the heretic, with the bad Catholic, and even with the brother in the same household. One may grow weary and exclaim, 'Why should I eat out my life in contention? I will return within myself.' But even there one will find that the flesh lusts against the spirit. Peace will not come until this corruptible puts on incorruption, and then only for the redeemed, because hell is the perpetuation of unresolved conflicts. Perfect peace is reserved for heaven, where there shall be no hunger nor thirst nor provocation of enemies" Roland H. Bainton, *Christian Attitudes Toward War and Peace* (Nashville: Abingdon Press, 1960), pp. 91-92.

[794] John Wesley: "Instead of repining at your not being wholly delivered, you will praise God for thus far delivering you. You will magnify God for what he hath done, and take it as an earnest of what he will do. You will not fret against him because you are not yet renewed, but bless him because you shall be; and because 'now is our salvation' from all sin 'nearer than when you' first 'believed' [citing Romans 13:11]. Instead of uselessly tormenting yourself because the time is not fully come you will calmly and quietly wait for it, knowing that it will come and will not tarry' [citing Hebrews 10:37]" from John Wesley, "Satan's Devices" (Sermon 42), II.5, edited by Albert C. Outler, Volume 2, *The Works of John Wesley* series (Nashville: Abingdon Press, 1985), II.5.

[795] Mark 13:35-37

[796] Judges 2:21-23; 3:4; Hebrews 13:20-21

[797] "If Satan were not continually molesting us with trials, with the persecution of our enemies, and the ingratitude of our brethren, we would become so careless and indifferent to all good works that in time we would lose our faith in Christ, resign the min-

"Show me your love and do not let those within your walls take your affections away from the very one who has redeemed your soul.

"Yes, let the sight of any Diabolonian heighten your love for me.

"I came once, twice, and thrice to save you from the poison of the arrows that would have brought your death.

"Stand for me, your Friend, my Mansoul, against the Diabolonians, and I will stand for you before my Father and all his court.[798] Love me against temptation and I will love you notwithstanding your infirmities.[799]

"O my Mansoul, remember what my captains, my soldiers, and my engines have done for you. They have fought for you. They have suffered for you. They have borne much at the Diabolonians' hands to do you good.

"If you hadn't my captains, my soldiers, my engines to help you, Diabolus would have made a hand of you.[800]

"My Mansoul, nourish those that bear my arms. When you do well, they will be well. If you do ill, they will be ill, and sick, and weak.

"Do not make my captains sick! If they are sick, you cannot be well; if they are weak, you cannot be strong; if they are faint, you cannot be stout and valiant for your King.

"Nor must you think always to live by your sense.

"You must live by my word. You must believe that even when I am away, I still love you and forever bear you upon my heart.[801]

"Remember, therefore, O my Mansoul, you are beloved of me. As I have taught you to watch, to fight, and to make war against my foes, so I command you to believe my love is constant to you.[802]

"O my Mansoul, how have I set my heart and my love upon you!

"Watch!

"I lay no other burden upon you, than what you already have.

---

istry of the Word, and look for an easier life" Martin Luther, *Commentary on Galatians*, trans. by Theodore Graebner (Digireads.com Publishing, 2019), Galatians 5:13; p.145.

[798] Matthew 10:32-33

[799] Psalm 103:3; Isaiah 53:3-4, 10; Matthew 8:17; Romans 15:1; 2 Corinthians 12:9-10; Hebrews 4:15

[800] The Hand – Among the last things Bunyan writes regards the hand under which Mansoul will go on to serve. Not just a part of the body, the hand biblically is a symbol of power and authority. In service to Diabolus Mansoul will fall under the hand of his deceptive and manipulative sociopathic evildoing. In devotion to Emmanuel the workings of Mansoul's hands will ever be in the service of a time-honored and eternal good. Thus, the image of the laying on of hands in consecration and ordination. Among Bible references to hand, see Daniel 3:15.

[801] John 17:20-28

[802] Text and Song Interactional: "Come as You Are" by David Crowder, released 2014

"Hold fast, until I come."[803]

PRAYER STARTER: *Bind us to your heart, dear God, and hold us close to your people. Help us be a strength and encouragement to one another. May we do nothing to tarnish the good you are working within us. As we await your fulfillment of our lives, keep us keeping on, with eyes wide open and ears attentively listening to your call.* [From here on continue with your own prayerful words.] *In Jesus' name, we pray. Amen.*

Your Hands Dirtied Doing Good

Years ago, as a young pastor, I remember Bishop Joseph Yeakel paraphrasing some lines from Rogers and Hammerstein's 1949 production of James Michener's *Tales of the South Pacific*. Upon peering into its source, the quotation was not exact, but the sense was clearly the same.

Bishop Joe proclaimed: "You've got to be carefully taught to love, to hate, before your sixes and your sevens. You've got to be carefully taught to love, to hate." The actual words followed a line by Lieutenant Cable positing racism as something not born within one, but something developing afterwards.

At the time, there was a significant protest over the message of the musical, but the producers remained insistent about its presentation.

As the years unfolded, the Bishop's message remained with me. By the time I had been ten years in pastoral ministry, I had the blessing of traveling to Israel – the first time of five separate occasions.

My first travel time was a basic Bible Lands tour into Israel and Jordan that my wife and I enjoyed in 1987. How fascinating to pass out into the Jordanian desert, enjoy baklava saturated with crystal-clear honey, and visit Petra, an ancient city carved out of rock.

By January 1989, I was invited to participate in a factfinding mission, which coincided with the time of the First Intifada.[804] Our mission was called a Journey toward Understanding. Led by Bishop Forrest Stith and the Reverend Dr. William Pegg, we met various people of Israeli, Palestinian, UNRWA (United Nations Relief and Works Agency), political, religious, and business backgrounds.

During any trip to Israel, people might visit the Church of the Holy Sepulcher, one of the holiest sites in Christendom. The site of this fourth-

---

[803] Proverbs 4:4; Titus 1:9; Hebrews 3:6; Revelation 2:24-25

[804] From Arabic about the 1987-1993 and 2000-2005 uprisings, rebellions, initially intended nonviolent; also applied to Matthew 10:14; Mark 6:11; and Luke 9:5, meaning "a shaking off the dust" from one's feet.

century church, now within the walls of Jerusalem, was, at the time of Jesus' crucifixion and resurrection, outside the walls.[805] Sadly, this shrine now sacred to six branches of the Christian faith[806] has not escaped a share of aggravating tensions.

For instance, a fight broke out with its resident Orthodox and Catholic congregations in the mid-1800s and sparked the Crimean War.[807] The British artist William Holman Hunt, who spent considerable years in Palestine, wrote of passing through Crimean War territory upon returning home: "The spectacle of Christian nations contending in blood together in Crimea was of humiliating sadness."[808] Moreover, no fewer than three decades later, pilgrims observed the Ottomans having to post custodians at the entrance of the church to keep any congregants and visitors from provoking further discord.[809]

While preparing for my second trip to the Middle East, which was the Journey toward Understanding, I learned of the Palestinian priest Abuna Elias Chacour,[810] an Eastern [Melkite] Christian in communion with Rome, later Archbishop, whose life story, and humble, insightful, and compelling message and mission for reconciliation and peace is told in his *Blood Brothers* and *We Belong to the Land* – expounding a life spirited forward by Jesus' Beatitudes.

A few years afterwards, my oldest son, Jonathan, and I, and still later, my wife Beth and daughter, Keryn, on another journey, engaged in Volunteer in Mission experiences in Abuna's village of Ibillin, a short distance from Haifa near Upper Galilee. After a gap of still another number of years, I was back in Israel – this time, with another son, Jared, a pastor – working for five weeks upon the Tel Gezer archaeological dig. Moreover, my pastor son, my wife, and I returned to Israel with our church people on still another journey divided between a stay in Abuna's Palestinian village and a tour of Bible Land sites in other parts of Israel.

---

[805] Matthew 27:39; John 19:20; Hebrews 13:12

[806] Denominations therein sharing property: Greek Orthodox, Roman Catholic, Armenian Apostolic; and to a lesser degree, Coptic Orthodox, Syriac Orthodox, and Ethiopian Orthodox

[807] Crimean War, 1854-1856, with causalities totaling 900,000, death primarily due to terrible living conditions

[808] W. Holman Hunt, *Pre-Raphaelitism and the Pre-Raphaelite Brotherhood*, Vol. 2 (London: Macmillan and Co, Limited, 1905), 82.

[809] Bertha Spafford Vester, *Our Jerusalem: An American Family in the Holy City, 1881-1949* (Garden City, New York: Doubleday & Company, 1950), 87 [especially refer to Bibliography reference for a brief summary of the experience and impact of the Spaffords' lives].

[810] Abuna is a term of endearment for a priest

On two of these journeys to the Middle East,[811] I had the opportunity to visit two refugee camps – one in Jordan and the other in Israel. It is hard to imagine the living conditions that people of several generations jammed together in close and meager confines were impelled to endure. As our group walked along the muddy streets of the Jordanian camp, I can never forget a colleague who exclaimed: "We walk around. Take a few pictures. Get on our bus and leave. It just doesn't make sense." Still another colleague remarked regarding an endurance she envisioned as "the triumph of the human spirit!"

There was a book among those for our Journey toward Understanding. Certainly, there were many resources from both Jewish and Palestinian backgrounds I found awakening, disturbing, and enriching across the years. However, there was one that some might pass off as old and outdated today. But really? We still can draw from its basic message. What I am thinking of is *The Yellow Wind,* by a young (at the time) Israeli novelist, David Grossman, given a three-month assignment to head into the West Bank to view "one of the most tormented issues in world politics" [from the book cover]. In one chapter, Grossman cites a study conducted by Dr. Yoram Bilu, a psychology instructor at Hebrew University, probing the dreams of eleven-to-thirteen-year-old Arab and Jewish children. My gathering a few of Grossman's informational pieces appear in the indentation as follows:

> Seventeen percent of the Jewish children's dreams pertained to meeting an Arab. Thirty percent of the Arab children's dreams pertained to meeting a Jew. No one could be identified by a name or personal appearance. The individuals fell under some ethnic identity (Jew, Arab, Zionist, etc.) or value-laden word (terrorist, oppressor, etc.). The Jewish children studied portrayed the Arabs as criminals, had trouble dealing with life's constant struggle, and were left to find release in their imagination and transference. A basic plot for the Arab children saw Zionist soldiers surrounding the house, which had permeable walls, and, in time at the betrayal of a neighbor, they found the child for whom they were searching. All in all, most of the dream interactions were aggressive, violent, and resulted in death. In the end, Grossman concluded his poignant six-page summary with what did not come into view among the thousand dreams of the Jewish and Arab children. There was not one dream that indicated a longing for peace.[812]

In a parallel concern, I reach back earlier than David Grossman to Dorothy Thompson, 20th-century journalist, and daughter of a British emi-

---

[811] The 2nd and the 5th

[812] David Grossman, *The Yellow Wind*, trans. From the Hebrew by Haim Watzman (New York: Farrar, Straus and Giroux, 1988), 29-33.

grant Methodist Episcopal pastor, notably the first woman to hold a major oversees news post. Following World War I, her territory embraced an area spanning the former Austro-Hungarian Empire. Dubbed the First Lady of American Journalism, Thompson, "a legend in her own time" according to Marion K. Sanders, one of her biographers,[813] was a strong critic of Adolph Hitler, years before the United States came to acknowledge the evil in which Hitler was engaging. In fact, Thompson was among the first journalists Hitler expelled from Nazi Germany nearly a decade before America entered World War II. Her book, *I Saw Hitler,*[814] was a graphic prophecy of the malevolence she discerned in this latest political sensation.

After World War II, Dorothy Thompson and her husband toured the Nazi extermination camps. On the one hand, the barracks, the gas chambers, and the dreadful crematoria and, on the other hand, the image of Nazi exterminators as "happy family men, devoted to their wives and children, appreciative of music, and the arts,"[815] were sickening contrasts to Thompson and her husband who, by the way, was a concentration camp survivor himself. Subsequently, Thompson and her husband traveled to the Middle East. Although for years a supporter of Jewish Zionism, what she saw by the late-1940s did not seem right concerning what she saw happening to its area Palestinian people. Consequently, the articulation of this concern brought the removal of Thompson from major news syndicates and magazines, wherein previously she had a readership of some eight to ten million people. After the removal, though, she continued writing for *The Ladies Home Journal*. For another of her biographers, Thompson would go down in history dubbed American Cassandra, after a woman during the Greco-Trojan War, noted for her ominous concerns that people would not comprehend until too late.

The life of the 1600s British Civil Wars soldier, John Bunyan, was a stirring example of one who wanted to share the message of being at peace with God and a blessing for all to whom he could minister. His message, rooted deeply in the recognition of God's grace, was not that of people battling one another in a war that took lives. His message was a reawakening to a different kind of war, a holy war, where the challenges between good and evil were what was battling around and within each and every person.

Any comprehension of the seriousness of such a warfare begins with a reawakening to God's voice within oneself! It comes with a recognition

---

[813] Marion K. Sanders, *Dorothy Thompson: A Legend in Her Time* (Boston: Houghton Mifflin Company, 1973).

[814] Initially the March 1932 issue of *Cosmopolitan*

[815] Peter Kurth, *American Cassandra: The Life of Dorothy Thompson* (Boston: Little, Brown and Company, 1990), 374.

of the spiritual dynamics that tear at one another and cast a devastation throughout life. John Bunyan did not come to this comprehension immediately. It was mulling in and around his heart for years. But then, what a legacy he left us![816]

My heart goes back to God's promise to Abraham and Sarah that they would be blessed, yes, and that all the world would be blessed through them.[817]

The Lord Jesus deepens our sense of this blessedness in the Sermon on the Mount. Living the Beatitude faith, as Abuna Elias Chacour[818] would put it, is not a passive just-let-me-feel-good religion. It is an active faith as appears in the following portion of Abuna's compelling writings.

> "Blessed" is the translation of the word, *makarioi*, used in the Greek New Testament. However, when I look further back to Jesus' Aramaic, I find that the original word was *ashray*, from the verb *yashar*. *Ashray* does not have this passive quality to it at all. Instead, it means "to set yourself on the right way for the right goal; to turn around, repent; to become straight or righteous."

> How could I go to a persecuted man in a Palestinian refugee camp, for instance, and say, "Blessed are those who mourn, for they shall be comforted," or "Blessed are those who are persecuted for the sake of justice, for theirs is the kingdom of heaven"? That man would revile me, saying neither I nor my God understood his plight, and he would be right.

> When I understand Jesus' words in the Aramaic, I translate like this:

> Get up, go ahead, do something, move, you who are hungry and thirst for justice, for you shall be satisfied. Get up, go ahead, do something, move, you peacemakers, for you shall be called children of God.

> To me this reflects Jesus' words and teachings much more accurately. I can hear him saying, "Get your hands dirty to build a human society for human beings; otherwise, others will torture and murder the poor, the voiceless, and the powerless." Christianity is not passive but active, energetic, alive, going beyond despair.[819]

---

[816] Text and Song Interactional: "Goodness of God" by Jenn Johnson, released 2019

[817] Genesis 12:3

[818] Abuna Elias Chacour's Prophet Mar Elias School in Ibillin, Israel, is notable for its drive to be an educationally safe place for Jewish, Christian, Islamic and Druse people to learn in a holistic environment.

[819] Elias Chacour with Mary E. Jensen, *We Belong to the Land: The Story of a Palestinian Israeli who Lives for Peace and Reconciliation* (New York: HarperCollins, Publishers, 1990), pp. 143-144.

Though John Bunyan and Elias Chacour are separated by many years, and a considerable difference in life experiences, however, there is a point where Chacour would echo Bunyan.

The good Lord God's grace is not something I consume for myself. It, as well, is something I live out for the good of others.

Let it be so!

The Master Craftsperson

Hebrews 11:10: For he loked for a citie hauing a fundacion, whofe buylder and maker is God (GEN, 1560)

For he looked for a city having a foundation, whose builder and maker is God (GNV, 1599).

In 1969 Ralph Carmichael and Kurt Kaiser produced a folk musical about God, *Tell It Like It Is*, in which appeared the song "Master Designer"[820] singing the praises of the richness and beauty of God's wonderful creation.

Nearly three hundred years before that, in 1682, John Bunyan in *The Holy War* brought to imagination a picture-perfect world Shaddai fashioned for Mansoul within the "famous continent of Universe." The story began with the creative and sustaining plan that God had for Mansoul (a.k.a. humanity) from time primeval. Despite Diabolus's effort to bring ruination to the world, God ultimately would not be foiled but eventually would accomplish a redemptive plan on into eternity.

As Bunyan kept identifying himself as a tinker throughout his life, let us respectfully turn to a possibly mundane analogy regarding God as a craftsperson. I know this is an uneven analogy. Such a comparison between a human being and God is not where I want to stay very long. To aid in the understanding, though, Scripture provides a jumpstart as in Proverbs 8:27-29, David Wilkinson, a British Methodist minister and research astrophysicist, points to the wisdom undergirding God's creative handiwork:

Wisdom is before the Universe and fundamental . . . to the whole creative process, and in particular of ensuring the stability and continuation of creation. Wisdom is key to the continuous process of fashioning creation into a world that is intelligible, orderly and good. The images of architect and builder give a picture of a well-structured creation.[821]

---

[820] Text and Song Interactional: Ralph Carmichael and Kurt Kaiser, "Master Designer" in *Tell It Like It Is: A Folk Musical about God*, released 1969.

[821] David Wilkinson, *The Message of Creation: Encountering the Lord of the Uni-*

With the Greek words in Hebrews 11:10, we draw upon the images of God as builder and maker. It was a destiny for which Abraham and Sarah were steadily and patiently waiting in spite of their earthly disappointments.[822] The word τεχνίτης (technitēs), found here and in Acts 19:24, 38, carries the sense of God as the designer, artisan or architect of the realm that all the people of God would hope to enjoy. The Greek word δημιουργὸς (dēmiourgos), which appears in this place alone in the New Testament, carries the idea of one working for the good of a whole community, such as a public workman, a constructor – in ancient Athens, a position that had a proud ring to it. However, the destination to which Abraham and Sarah were pressing was not in building an earthly commonwealth, temporary as that would be, but a destiny that had eternal foundations![823]

In terms of this world, though, God, the "Master Designer," who, as we affirm, brought all that we have into being, has blessed us with a diversity and an abundance intended for the good, constructive, artistic, and life-giving use of us all. Until eternity dawns, though, how much more have we kept faith with that which weighs upon us? Consequently, we need a reawakening to the importance, beauty, and refreshment of this realm God fashioned for us!

In the January / February 2022 *Smithsonian Magazine*, Jonny Diamond, in "The Old Man and the Tree," draws attention to the mission in which retired software developer, Bob Leverett, has engaged traipsing the forests of New England searching for "big trees." With the enthusiasm as catchy as an "old Southern senator" engaging in a filibuster or "itinerant preacher" delivering an evangelistic sermon, Leverett reaches scientists, forest managers, college professors, lovers of nature and others with something that, in part, could help turn us from the downward spiral of misusing, or even missing out on using, our good resources. It regards preserving these one hundred to one hundred and fifty years old and older monoliths in existent "old-growth forests." It is because these old trees

verse, Bible Themes Series, ed. Derek Tidball (Downers Grove, Illinois: InterVarsity Press, 2002), 85.

[822] Archibald Thomas Robertson, *Word Pictures in the New Testament*, vol. 5, *The Fourth Gospel, The Epistle to the Hebrews* (Nashville, Tennessee: Broadman Press, 1932, 1960), 422.

[823] F. F. Bruce, *The Epistle to the Hebrews: The English Text with Introduction, Exposition and Notes* (Grand Rapids, Michigan: Wm. B. Eerdmans Publishing Co., 1964), 297-299.

draw more toxic carbons from the environment than the younger trees do, thus helping to bring a refreshment and ecological renewal to our planet![824]

In Bunyan's way of expression, Emmanuel's wresting Mansoul from Diabolus's clutches and *newly modeling* the town, was, even as we think of good stewardship, bringing such a place away from its toxic backwaters and *toward* what was initially intended good.

I grew up on the edge of a farm, my Grandpa's farm, wherein there was a small sawmill. I played around that sawmill. I observed how painstakingly my Grandpa, a skilled saw sharpener, could file and set the teeth in all types of blades – including the large circular ones for the mill. I watched and I sometimes helped the grown-ups mill the logs drawn from the flatlands and mountains amidst where we lived. They would then lay the sawn boards out in stacks, with stickers in between to air dry and season the lumber. I carry the pride of that in my heart and mind throughout the years to this very day.

I am no master craftsman. Far from it! Still, memories of my grandfather and growing up around his sawmill planted seeds of an interest in my heart. I also discovered that working with wood does not stop at an interest. It requires a commitment to a step-by-step process, a continual exercise of patience, a skill in using various types of tools, an awareness of the nature of each species of wood with which one is working, a studied carefulness in preparing the pieces (you measure twice and cut once), the sequencing in which the project is accomplished, an artistic bent, a willingness to keep on trying, and a stewardship of resources – thus, a replenishing of them.

Much as with any carpenter or cabinet maker, the tinker faces a learning curve and carries a sense of it through life! Some of the imagery in which Bunyan had worked may have slipped into his preaching, like "strike the iron while it is hot," and helped, to his people's delight, hammer home a point.

In another way of stating it, any craft that is done well takes discipline, a faithful work ethic, patience, practice, a vision, a pride in what you are doing, and a commitment to the people one is serving. Furthermore, I'm sure that Bunyan, as a tinker, did not automatically plop into his trade. He grew up around and into it, with his father being a tinker as well.

I once observed a tinker's anvil put on view in Bunyan Meeting House and Museum in Bedford, England. Shaped quite differently than a blacksmith's anvil, the tinker's anvil was, I noticed, still large, had a long horn,

---

[824] Jonny Diamond, "The Old Man and the Tree," *Smithsonian Magazine* Vol. 52, No. 09 (January / February 2022), 34, 38.

and was undoubtedly heavy! I can only imagine the tinker lugging it around.

To keep with the analogy of wood crafting, though: red oak, a popular mainstay in fine cabinetry, is a hardwood with which other woods are often compared. Working with sassafras, a softer wood which has the appearance of ash, produces a fragrance of root beer. Butternut, another softer wood, at times called white walnut, approaches the beauty, but without the toxicity, of black walnut. There is an attractive hardwood, chechen, a.k.a. black poisonwood, found around the Caribbean and Gulf of Mexico. It must be safely harvested at an appropriate time because it secretes a toxic sap like poison ivy. Then, there is canarywood, a lovely wood – one of my favorites – that displays a multicolor array of purple, orange, brown, and yellow grains, black markings, and splashes of red. This beautiful wood is so abundant in its native lands, from Panama south and through Brazil, it is sometimes used for construction timbers and railroad crossties. The wood in service from each type of tree – over 60,000 known species throughout the world – has its own respective nature, sacred place, and beneficial uses.

As I mention these types of wood used in woodworking, I am only scratching the surface. What an amazing array of the flora the Lord God Shaddai has fashioned throughout His awesome creation!

As there is a respect for life and an understanding when dealing with any individual type of wood, there is a vision, sensitivity, patience, and hopefulness when it comes to dealing with conditions surrounding people's souls.

A principal part of Bunyan's theology is a realization of God's grace! What if, in dealing with people, while centering upon some of Bunyan's character names, the tradesperson was to fashion a work with the help of Patience, Promise, Skill, and so on, instead of the insincerity of the Forget-Good, the High-mind and the Heady self-centering of the Diabolonian sort?

Quite frankly, the world would be a more redemptive, safe, and gracious place – quite as God intended it – and will eventually bring it forth to be! Thus, this is what comes across in Bunyan's allegory.[825]

One of the most intriguing stories in the Bible and, consequently, revealing some of the best and worst of human nature, is the parable of the

---

[825] "Allegory, in some sense, belongs not to medieval man but to man, or even to mind, in general. It is of the very nature of thought and language to represent what is immaterial in picturable terms. What is good or happy has always been high like the heavens and bright like the sun [although] evil and misery were deep and dark from the first" C. S. Lewis, *The Allegory of Love: A Study in Medieval Tradition* (New York: Oxford University Press, 1936; Paperback, 1958), 44.

trees in the book of Judges. It tells how, one day, the vines, shrubs, and trees were conversing with one another as to which among them would be the chief. The olive tree, grape vine, and palm tree were busy doing just what they were intended to be doing. Meanwhile, the thornbush (a high-minded character in the allegory), ascribing to be the great potentate, would strut forward posing himself best suited for the job – even to the point of edging out the majestic cedars of Lebanon. Most significantly, Bunyan, mindful of this allegory, deems Diabolus the lowly bramble in his *The Holy War*.[826]

The character Willbewill in Bunyan's story gets caught for a while in the clutches of that bramble Diabolus's control. In the beginning, as he shifted away from Shaddai, there was "no one like Willbewill to trumpet the brave nature, wide conduct, and great glory of Diabolus – his illustrious lord and valiant prince – as he traipsed about Mansoul." However, as this kingdom that Diabolus had stolen from Shaddai was captured by Emmanuel, with Willbewill being taken prisoner of war, Willbewill acknowledged his own sinful rebelliousness. God's amazing grace appeared as repentant Willbewill and the other Mansoulian people were graced with forgiveness. In turning back to Shaddai and Emmanuel, Willbewill became one of the most responsive and effective Mansoulian leaders. Oh, he wasn't perfect. He still had his fumbles. Notwithstanding, his heart was set upon a different base and he became a strong and fascinating example of a transformed life!

In woodworking, there are interesting examples of redemption. Consider the maple, for instance. There are times that any number of maple trees may struggle with difficult growing conditions or suffer infections brought on by some invasive insect or fungus. However, the wood from such trees in the hands of the sawyer, millwright, and master craftsperson can take on a lovely appearance. Such, to mention two, are the circumstances pertaining to birdseye maple and ambrosia maple. The skilled craftsperson draws from their possibilities something good and beautiful. How much more the marvelous, gracious, and redemptive through the power of God![827]

In one of the churches in which I served as the pastor for fifteen of my forty years in full-time ministry, there was a layperson, Grant Amey, a schoolteacher, who would come across some badly broken, dented, and discarded pieces of furniture set out at the curb for garbage and would re-

---

[826] In Judges 9:1-57 Jotham, the youngest son of Jerub-Baal (Gideon), calls his assassin brother, Abimelek who murdered his seventy brothers, a bramble, morally and dangerously unfit to hold leadership in Shechem.

[827] Text and Song Interactional: "It Is Well," Bethel Song; Kristine DiMarco, featured artist, 2014

habilitate them. I think, especially, of a severely damaged marble-top table drawn from the ruin of our 1984 church fire. The table's being retrieved from the devastation, Grant, through a lot of hard, creative, thoughtful work, brought the table back to its distinctive life, beauty, and usefulness. A rebirth! Then, after the refinishing, the table was set in the atrium just outside of the newly rebuilt sanctuary.[828]

In a lovely book, *The Soul of a Tree: A Woodworker's Reflections*, George Nakashima presents an engaging volume of text, color photography and drawings on the topic of the tree.

> We are left in awe by the nobility of a tree, its eternal patience, its suffering caused by man and sometimes nature, its witness to thousands of years of earth's history, its creations of fabulous beauty. It does nothing but good, with its prodigious ability to serve, it gives off its bounty of oxygen while absorbing gases harmful to other living things. The tree and its pith live on. Its fruits feed us. Its branches shade and protect us. And, finally, when time and weather bring it down, its body offers timber for our houses and boards for our furniture. The tree lives on.[829]

Such is the gift, and abundantly more, with which the creator God graces our world, "the continent of Universe!" – indeed, an appreciation through which we need to come to a reawakening ourselves.[830]

One of the earliest Christian beliefs is God's working upon and within our lives to fit us for heaven.[831] God, the master craftsman, at work in the human soul, casts such a bountiful and beautiful work through the various ages and stages of life. And yes, no matter what we have been through![832]

---

[828] Grant Amey, co-chair with Margaret Fairhead, led the 1986-1988 Building Committee at Faith United Methodist Church, Lancaster, NY, through the 1987 rebuilding of the sanctuary following the 1984 fire. Lardon Construction, Blasdell, NY, was the general contractor.

[829] George Nakashima, *The Soul of a Tree: A Woodworker's Reflections*, with an introduction by Dr. George Wald (New York: Kodansha USA Publishing, LLC, 1981, 2011), p. 81

[830] Text and Song Interactional: "10,000 Reasons" by Matt Redman, released 2013

[831] As highlighted previously: "The crucifixion and resurrection of Christ are absent from the chronological narrative [of *The Holy War*], but present in the message. While the Bible narrates God's redemptive work for man, *The Holy War* is largely the narrative of humankind's response to God's redemptive work" Daniel V. Runyon, "John Bunyan's Master Story: The Holy War as Battle Allegory in Religious and Biblical Context" (Published version of Ph.D. dissertation, Lampeter, Wales: Edwin Mellen Press, 2007), 237-238.

[832] "The Scriptures present Christ in a twofold aspect. First, as a gift. 'He of God is made unto us wisdom, and righteousness, and sanctification and redemption.' (1 Cor. 1:30.) Hence my many and grievous sins are nullified if I believe in Him. Secondly, the Scriptures present Christ for our example. As an exemplar He is to be placed before me only at certain times. In times of joy and gladness that I may have Him as a mirror to reflect

In the first Psalm, most fittingly an entry point to the whole book of Psalms, there is the lovely image of a tree planted by the water.[833] In John's Gospel, Jesus directs the Samaritan woman to the living water with which her life can be eternally refreshed.[834] In the book of Revelation, there is a magnificent reference to a tree whose leaves are for the healing of the nations.[835]

As Bunyan's *Holy War* reaches an end, the Mansoulians await the consummation of their faith. They are still in that time in between Mansoul's creation and heaven's ultimate fulfillment. Yet, the importance of their staying alert and true to their daily responsibilities has not come to an end. Drawing insights from what U. Milo Kaufmann designated the "two-way quest," Daniel V. Runyon points out:

> By returning Mansoul to the world to do battle with sin [...] The people of Mansoul are back where they began, but there is a qualitative difference at the new beginning. Experience results in wisdom, contentment, and new levels of moral and intellectual development that make them willing to suffer, and in their willingness to hold fast, they are a new creation.[836]

Also, in that time in between creation and heaven's ultimate fulfillment, there is another fascinating image from the book of Revelation in the Bible. It comes from the Spirit's message to the church at Laodicea.[837] In this regard we shift from the metaphor of woodcraft to that of water.

With the location of Laodicea in southwestern Turkey, I come to an allegory I can draw from the geographical location of not only this but another two Biblical cities. These three cities lay in somewhat of a triangular frame, with each being roughly seven miles apart. In Biblical times, the cities were Hierapolis, Colossae, and Laodicea – all associated in one way or another with the Apostle Paul.

A spa city from ancient times, Hierapolis was notable for its carbonate spring waters – soothing and thermal – cascading down the mountainside of Pamukkale, which, in Turkish, means "cotton castle." At another vertex, Colossae was known for its cold, refreshing drinking waters. Then,

---

upon my shortcomings. But in the day of trouble, I will have Christ only as a gift. I will not listen to anything else, except that Christ died for my sins" Martin Luther, *Commentary on Galatians*, trans. by Theodore Graebner (Digireads.com Publishing, 2019), Galatians 5:8; p.139.

[833] Psalm 1:3

[834] John 4:10-15

[835] Revelation 22:2

[836] John Bunyan, *The Holy War* Annotated Companion to *The Pilgrim's Progress*, ed. Daniel V. Runyon, (Eugene, Oregon: Pickwick Publications, 2012), xxvii

[837] Revelation 3:14-22

there was Laodicea, as noted in the Book of Revelation, which had its putrid lukewarm waters.[838] Quite a conglomeration of images!

Reflecting on this triad of cities and their respective kinds of water, let us draw an analogy of people living out in various ways and with various ends in heart and mind.

The Spirit in the Revelation speaks of the lukewarm waters of Laodicea as so nauseating that should one unwittingly take a gulp; the person would spew it out of his/her mouth.

For the other two types of water, could the Spirit be bringing forth still other analogies? Interestingly, the wording is: "I would that you were cold or hot!"

Let us imagine the Spirit saying to the God-beloved Mansoulian Christians as well as any of us today: I would wish that your life would manifest a healing warmth or cold refreshment, thus good for yourself and a blessing to others![839]

---

[838] Robert H. Mounce, *The Book of Revelation* (Grand Rapids, Michigan: William B. Eerdmans Publishing Company, 1977), 125-126.

[839] For the helpful fact-checking and proof reading of this chapter, I am especially indebted to Kevin Foley, who served as head of Civil Engineering Technology at Rochester Institute of Technology, with degrees in wood products engineering and in construction engineering; and to Joyce Foley, public schoolteacher, whose majors were in English and in Elementary Education with an emphasis on Early Childhood.

Appendix Number One

Some Reflections on the Psychological Dynamics

Abby Manzella, Wellness Counselor
Licensed Master of Social Work

The 1682 novel, *The Holy War* by John Bunyan was written as a powerful allegory on the emotional battles we face between "good and evil." He showed us many characters that can help or hinder when a challenge arises and how God always remains consistent as a source of unconditional love. Bunyan truly had a gift for weaving the timeless principles of Scripture into a narrative to help the reader connect to the Word.

In the rewritten book, *The Holy War: A Reawakening*, the author included a biography of John Bunyan to provide remarkable insight on who Bunyan was, and how his life's journey impacted the writings of the novel. The history of Bunyan gave such a personal connection to the village of Mansoul and the battle between good and evil. Bunyan grew up during a tumultuous time in England, during the Civil Wars, where he witnessed governmental, economical, and psychological hardships. One of Bunyan's most significant battles was at the age of sixteen, when his mother and sister passed within a month of each other. This traumatic event changed the course of this young man's life. Out of this tragedy, and many others, came the evolution of the good and evil characters written into the novel.

In hindsight, Bunyan was able to discover that many of his (and others') problems had a spiritual base. When looking at himself and these others, the internal battles that are faced daily can be redeemed and resolved by using God's word and Scripture to heal old and new wounds.

I enjoyed reading this because of the profound use of symbolism to address the internal "battles" faced by humans. As a counselor, I appreciated the "Holy War" for the battles that occur often when challenged by the environment as well as the "Diaboluses" speaking into our ears, tempting us to lose our focus on God's word. The additional biography of John Bunyan and the biographical reminiscences of the present-day author as craftsman helped to intensify the meaning. As with Bunyan and the author,

God is seen as the Craftsman/Designer constantly seeing something better unfold. I walked away from the book understanding God knows the weakness of humans, exercises forgiveness and sees what will come from the challenge.

One of the statements that echoes in my ear is, "out of pain and suffering comes a person who is better than before." Also, "if we listen to the music of 'holy wars' without the full symphony of Scripture, we will likely distort both" (Heath Thomas, 11/21/2011).

A couple diagnostic issues I find helpful for understanding John Bunyan's *The Holy War* relate to Narcissistic Personality Disorder (NPD) and Borderline Personality Disorder (BPD).

Narcissistic Personality Disorder (NPD) – people who are in love with an idealized, grandiose image of themselves. And they're in love with this inflated self-image precisely because it allows them to avoid deep feelings of insecurity. NPD involves a pattern of self-centered, arrogant thinking and behavior, a lack of empathy and consideration for other people and an excessive need for admiration. Often these types of people are described as cocky, manipulative, selfish, patronizing, and demanding. Some characteristics are:

1. **Need for constant praise and admiration** – A narcissist's sense of superiority is like a balloon that gradually loses air without a steady stream of applause and recognition to keep it inflated. They need constant food for their ego, so they surround themselves with people who are willing to cater to their obsessive craving for affirmation.

2. **Exploits others without guilt or shame** – Lacking empathy. They view people in their lives as objects to serve their needs.

3. **Frequently demeans, intimidates, bullies, or belittles others** – Narcissists feel threatened whenever they encounter someone who appears to have something they lack. Their defense mechanism is contempt. The only way to neutralize the threat and prop up their own sagging is to put those people down. (www.helpguide.org)

Engaging conversation on Narcissism, see the following chapters: "Spoiling Goodness" (pp.49-55), "The Coming of the Prince Emmanuel," "The Battle for Mansoul, "and "The Conquest" (pp. 86-104), which supply many contrasting reflections on Diabolus and Emmanuel.

Borderline Personality Disorder (BPD) – A condition characterized by difficulties regulating emotion. This means that people who experience

BPD feel emotions intensely and for extended periods of time, and it is harder for them to return to a stable baseline after and emotionally triggering event. Some characteristics are:

1. Inappropriate, intense, or uncontrollable anger

2. Frantic efforts to avoid real or imagined abandonment by family or friends

3. Gas-lighting – A form of manipulation that occurs in abusive relationships. It is an insidious and somewhat covert type of emotional abuse where the bully or the abuser makes the target question their judgments and reality. This technique undermines the target's perception of reality. Gas-lighters are habitual and pathological liars. Lying is the cornerstone of their destructive behavior. Even when you know they are lying, they can be very convincing. When called out or questioned, they will use kind and loving words to try to smooth over the situation.

4. Splitting – All or nothing dichotomy ("black and white, good or bad"). Its widely believed to be a self-defense mechanism against feelings of hurt, rejection, or abandonment. (www.verywell-health.com)

Further Thoughts:

In the Bible, God is portrayed as an all-powerful being, who is holy and good, and who is committed to "eradicating sin and renewing creation." God's Holy Wars are his battles to reconcile all sin of the world through Jesus.

An example of this is the Biblical story where God fights for Israel to secure his land for his people. For Israel's God to show the other gods of the nations were false, God had to demonstrate his power in a way that was profound. Those who believed were to receive eternal blessings from God.

Another example would be the story of Canaan. God did not punish the people immediately, but gradually (over four hundred years). "His mercy extended long because his grace and compassion are long."

"Ephesians reveals that God's kingdom will be established not through coercion, but through sacrificial love, in the manner of Christ" (Heath Thomas 11/21/2011).

Abby Mansella, Wellness Counselor
Licensed Master of Social Work

Appendix Number Two

Some Reflections on the Trial Scenes

Lynda Ashbery Dodd
Trial Attorney, Dayton, Ohio

[In Bunyan's The Holy War, there are two trial scenes.] The line that stands out to me the most, which is descriptive of both trials is: "Lord Willbewill thought it more honorable to the Prince, more comfortable to Mansoul, and a discouragement to the enemy, if a fair trial be the structure with which to deal with the prisoners" ("Another Day in Court," p. 198).

The procedures described thereafter demonstrate only seeking the appearance of a fair trial. The description appears to start well. The jury was empaneled, and witnesses were sworn. But this was hardly an impartial jury. The same jury was used that had been used in the first trial. As with the first trial, even the names of those on trial and the witnesses foretell the desired outcome of the trial. Imagine a present-day prosecutor renaming the Defendant on trial as the "Lying rotten good for nothing thug" and renaming the State's witnesses and "Speakers of Truth and Justice." Nor is there any jury deliberation. The Judge issues rulings making the Court's opinions clear before the jury deliberates. The expected verdict, and sentence, are obvious. Per the introduction, this is exactly the world Bunyan lived in, a world where jurors who acquit when they should have convicted are fined! This is wholly opposite of a justice system where the Court instructs the jury: If, during the trial, the Court said or did anything that you consider an indication of the Court's view of the facts, you are instructed to disregard it" (Ohio Jury Instruction 207.3). Similarly, a justice system such as Mansoul's which strives only for the appearance of propriety is far different than a justice system in which, when operating as it should, the court and counsel strive to avoid even the appearance of impropriety.

In your closing pages, you write that any craft done well takes discipline, faithful work ethic, patience, practice, and commitment (p. 219). What resonates with me in this story is that it is so easy to settle for the appearance of these things. Mansoul's willingness to settle for the appearance of a fair trial, the appearance of justice, was at the first trial a signal that they were not wholly on the right track and were vulnerable to back-sliding (pp. 118-128).

Similarly, when we settle for the mere appearance of faithful work ethic, the mere appearance of conscientious discipline, etc., we are settling for less that we are intended to be. We desperately are in need, every day, of that new day dawning.

Lynda Ashbery Dodd, Trial Attorney
Montgomery County, Ohio

Appendix Number Three

Some Reflections on the
Holy War Itself

Reverend Dr. J. Paul Womack, Chaplain (Colonel)

This reflection is not designed to offer a literary criticism of Bunyan's allegorical work, *The Holy War*. Others more competent than I can provide insights into this work as a work of literary art in terms of narrative, character development, plot, drama, and so forth. My response, rather, is as a mostly twentieth century post-enlightenment pastor and former United States Army Chaplain, and it is that context which shapes the following points of view.

I assume in his musings on the spiritual development and growth in the Christian faith (or his version of the Christian faith) of the individual and society, it would have been difficult for Bunyan to avoid the military/spiritual warfare metaphor. As Duane Priset has noted, the reality of warfare was present not only in Bunyan's life but the society at large. That Bunyan took over the metaphor of warfare or struggle is not surprising, and his use of the metaphor apt for those who shared his historical context. My questions, however, reflect my time and my place in history.

It is for historians to evaluate the various complexities that played a role in the wars of Bunyan's era – economic, ethnic, imperialistic, cultural, and religious aims. It is, of course, easy to reduce such complexities to simplistic categories of truth versus falsehood, the good versus evil, the Godly versus the ungodly, the hosts of heaven aligned against the forces of the Evil One. In my experience, however, conflict between humans is not reducible to such binary categories of good versus evil. The power to destroy, not only the "enemy" combatant, but the collateral damage to a descriptive category we used in Vietnam, "innocent civilians," is too vast, powerful, and destructive to justify the use of the warfare metaphor as a tool or word symbol to indoctrinate the present generation in the processes of spiritual development and/or coming into faith. My fear is that the individual and the individual's society, indoctrinated in such a fashion, can too easily use "war" as the dominant means to "win" the struggle. Whether the metaphor enters religious discourse from the secular or infects the secular from the language of faith, "warfare" becomes the primary tool for resolution and is always "on the table," requiring the use of vast resources to militarily ever be at the ready.

Following the Trinity Explosion of the first atomic bomb, Manhattan Project Director J. Robert Oppenheimer quoted from the *Bhagavad Gita*: "I have become Death, the destroyer of worlds" (Chapter 11, verse 32). This sobering assessment pierces the innocence of warfare's metaphor.

Related to the binary simplification of good/evil or right/wrong is the possible truth that there is never any pure evil or good in humans or humanity. In the Wesleyan tradition, this insight serves to humble the pride of the righteous and their vanity. Redemption would not be possible if there was not some inkling of heart or mind that could be persuaded to the "good" – the kind or generous or compassionate – and thus grow in those virtues. This does not mean that there are no systemic expressions of evils in the human community. It does suggest that the efforts to counter such evils often risk reflecting that which is opposed. Soldiers are often haunted for the rest of their lives by moral pain in spite of efforts on the part of well-meaning supporters to justify their actions with comments like "thanks for your service" or the narratives that necessary actions were required to "save the world for democracy" (See Peter Marin's essay, "Living in Moral Pain" in *Freedom and its Discontents*, 1995). It is my conclusion after tours of duty in three wars (Vietnam, Desert Storm, and Operation Iraqi Freedom) that moral pain is a price paid to exist and to engage the elusive quest for the true and the beautiful and the good in a morally ambiguous world. I fear Bunyan's work, however masterful as literature it may be, fails to grasp this harsher reality to our conflicts, no matter how righteous we perceive our cause to be. Sadly, I have witnessed hearts that grow vengeful or hateful and become the very evil one struggles against.

The 20th century American theologian Reinhold Niebuhr, in his classic work *The Irony of American History*, states well the path for spiritual transformation (at least for me). He writes,

> Nothing that is worth doing can be achieved in our lifetime; therefore, we must be saved by hope. Nothing which is true or beautiful or good makes complete sense in any immediate context of history; therefore, we must be saved by faith. Nothing we do, however virtuous, can be accomplished alone; therefore, we are saved by love. No virtuous act is quite as virtuous from the standpoint of our friend or foe as it from our standpoint. Therefore, we must be saved by the final form of love which is forgiveness.

My point: regardless of the literary genius of Bunyan, as exemplified in the allegorical *The Pilgrim's Progress*, and *The Holy War*, the warfare metaphor is not adequate or sufficient, or even moral, in a time that calls for peace-making and nonviolence. Our personal and social spiritual growth is best nurtured by the Howard Thurmans, the Martin Luther Kings, the Gandhis, or the Thomas Mertons of history.

In brief, the struggle is real, but the metaphor used by Bunyan is inadequate to the needs of our time.

Reverend Dr. J. Paul Womack
Military Chaplain (Colonel)

Questions for Individuals and Groups
For Reflective Moments and Discussion

Entry Pieces

What is a reawakening? A reawakening from what? And a reawakening into what?

What are your thoughts and feelings about Biblical war and battle stories?

How do you account for the presence of evil invading a world that was intended to be good?

To a considerable extent there is conflict, war, misplaced people, and suffering somewhere in the world. What enflames people against each other? What promotes understanding and compassion?

Starting with Matt Redman's "10,000 Reasons (Bless the Lord)," there are various song titles placed amidst the footnotes. Each one is marked as a *Text and Song Interactional*. Interact with any parts of the story through the "eye" of one or more of these songs. Does the selected song(s) help you sink your thoughts deeper into the story and provide a helpful parallel, contrast, added dimension, or what?

- pp. 4-5, 222: "10,000 Reasons (Bless the Lord)" by Matt Redman, released 2013

- pp. 14-16: "Where Have All the Flowers Gone" by Kingston Trio; Peter, Paul, and Mary; and Katarina Witt (figure skater), Lillehammer 1994

- pp. 47-48: "A Mighty Fortress Is Our God" by Martin Luther

- p. 63: "World Needs Jesus" by River Valley Worship, released 2014

- p. 81: "Remind Me Who I Am" by Jason Gray, released 2011

- p. 85: "Battle Belongs" by Phil Wickham, released 2021

- p. 100: "I Still Believe in Christmas," by Anne Wilson, released 2021

- p. 110: Text and Song Interactional: "He Has Come for Us (God Rest Ye Gentlemen)," a remake of a classic Christmas song, by

Meredith Andrews, released 2017

- p. 113: "Cornerstone" by Hillsong Worship, released 2012

- p. 131: "Holy Spirit," by Francesca Battistelli, released 2014

- p. 138: "Slow Fade" by Casting Crowns, released 2007

- p. 143: "Move (Keep Walkin')" by Toby Mac, released 2015

- p. 149: "In the Eye of the Storm" by Ryan Stevenson and Gabe Real, released 2015

- p. 163 "Fires" by Jordan St. Cyr, released 2021

- p. 164: "Haven't Seen It Yet," by Danny Gokey, released 2019

- p. 186: "Help Is on the Way (Maybe Midnight)" by Toby Mac, released 2021

- p. 189 "The Battle Belongs to the Lord" by Jamie Owens-Collins, sung by Petra and others, released 1989

- p. 193: "Almost Home" by MercyMe, released 2021

- p. 195: "Your Great Name" by Natalie Grant, released 2010

- p. 206: "Light of the World (Sing Hallelujah)" by We the Kingdom, released 2021

- p. 207: "Waymaker" by Michael W. Smith and Vanessa Campagna, released 2019

- p. 208: "Enough" by Natalie Grant, released 2015

- p. 209: "Scars in Heaven" by Casting Crowns, released 2021

- p. 209: "Fear No More" by Building 425, released 2019

- p. 211: "Come as You Are" by David Crowder, released 2014

- p. 216: "Goodness of God" by Jenn Johnson, released 2019

- p. 217: "Master Designer" by Ralph Carmichael and Kurt Kaiser, released 1969

- p. 221: "It Is Well," Bethel Song, by Kristine DiMarco, released 2014

Are there any other songs or song types that better fit your likings? Please feel free to build your own playlist for interaction purposes.

On March 11, 2020, the World Health Organization (WHO) declared Covid-19 to be a pandemic. Consider the songs released in 2020 and 2021. Mull over their messages within the context of this worldwide pandemic. How does a reexamination of these songs and Bunyan's story speak to hearts today?

Check out the good angel and bad angel passage from the early church-era *Shepherd of Hermas*. Describe a helpful response or decision-making process you would use when facing conflicted choices. See pages 11-12, 63.

How do any individual or collective sufferings affect a breakdown in relationships?

How do you minister to individuals who have experienced conflict and/or war?

What was it like interacting with a veteran describing his/her experience of war?

When is the time to talk or not to talk about something sensitive?

How would you describe sensitivity?

What is insensitivity?

A Bunyan Biography

What passes through your mind when hearing of someone facing arrest or a court trial?

Depending upon the political and/or sociological dynamics of any one place in time, what happens when a trial seems the semblance of a trial and not really the accomplishment of justice, restitution, and rehabilitation?

What is the burden of evidence in order to discern one has engaged in criminal behavior?

What is the meaning of deemed innocent until proven guilty?

How would you describe justice? Justice in what? Justice for whom?

In less than three months, fifteen-year-old Bunyan experienced the loss of his mother, the loss of his sister, and the gaining of a stepmother. What goes on amid such life changes in such a brief period?

During Britain's Civil Wars the fighting went on between the Cavaliers and Roundheads. Who were these people? What were they fighting for?

In his early adult years, Bunyan could be quite a vulgar and flappable person. Some years later he would be recounting his life story as *Grace Abounding to the Chief of Sinners*. What do you envision God could do with such a sinner?

How does the memory of what a person once *was* get in the way of the hopes for what a person *can yet become*?

At the age of twenty, Bunyan married one of whom we are given no name. How is it that history and biography sometimes leave us with empty blanks?

The impact of this nameless wife lives on with two books brought into marriage – *The Plain Man's Pathway to Heaven* by Arthur Dent and *The*

Practice of Piety by Lewis Bayly – her wedding dowry. Try to recall some-one or something that has impacted your life although the identifying de-tails have not been articulated, have slipped away, or become lost.

Given a few passions which drew Bunyan's attention – the game of Cat, bellringing, dancing with the village girls, Bible study, worship – were any of these meaningless affairs, sinful diversions, occasional commitments, or innocent enjoyments?

Overhearing some godly women in Bedford discussing their spiritual experiences caught Bunyan's attention. This eventually led Bunyan to meet their pastor, John Gifford, who, as well, reached into Bunyan's heart. Draw together two or three moments in your own life that you can look back upon with similar life-shaping significance.

While coming to a spiritual awakening, Bunyan happened upon a book in a rather tattered condition. It was a copy of Martin Luther's *Commen-tary on Galatians*. The find became a noteworthy influence upon him. Have you ever had some "unexpected finds" that have made a difference in your life? Share what, when, and how.

In one steady progression of experiences, Bunyan started sharing his personal testimony in public gatherings, eventually got into preaching sermons, which, without the sanction of the established church, ran him amuck the laws of the land. What do you think lay beneath Bunyan's mo-tivations in these regards?

The morning after Bunyan's arrest, Magistrate Wingate wanted to know what dirt could be gathered regarding those who hung around Bun-yan's preaching. The constable clarified that he had detected none. What does it feel like when one gets hit with misrepresentation? How does one deal with that?

John Bunyan was jailed because of devilishly abstaining from com-ing to an established church to hear the divine services. Instead, it is said, he participated in his own unlawful conventicles to the great disturbance of good citizens. What at close range or in the long run was the focus of such disturbances? What would you deem serious or trivial regarding such judgements?

Some of Bunyan's friends stopped the constable escorting Bunyan to Bedford County Gaol (jail). The friends were hoping something could be resolved. So, heading back to the Magistrate's home, who should Bunyan meet but William Foster, lawyer, who, seeming to be such a syrupy fellow, played Bunyan with his words! How does one save face or act graciously amidst unexpected encounters?

As Bunyan was leaving the Magistrate's house, he was about to say to Foster that he was carrying the peace of God with him. However, he checked his tongue and held his peace. What do you know of checking your tongue, holding your peace, and refraining from the so-called last word? Is such a check a frustration or blessing?

Bunyan lived at a time when people who carried a Bible to church and not *The Book of Common Prayer* were fined, arrested, or transported. What do you perceive beneath such a decree?

Praying with the help of a prayer book or praying extempore prayers? What is distinctive to each? What are the limitations of each?

Bunyan spent three months in jail, which stretched into six years, which went on into twelve years, before he was formally released. This jailing was in the county jail which could hold sixty or so prisoners. What if you didn't know (or hardly knew) someone who had been arrested? What would be your first thought?

What happens as people get caught up in disparaging stories regarding people with whom they have little or no acquaintance?

What effect do you imagine Bunyan's imprisonment had on his family? A newlywed wife? The children of a former marriage? The oldest child, Mary, blind?

Able to keep busy, Bunyan, like the Apostle Paul, ministered during his time in jail. He published books with the help of supportive publishers. Some of the jailers were friendly to his cause; others weren't. He made "long Tagg'd Lace" (shoelaces) to support his family. At times, the only one allowed to visit him was his blind daughter Mary. How would you reconcile yourself to any of these doings if you were in a position like Bunyan?

There was a time his wife, Elizabeth, persisted face to face with an intimidating cadre of magistrates. In the height of frustration, she railed at the gentry lawyers something that struck a well-remembered chord to almost anyone privy to the incident. "Because he is a tinker and a poor man, therefore, he is despised and cannot have justice!" How, if you were there, would a rejoinder like that hit you?

The years weighed heavy upon him. Bunyan, a prisoner of conscience, was not released until twelve years of incarceration had passed. During imprisonment he faced any number of grim fears and consequences – e.g., lost years of life, fear of deportation, fear of hanging . . . How would you fill in the dots?

As John Bunyan neared the end of these twelve years in jail, the Bedford congregation approved him as their pastor. What drew a congregation to call for such a person as their minister?

Eventually John Bunyan, the tinker, came to be called "Bishop Bunyan." In one regard, the accolade was in earnest. In another regard, the accolade was in jest. How do you face what seems a note of respect, but then–tongue in cheek–feels as if it is not?

What attracts your attention to Bunyan and brings about your respect for Bunyan?

Bunyan authored a number of books before *The Pilgrim's Progress* (Christian's journey) in 1678 and *The Holy War*, in 1682, which most brought him to distinction. Aside from these, he probably would have lived and died an unknown. A known or an unknown – what brings the measure of a life?

How as John Owen expressed it, do you explain Bunyan's ability to touch people's hearts?

Although you may not have read Bunyan's *The Life and Death of Mr. Bad Man*, which came out in 1680, how would you draw your own portrait of a Mr. Bad Man?

In course of time, Bunyan comes out with the story of Christiana and Mercy, the second installment to *The Pilgrim's Progress*, 1684, which, in one regard, helps bring to expression the feminine side of a journey allegory. How, in Bunyan's biographical sketch and his *The Holy War*, a battle allegory, do you see men, women, and children peopling the stories?

By the time Bunyan's life neared its end, it seemed there came a shift in British politics that Bunyan never found completely settled for the Nonconformist before he died. How does one continue to live in faith when one's dreams, one's callings, and one's commitments still await a consummation?

In the year he died, Bunyan published six books (the last one, posthumously). With the first of these six, *The Jerusalem Sinner Saved*, Bunyan raises the point: "It is because Christ shows mercy to the vilest that Satan rages so strongly." How does such a remark bespeak a sense of God's grace?

The Holy War

What is your visualization of paradise?

How would you describe the creation of Mansoul?

How would you define the word *soul*?

Bunyan's writings are rich in Biblical reference points and allusions. How or how not does Bunyan's storytelling help one experience the Scriptures?

How would it be to live in a place as Shaddai's Mansoul, where, at least initially, you would be secure against anyone with an ill-will who would try, but fail, to thrust themselves upon you?

How do you fathom a presence of evil in a world brimming with so much good?

What gets lost in Mansoul?

Discuss your comfort and discomfort levels when talking about evil.

How would you start building a working understanding of the literary genre of allegory?

Preparing to capture Mansoul, Legion, one of the devils in Bunyan's allegory, advised his evil comrades to "assault them in all pretended fairness, covering our intentions with all manner of lies, flatteries, delusive words […] and especially if, in all our lies and feigned words, *we pretend great love*" (italics mine). What do we have going on here?

What lay beneath a smooth and subtle front leading into a relationship built on deception?

How does one sense or recognize the presence and play of deception?

How does one guard against falling for a lie?

How does one maintain a reputation of truth and integrity?

Ill-pause is a beguiling character that Diabolus – the key Satanic figure – brings along for difficult occasions. Scottish preacher Alexander Whyte refers to Ill-pause as Diabolus's varlet and orator.

> When you were moved to terror and to tears under a Sabbath, or under a sermon, or at some deathbed, or on your own sick-bed – Ill-pause got you to put off till a more convenient season your admitted need of repentance and reformation and peace with God.[840]

Ill-pause's watchword is "Delay, Delay, Delay!"

How does a delay bring on an unfortunate or destructive result in life? On the other hand, could a delay have a constructive result, as well?

The basic meaning for the word "varlet" is of one acting as an attendant or a servant. An archaic definition is that of a dishonest or unprincipled person. However, there is quite an array of synonyms describing a varlet: e.g., knave, rapscallion, rogue, scoundrel, scallywag, villain, rascal.

To play a little game with such a word, pose as a protagonist faced with the plight of dealing with the antagonist – a varlet.

---

[840] Alexander Whyte, *Bunyan Characters – Third Series* [Public Domain] (Astounding-Stories.com, 2015), 41

Early in Bunyan's story, we meet Willbewill. Throughout the whole story he appears in many different contexts. First, he holds a significant place in Shaddai's Mansoul. He then falls for Diabolus's ploy and lands quite a position. Later, Willbewill is captured by Emmanuel and, becoming repentant, commits himself to Emmanuel's side and, would you believe it, is elevated to a high position in Mansoul, as well. How do you make sense of what initially seems such a teetertottering life?

Consider Mr. Tradition, Mr. Human-Wisdom and Mr. Man's-Invention who join up with Shaddai's army. Potentially good words – Tradition, Human-Wisdom, and Man's Invention – but they come to a point in which Bunyan features them in a bad light. They are captured on the battlefield and do an easy shift into Diabolus's army. Opportunists? Slick characters? Slippery individuals? Turncoats? What are they? Describe the good and not so good in each.

Bunyan has an extensive piece introducing us to the Recorder who initially falls for some of Diabolus's ploys. To assure the Recorder's occasional remembrances are kept away from the people's thinking of what they had lost regarding their time with Shaddai, Diabolus would step forward to shift, twist, and reframe the Recorder's outcries into some patronizing "you know how such a guy can sometimes be." How do put-downs – even politically – shade our conceptions of one another?

Suggest what you see in name and nature behind any of Bunyan's characters: Forget-Good, Carnal-Security, Insatiable, Desires-awake, True-heart, Think-well, the Lord Chief Secretary, God's-Peace, or another.

Loth-to-Stoop, notably a stiff old gentleman, was trying to barter with Emmanuel a place for Diabolus to maintain a foothold, big or small, in Mansoul. Loth-to-Stoop engages Emmanuel in quite a lengthy provocation. You may want to remind yourself of the script first. How would you describe such a fellow in any setting today?

In a series of military campaigns, skirmishes, and battles, Emmanuel's armies win back Mansoul. It seems as if the story is over. But is it? What is it like when, in similar ways, you cannot assume a matter resolved or a battle completed?

What do some flags of Bunyan's various color coding – e.g., white, red, black, etc. – convey throughout the story?

At the time that Emmanuel conquered Mansoul, the conquered people struggled to get a sense of how he might deal with them in that they were unable to read his countenance. What goes on as you look upon the face or into the eyes of another and try to detect the person's attitude of yourself?

With Emmanuel's presence, Mansoul had it good, but then lost out - how?

After losing fellowship with Emmanuel, Mansoul kept reaching out to Emmanuel with a petition seeking his mercy. Answers hung in suspension. How'd you feel left hanging for help?

Some did not want Mr. Good-Deed to be the one to carry their petition seeking mercy to Emmanuel. In what regard would the good deed of a good-deed-do-er fall short? What lay beneath the feeling that someone would be undependable and insincere?

Desires-awake and Wet-Eyes did not want to seem as an intrusion or even one engaging in surfacy talk as they approached Emmanuel. In our world, what would seem intrusive? What would seem like surfacy talk?

In "A Day in Court," Mr. Hard-Heart and Mr. False-Peace are two contrasting characters who wind up facing the same series of interrogations. The one is so hard-hearted that he does not really care. The other says he cares so much that he smooths over anything. How do you figure the comparative and contrasting natures of these two?

That was incredible! Mr. Incredulity broke out of jail. Play with the words incredible and incredulity. What is the nature of incredibility? Can we be too serious? Can we not be serious enough?

How do people know to whom you belong?

Emmanuel commissions a new captain, Captain Experience, drawn from the Mansoulian community itself. How does experience interact with Scripture, tradition, and reason to enrich and strengthen one's faithful endeavors?

Identify the Lord Chief Secretary sent from Shaddai's house. Review the descriptors and suggested Scripture connections. Discuss how or how not Bunyan is describing the Holy Spirit.

Going back to the beginning of Bunyan's story, is Ill-pause the *unholy spirit* upon whom Diabolus (Satan) depends? Compare, contrast, and discuss.

In Shaddai's and Emmanuel's Mansoul, two individuals in sequence hold the position of Recorder. First, there is Mr. Conscience. Then, after Emmanuel wins back Mansoul, there is Mr. Knowledge. At this time, though, Mr. Conscience is moved to a key position as a teacher paired in a secondary role to the Lord Chief Secretary. How would you describe the business of "the Recorder" in each setting?

As St. Paul draws attention in Ephesians 4:30, how does one grieve the Holy Spirit?

Godly-Fear, invited to a banquet by Carnal-Security, is set up to feel quite out of it! Describe what it is to feel isolated, alone, played upon, and lost in a group.

What is it like to have a message pressing upon your heart and mind and you are struggling to know how and when to give it? What kind of message would that be?

Sermon-smitten and sermon-sick – a good thing?

After having drifted off in relationship to Emmanuel, the Mansoulian people were struggling with a grave and long-lasting illness, but not the Diabolonians. Consequently, the Mansoulian weaknesses seemed to be the enemy's strengths. How does it go when other people's lives seem to run so easy but your's does not?

Where is God when it hurts?

What about when it hurts again, and again, and again?

Incredulity, getting back into Diabolus's lair, becomes commanding general of an army of twenty thousand Doubters. Saying something is "incredulous!" prefaces doubt. What function does doubt play in the demolishing of or even the strengthening of a faith?

It is noted several times throughout the story that Diabolus's forces have the advantage in field work and night work. Aside from a military context, what spiritually speaking could the metaphors of field work and night work mean?

In the second frame of the war, Diabolus drifts from depending totally on the Doubters to putting more confidence on the Blood-men. Try to distinguish between the two. How would you describe facing an army of Doubters? How would you describe facing an army of Blood-men?

Apollyon argued that it was better to make Doubters political leaders instead of soldiers. Toss that idea around. How does fostering, cultivating, engaging in doubt play out in daily life, civic engagements, and politics? How is there or how is there not a razor's edge between doubt and confidence?

Professor Daniel V. Runyon describes Willbewill as Bunyan's "most fully developed" character. It is quite a developmental journey from being a "slippery and depraved pawn of Diabolus" to what he eventually became back in the service of Emmanuel. However, as Runyon says, "the most profound thing in a person is his will, not sinful tendencies, so that once Willbewill recognizes his error and experiences forgiveness from Emanuel, he is able once again to follow his nobler instincts."[841] What is your view of sin, coming-to-an-awareness, and transformation?

---

[841] Daniel V. Runyon, "John Bunyan's Master Story: The Holy War as Battle Allegory in Religious and Biblical Context" (Published version of Ph.D. dissertation, Lampeter, Wales: Edwin Mellen Press, 2007), 174, 129, 213

As Bunyan's allegory concludes, the Mansoulians still face Diabolonians in their midst. How does one account for Emmanuel having been victorious and evil still lurking in the background?

In this frame of time, how is the fulfillment of one's faith completed and not completed?

Discuss how Bunyan's own experience of arrest and imprisonment surface, color, and/or provide an underlayment to what comes across in *The Holy War*.

Throughout this rendition of Bunyan's *Holy War*, there are several Pen and Ink Drawings done by Kaitlyn E. Priset, a high school senior. Express how these art pieces help bring forward and illustrate various aspects of the story?

• p. 55 Pen and Ink Drawing Depicting Diabolus

• p. 79 Pen and Ink Drawing Depicting Ill-pause

• p. 94 Pen and Ink Drawing Depicting Loth-to-Stoop

• p. 150 Pen and Ink Drawing Depicting Cerberus, the Dog of Hell-gate

• p. 167 Pen and Ink Drawing Depicting a Sally Port

• p. 184 Pen and Ink Drawing Depicting 17th-century Military Weapons

• p. 199 Pen and Ink Drawing Depicting Mr. Diligence during a Nightwatch

• p. 262 Pen and Ink Drawing Depicting the Tree of Life whose Leaves are for the Healing of the Nations

At different parts of the story, two characters, Prywell and Diligence, come across as spies or eavesdroppers. They pose to be factfinders or secret service or central intelligence agents. How do you regard the roles they play in the story?

Suggest how *The Holy War* may detail the story of salvation from Genesis to Revelation.

What touches of humor do you detect throughout Bunyan's story?

What does Bunyan regard as serious pertaining to our lives?

Express how Bunyan's work is a manual upon spiritual warfare.

What constitutes the nature of spiritual warfare?

In Ephesians 6:12, the Apostle Paul writes: "Our struggle is not against flesh and blood, but against the rulers, against the authorities, against the powers of this dark world and against the spiritual forces of evil in the heavenly realms" (NIV). Describe how Bunyan expounds this reality?

Describe how poignantly Bunyan exposes a struggle with a "dark world"?

How does Bunyan define "the spiritual forces of evil"?

How do you relate to allegory as a literary device?

For a Wrap-up

What do you read into a Middle Eastern child's or any children's dream-world when and where there is nothing indicating a longing for peace?

What does peace look like to you?

If when trying to defeat the beast, one becomes the beast, then the beast has won (a paraphrase of Roland Bainton). What does something like that say?

In a totally different frame than John Bunyan's time, Abuna Elias Chacour talks about getting our hands dirty doing good. Upon unearthing such a statement, what does it say?

What do the Beatitudes do for your Christian calling and life? Refer to Matthew 5:3-12.

Hot water, cold water, lukewarm water: "I would thou wert cold or hot" (Revelation 3:15 King James Version). Describe your understanding of these images from the book of Revelation.

How would you frame the place of God in creation, as Hebrews 11:10 puts it, with God as the creator, maker, and builder of all that was, is, and is to be?

In what way does Bunyan's story bring one to a reawakening?

What is the function of God's grace in our lives?

An Annotated Bibliography
Helpful Resources

Dr. John Owen, Nonconformist intellect, Oxford administrator and divine, and an older contemporary of John Bunyan, once told King Charles II he would willingly exchange his great learning for the tinker's power of touching people's hearts! (Brown, 382)

Bainton, Roland H. *Christian Attitudes Toward War and Peace: A Historical Survey and Critical Re-evaluation.* Nashville, Tennessee: Abington, 1960. An extensive and richly detailed examination and delineation of the concepts of just war, crusade, and pacifism from ancient times to modern times by a notable church historian.

Bible Gateway, a division of The Zondervan Corporation, 3900 Sparks Drive SE, Grand Rapids, MI 49546 USA. https://www.biblegateway.com. An easy-to-use and efficient way to retrieve Bible references, words, and phrases in more than two hundred versions of the Bible and seventy languages. For my frame of research utilizing this tool, the 1599 Geneva Version and the 1611 King James Version have been primary resources.

The 1662 Book of Common Prayer, International Edition. New Material and Updated Language by Samuel L. Bray and Drew Nathaniel Keane. Downers Grove, Illinois: InterVarsity Press Academic, 2021. An ecclesiastical classic programmatically and structurally rich in scheduled Bible readings, liturgical guidance, a monthly read-through of the Psalms, and crafted prayers, *The Book of Common Prayer* holds between its covers an extraordinary expression of the Protestant doctrine of grace and a wealth of spiritual resources culled from the wisdom of its past and present centuries. On the other hand, John Bunyan, as articulated in *Praying in the Spirit*, insisted on a more free-flowing and extemporaneous approach to worship, prayer, and sharing the faith. And yet, the general confession for morning prayer in The Book of Common Prayer seems responsive to what Bunyan sought to bring across in *The Holy War*.

Almighty and most merciful Father, we have erred and strayed from thy ways like lost sheep. We have followed too much the devices and desires of our own hearts. We have offended against thy holy laws. We have left undone those things which we ought to have done; And we have done those things which we ought not to have done; and there is no health in us. But thou, O Lord, have mercy upon us, miserable offenders. Spare thou those, O God, who confess their faults. Restore thou those who are penitent, according to thy promises declared unto mankind in Christ Jesu our Lord. And grant, O most merciful Father, for his sake, that we may hereafter live a godly, righteous, and sober life, to the glory of thy name. Amen. (*International Edition* 2021)

Brown, John. *John Bunyan: His Life, Times and Work*. London: Wm. Isbister Limited, 1885. A standard, richly detailed Bunyan biography and treasure trove of information from a notable minister who, for twenty years, pastored Bunyan's Meeting, in Bedford, England. The book features an abundance of characters engaged in Bunyan's life, various shifts in 17th British government positions, several line drawing illustrations, and helpful summations of Bunyan's many writings.

Bunyan, John. *Grace Abounding*. Edited with Introduction and Notes by John Stachniewski with Anita Pacheo. New York: Oxford University Press, 1998. Published in 1666, among the first of Bunyan's most notable writings, and penned while he was jailed in Bedford County Gaol.

Bunyan, John. *The Holy War* Annotated Companion to *The Pilgrim's Progress*, ed. Daniel V. Runyon. Eugene, Oregon: Pickwick Publications, 2012. A nicely readable presentation of Bunyan's *Holy War* allegory, featuring cross-references to *The Pilgrim's Progress*, clarifying insights regarding the presence of Bunyan's marginal notes, pertinent footnotes of selected Bunyanesque life and literary facts, and substantial scriptural and content / character indexes.

Bunyan, John. *The Holy War: The Battle for Mansoul*. Edited by Catherine Mackenzie. Geanies House, Fearn, Tain, Ross-shire, Scotland, Great Britain: Christian Focus Publications, 2008. Reprint, 2013 and 2018. A helpful rendering of Bunyan's text, with many Scripture connection points and other enhancements, including a Further Study Section; Life Summary: John Bunyan; Holy War Dictionary; Unusual Phrases; and Positions of Authority.

Bunyan, John. *The Pilgrim's Progress*. Edited with Introduction and Notes by Roger Sharrock. New York: Penguin Classic Reprint, 1987. A standard work from one who would be considered one of the foremost Bunyan scholars who also has helpful end notes related to the text.

Chacour, Elias with David Hazard. *Blood Brothers*. With a foreword by James Baker III. Grand Rapids, Michigan: Chosen books, A Division of Baker Book House, 1984, 2003. The moving life story of a Melkite (an Eastern Christian Church in Communion with Rome) pastor, affectionally known as Abuna, in the Palestinian village of Ibillin. Eventually Chacour became Bishop and then Archbishop. A moving, must read!

Chacour, Elias with Mary E. Jensen. *We Belong to the Land: The Story of a Palestinian Israeli who Lives for Peace and Reconciliation.* New York: Harper San Francisco, 1990. An augmentation of Father Chacour's life story which contains information not initially realized within Chacour's *Blood Brothers.* Especially note Chacour's interpretation of Jesus' Beatitudes actively. In 1994, Chacour, a Nobel Peace Prize nominee, was honored with the World Methodist Peace Award.

Christensen, Mark, narrator. *The Holy War: Made by Shaddai upon Diabolus for the Regaining of the Metropolis of the World* (Bunyan Updated Classic, Book 2). 2020. An audio book version packed with Scripture reference points throughout the story and closing with a substantial biographical presentation of John Bunyan's life.

Contemporary Christian Music, Christian Rock. Selected song titles with names of performers as aired and heard in 2021. https://www.siriusxm.com/themessage. Coming across songs aired by *SiriusXM 63 The Message*, I, at times, found myself drawn to ones which could highlight aspects of Bunyan's story for listening, reflection, and discussion. The songs are indicated in footnotes marked "Text and Song Interactional" throughout the story. Listening experiences and, in some cases, video presentations are possible through Internet searches.

Diamond, Jonny. "The Old Man and the Tree." *Smithsonian Magazine* Vol. 52, No. 09 (January / February 2022): 34-43, 118. As a magazine cover story, "Finding the Oldest Tree: The discovery of ancestral U.S. forests and their vital role in our future," Jonny Diamond draws attention to one man Bob Leverett's ventures rummaging through still existent old-growth New England forests. Acknowledging the "serene effect on the human soul" of such ventures, Leverett goes on to point out the ecological value of the old trees for cleansing and healing the environment. A fascinating article underscoring the significance of responsible stewardship of life's resources that is enriched with colorful photography by David Degner.

Doherty, Kathleen M. and Cornog, Mary W., editors. *Merriam Webster's Reader's Handbook.* Springfield, Massachusetts: Merriam-Webster, Incorporated, 1997. A helpful, easy-reference guide when it comes to bringing into focus, understanding, and definition various literary terms and styles.

The Geneva Bible, a Facsimile of the 1560 Edition. Introduction by Lloyd E. Berry. Peabody, Massachusetts: Hendrickson Publishing, 2007. Considered the Bible of the Protestant Reformation and, along with the King James Bible of 1611, was among the two English translations accessible and spiritually nourishing to John Bunyan.

Grossman, David. *The Yellow Wind*. Translated from the Hebrew by Haim Watzman. New York: Farrar, Straus and Giroux, 1988. A thoughtful and disturbing examination of the relationships, tensions, and conflicts in one of the most sensitive, war-torn, and unresolved corners of the world.

Gulliver, John P., ed. *The Complete Works of John Bunyan, with an Introduction*. Philadelphia: Bradley, Garretson and Co., 1872. A handy compendium of John Bunyan's writings in rather fine print, with an insightful introduction regarding Bunyan's life, preaching, and inspiration from God at the front of the book; ten pages in the table of contents; and then the writings themselves.

Henry, Matthew. *Commentary on the Whole Bible*. Old Tappan, New Jersey: Fleming H. Revell Company, modern reprint from 1712 edition. A younger contemporary of John Bunyan and a Nonconformist minister. It is worthwhile to plumb the devotional richness of Henry's writings for comparison with Bunyan's reflections.

Irving, Washington. *The Legend of Sleepy Hollow and Other Stories from The Sketch Book*, with an Introduction by Wayne Franklin (New York: Signet Classics by Penguin Group, 1961, 2006), 36-55, 79-85, 338-369. Most known for its "Rip Van Winkle" and "The Legend of Sleepy Hollow," Washington Irving's *Sketch Book*, as from the pen of an American observer abroad, is a fascinating chronicle of human interest, observation, and insight. An astute, sensitive, and entertaining chronicler, Irving brings us beneath the surface of life to perceive people's attentiveness, lack thereof, crust of pride, and contrasting humility. Especially consider "The Art of Bookmaking" and "The Mutability of Literature."

Gerhard Kittel and Gerhard Friedrich, editors. *The Theological Dictionary of the New Testament*, 10 volumes (10th being an index volume compiled by Pitcomb). Translated by Geoffrey Bromiley. Grand Rapids, Michigan: Wm. B. Eerdmans, 1964 – 1976. In-depth, expansive, scholarly articles regarding the New Testament Greek words in the Bible, with attention to etymology, insights, and developmental understandings throughout the various stages of literary history. The best translations across the years rely on the most up-to-date insights and discoveries in translation history. Although Kittel is a modern resource, it helps to derive a foundation for getting back into basic scriptural images and understandings.

Kurth, Peter. *American Cassandra: The Life of Dorothy Thompson.* Boston, Toronto, London: Little, Brown and Company, 1990. Basking in a flourishing journalistic career the years between the First and Second World Wars, Dorothy Thompson, the daughter of a Methodist Episcopal pastor and regarded the First Lady of American Journalism, was a significant voice advocating a prophetic concern for the European Jews suffering Holocaust and then, in the Post World War II era, drew early attention to the Middle Eastern Palestinian concerns. Kurth's book is a masterpiece of careful research, insight, documentation, and story, bringing to light the poignant account of a significantly forgotten voice!

Lewis, C. S. *The Allegory of Love: A Study in Medieval Tradition.* New York: Oxford University Press, 1936; Paperback, 1958. As an informational classic among Lewis' many writings, *The Allegory of Love* is an in-depth examination of the ancient and medieval underpinnings of allegory, bearing depths of insight on the best and worst examples, as it helps people understand the "material in picturable terms." Thus, Bunyan's journey allegory and battle allegory are situated in their respective wider literary backgrounds.

Lewis, C. S. *The Chronicles of Narnia* (individually titled in a series of seven). New York: HarperCollins Children's Books, 1950 through 1956. Interestingly, there are many thoughts that can relate to one another in Bunyan's *The Holy War* and Lewis's *Chronicles of Narnia* children story classics. A few are footnoted throughout the text.

Lewis, C. S. *The Screwtape Letters.* C. S. Lewis Pte. Ltd, 1942. Reprint, New York: HarperCollins, 2001. During World War II, Lewis's imaginary, insightful attempt of an experienced worldly-wise old devil, Screwtape, to enlighten his novice nephew demon, Wormwood, in the subtlety and intended successfulness of temptation.

Luther, Martin. *Commentary on Galatians.* Translated by Theodore Graebner. Digireads.com Publishing / Neeland Media LLC, 2019. From the time John Bunyan happened upon a tattered copy of Luther's *Commentary on Galatians*, Bunyan came to a helpful understanding of the difference between Law, Gospel and God's grace as understood by Luther, in contrast to the scholastic method, monastic practice, and as understood by Anabaptist and Roman theologies held in his day.

Martin, Walter, Jill Martin Rische and Kurt Van Gorden, *The Kingdom of the Occult.* Nashville, Tennessee: Thomas Nelson, 2008. An extensive exploration in the theological realm of apologetics on Satan and the occult in many historical, Scriptural, and contemporary contexts.

Meier, Eric. *Wood! Identifying and Using Hundreds of Woods Worldwide.* Published book from The Wood Database and a Web site, www.wood-database.com, 2016 by Eric Meier. Among the many practical books on woodworking, Meier's is a detailed guide to the characteristics, uses, and sometimes toxicity of hundreds of woods throughout the world. It is an excellent primer with colorful information that helps bridge the gap between scientific and craft-oriented knowledge to foster an appreciation of one of the earth's most fascinating natural resources. A good primer highlighting facts on over 350 woods, there are: 100+ full-page profiles, 100+ half-page profiles, and nearly fifty pages of general information.

Mounce, Robert H. *The Book of Revelation.* Grand Rapids, Michigan: William B. Eerdmans Publishing Company, 1977. If a Bible commentator's task is to gather and sift information that fits the commentator's purpose and brings enrichment to the reader, Mounce's is among the best, most balanced and helpful resources on the Apocalypse. Especially interesting is his treatment of the geographical and historical backgrounds of the seven churches at the beginning of the book. A fascinating example, for instance, Mounce culled from other scholars is his description of the waters of Colossae, Hierapolis, and Laodicea.

Mounce, William D., gen. ed. *Mounce's Complete Expository Dictionary of Old & New Testament Words.* Grand Rapids, Michigan: Zondervan, 2006. An easy-to-use and clearly written examination of the Hebrew and Greek vocabulary undergirding the English words to help bring clarity, depth, and understanding to one's study of the Bible.

Munson, Scott P. *A Gift from Saint George.* Indianapolis, Indiana: Dog Ear Publishing, 2015. A vivid, imaginative recounting of what soldiers Missing in Action during the Vietnam War faced, placed in a stage setting between heaven and earth, based on the author's gleanings from the experiences of close Marine and Army friends who fought in Vietnam. Traditionally, St. George is featured as the patron saint of soldiers. Tactically an angelic troop of historic notables – Hoover, Lee, Grant, Eisenhower – interact with one another throughout the story. Technically Munson's work is a *faction* which, according to the *Merriam Webster's Reader's Handbook*, is a work "based on fact but using the narrative techniques of fiction." A very moving account!

Nakashima, George. *The Soul of a Tree: A Woodworker's Reflections.* With an introduction by Dr. George Wald. New York: Kodansha USA Publishing, LLC, 1981, 2011. Nakashima's thoughtful and fascinating reflections on the tree provide a respectful and reverent side-trip into an aspect of an interesting and beautiful world fashioned for humanity to ultimately enjoy.

Pelttari, Aaron. *The Psychomachia of Prudentius: Text, Commentary, and Glossary*. University of Oklahoma Press, Norman, Publishing Division of the University, 2019. The *Psychomachia* by Aurelius Prudentius Clemens (348-413) of the early church and a contemporary of Ambrose and Augustine, is deemed a notable thematic and structural parallel to Bunyan's *The Holy War.* Having come from Calahorra, northern Spain, Prudentius first served as a lawyer, then provincial governor, spent time in imperial service at the time of Emperor Theodosius or his son Honorius, was a Roman senator, then a Christian poet / hymnist. Aaron Pelttari cites Prudentius's having written of the battle of Pollentia which occurred April 6, 402 (Easter), when the Roman General Stilicho turned away Alaric and the invading Visigoths. The central theme of *Psychomachia*, however, is in terms of seven battles featuring the conflict between virtue and vice carried on until the very end of time. Auaritia (greediness, avarice) is the root of all evils and Discordia (dissension, discord, strife) is the last of the vices. The *Aeneid* of the Roman Virgil is seen as a significant resource for much of Prudentius's vocabulary whereas the writings of the Apostle Paul are deemed a key to Prudentius's theology. An interesting twist happens with 1 Corinthians 13:13 where Paul's faith, hope, and love get rendered faith, hope and peace by Prudentius – probably because peace underscores the value of an unperturbed mind.

Reid, D. G. "Satan, Devil." In *Dictionary of Paul and His Letters*, ed. Gerald F. Hawthorne, Ralph P. Martin, and Daniel G. Reid. Downers Grove, Illinois: InterVarsity Press, 1993, 862-867. Substantial article on the various contexts in which the words for Satan, including Diabolus, appear in Biblical and extra-Biblical texts.

Runyon, Daniel V. "John Bunyan's Master Story: The Holy War as Battle Allegory in Religious and Biblical Context." Published version of Ph.D. dissertation. Lampeter, Wales: Edwin Mellen Press, 2007. As an experienced and scholarly guide mindful of the landscape of Bunyan's interpreters, Daniel V. Runyon devotes significant attention to exploring the roots and retelling of the master story: **Section I** focuses on the religious context in which *The Holy War* was written; **Section II** provides a detailing of its biblical context. In **Chapter 1, Section I** articulates the background history and theological streams beneath Bunyan's hybrid Puritan covenant theology with its distinct spiritual fervor; **2** The nature of progress allegory in *The Pilgrim's Progress* and battle allegory in *The Holy War*, parallel thoughts in 4th/5th century early church father Prudentius's *Psychomachia*, an allegory regarding the conflict of and for the soul, and Martin Luther on allegory as an effective teaching tool when scripturally resourced and artfully employed; **3** John Foxe's *Acts and Monuments of the Christian Martyrs* and the church's struggle against corruption within and enemies without, the nature of salvation history, and the Bible vital for understanding God's witness and work throughout the course of time; **4** A master story patterned by Scripture, the lenses through which one may engage a text (cluster, fantasy-theme, feminist, and generic criticism and, more significantly, ideological, metaphoric, narrative, pentadic and generative criticism),[1] inductive and deductive reasoning,[2] the limitation of trying to defend a faith by sheer argument, and Northrop Frye's seven phases of the biblical plot carried out in creation, revolution, law, wisdom, prophecy, gospel, and apocalypse; In **Section II, Chapter 5,** the scriptural underpinnings to *the Holy War*, Shaddai's creation of Mansoul and Diabolus's deceptive siege of the soul; **6** Law, wisdom, and prophecy primarily expressed through Old Testament texts and the need for God's intervention, the significance of prayer, and a word about millennialism; **7** Joseph in Genesis as a foreshadowing for Jesus, the coming of Emmanuel, the trial of the Diabolonians, Lord Chief Secretary as the Holy Spirit, Bunyan's understanding of the Trinity, the conscience to keep in sync with the Holy Spirit, God's work in believers throughout the challenges of life; **8** Apocalypse fundamentally *the destruction of evil and triumph of good*, Latitudinarianism as religion of reason and works, the smooth, conniving maneuvers of Carnal Security, a distracted Mansoul, the Prince of Darkness gaining ground and driving Mansoul into the castle for stronghold, sorting through the difference concerning election and free will, reaching out to the Lord Chief Secretary, Diabolus's plot to distract the town by engaging it in business, Emmanuel's coming, shifting from a defensive to an offensive war, the

---

[1] Some lenses through which Literature may be Analyzed: Ideological Criticism looks at the assumptions, beliefs, and values of an author and the culture his/her work represents; Metaphoric Criticism evaluates the effectiveness and meaning of symbols used to define reality; Narrative Criticism recognizes the meaning that can be derived from the way in which a story is organized; Pentadic Criticism distinguishes between motion and action (whether the players act or are moved); Generative Criticism is used when formally recognized methods of criticism listed are inadequate and the critic must generate his/her own units of analysis. Feminist Criticism is applied to *The Pilgrim's Progress* but not *The Holy War* which basically ignores gender issues. Daniel V. Runyon, "John Bunyan's Master Story: The Holy War as Battle Allegory in Religious and Biblical Context" (Published version of Ph.D. dissertation, Lampeter, Wales: Edwin Mellen Press, 2007), 97-100.

[2] Deductive reasoning, which tends to be subjective and prejudicial, moves from generalizations to support the particulars, whereas inductive reasoning first examines the particulars and then come to one's conclusion. Ibid., 103-104.

nature of despair, enemy doubters, enemy blood-men, and the persistence of evil; **9** The biblical version of the crucifixion and resurrection held but not developed in Bunyan, instead a sense of God's redemptive work, sifting thoughts upon an earthly millennium, more importantly the daily threat of sin, hope of life beyond the grave, and one's holding fast; **10** In conclusion, the care of souls, free to suffer and forgive, hope of a new heaven and a new earth, a progress allegory amidst a battle allegory, a master story that begins with creation and ends with the promise of recreation, England's Puritan epic!

Sheldrake, Philip, ed. *The New Westminster Dictionary of Christian Spirituality*. Louisville, Kentucky: Westminster John Knox Press, 2005. A handy, easily accessed, and scholarly reference guide to basic and carefully focused information on Christian spirituality, by a significant number of scholars on a range of topics such as allegory, election, soul, and many others.

The Shepherd of Hermas. Translated by J. B. Lightfoot. London: Macmillan, 1891; reprint, CrossReach Publications, 2017. *The Shepherd*, containing visions, commandments, and similitudes, was an early spiritual classic associated with Rome in circulation by the last half of the 2nd century. Considered divinely inspired by some, not canonical but useful in catechetical training by others, eventually *The Shepherd* suffered mixed reviews and a lessening in value. Niebuhr called it a good but dull novel. Mosheim called it a pious fraud. On the other hand, there were those who regarded it as truly historical and that Hermas sincerely believed what he was putting across. On account of the book's allegorical nature, it has been deemed the early church era's *The Pilgrim's Progress*. Moreover, Henry Wace and William C. Piercy in their 1911 *A Dictionary of Christian Biography* (448-453) respectfully noted its significance as a prophetic challenge to a church which by the writer's time had become corrupted and tainted with worldliness. Thus, *The Shepherd* holds accordance with Bunyan's *The Holy War*.

Tzu, Sun. *The Art of War*. UK: Arcturus Holdings Limited, 2018. An English translation of an ancient 6th century BC military manual that has been read, respected, and put into practice by such generals as Napoleon, MacArthur, Patton, and others throughout the centuries as well as present-day business, sports, and political leaders.

Unger, Merrill F. *Biblical Demonology: A Study of the Spiritual Forces Behind the Present World Unrest*. With an Introduction by Wilbur M. Smith. Wheaton, Illinois: Scripture Press Publications, Inc., 1952. An engaging treatment of the field of demonology, rich in Scripture connections and comparative insights from other belief systems, containing chapters on demon possession, magic, divination, necromancy, and other topics. Based on his Th.D. work at Dallas Theological Seminary, Unger exhibits a thorough knowledge of a serious subject. Many Bible students may know of Unger through his Bible Handbook, published in 1966, similar in scope to Halley's Bible Handbook, published in 1924.

Vester, Bertha Spafford. *Our Jerusalem: An American Family in the Holy City, 1881-1949.* With an Introduction by Lowell Thomas. Garden City, NY: Doubleday & Company, Inc., 1950. The story of the Horatio and Anna Spafford family who founded the American Colony of Jerusalem. Having lived in the Holy Lands through the years of the Ottoman Empire, World War I, British Mandate, World War II, and the establishment of Israel and, with graciousness, facing a cacophony of challenges, terrors, and political influences for nearly a century, the Spaffords sought to live at peace, in service, and in goodness toward all around them. In their early years, after suffering the tragic Mid-Atlantic sinking of the Ville du Havre in 1873, in which their four young daughters lost their lives (background to the hymn, "It Is Well with My Soul"), the Spaffords and those who gathered around them moved to Palestine to seek peace and healing in the land in which Jesus' walked. In turn, by extending compassion to its people, they continually came to bless and enrich the people in one of the most divided and divisive contexts on the face of the earth. World War I Field Marshal Edmund Allenby expressed admiration for them by lauding how they cared for "the wounded and sick, without distinction of creed or nationality, and in circumstances of peculiar difficulty, and even danger."[3]

Wesley, John. "Catholic Spirit" (Sermon 39). Edited by Albert C. Outler. Volume 2 in *The Works of John Wesley* series. Nashville: Abingdon Press, 1985. A timeless Wesley sermon, keyed from 2 Kings 10:15, where Jehu, "as mixed a character as he was," greeted Jehonadad with the classic line, "Is thine heart right, as my heart is with thy heart . . . give me thine hand."

Wesley, John. "The Great Assize" (Sermon 15). Edited by Albert C. Outler, Volume 1 in *The Works of John Wesley* series. Nashville: Abingdon Press, 1984. Interestingly, John Wesley preached this sermon, on Romans 14:10, in St. Paul's Church, Bedford, England, March 10, 1758, before the presiding Judge of Common Pleas, Sir Edward Clive. The High Sheriff of Bedfordshire, William Cole had arranged for the oc-

---

[3] Allenby, F. M., to Mrs. Vester, January 1924, in Bertha Spafford Vester, *Our Jerusalem: An American Family in the Holy City, 1881-1949* (Garden City, N.Y.: Doubleday & Company, Inc., 1950), 266.

casion – an interesting contrast to how John and Elizabeth Bunyan, almost one hundred years previously, had been treated by the legal system. Wesley, John. "Of Good Angels" (Sermon 71) and "Of Evil Angels" (Sermon 72. Edited by Albert C. Outler, Volume 1 in *The Works of John Wesley* series. Nashville: Abingdon Press, 1986. Citing a dearth of materials after New Testament times and the earliest centuries of the church, Wilbur M. Smith draws attention to several Christian leaders across the centuries who drew very little attention to the topic of demons. He included, for instance, John Wesley who, Smith said, devoted just one page to the subject. What Smith may not have known was that Wesley published no fewer than four untitled instalments of standard Christian thought on angels in the *Arminian Magazine*, January through April 1783, which, later, was titled: "Of Good Angels" and "Of Evil Angels."

Wesley, John. "Satan's Devices" (Sermon 42). Edited by Albert C. Outler, Volume 2 in *The Works of John Wesley* series. Nashville: Abingdon Press, 1985. This sermon, on 2 Corinthians 2:11, came through John Wesley's concern about people's confusion regarding the practice of holy living in general and the doctrine of Christian perfection.

White, Matthew. "The Turbulent 17th Century: Civil War, Regicide, the Restoration, and the Glorious Revolution. The British Library. Discovering Literature: Restoration & 18th Century. June 21, 2018. https://www.bl.uk/restoration-18th-century-literature/articles/the-turbulent-17th-century-civil-war-regicide-the-restoration-and-the-glorious-revolution A clearly written article available through an Internet search providing a helpful glimpse into the political and religious overview of Seventeenth-century England, Scotland, and Ireland, with cameo descriptions of the various kings and political leaders, religious crosscurrents and economic stressors analyzed by Dr. Matthew White, Research Fellow in History at the University of Hertfordshire.

Whyte, Alexander. *Bunyan Characters Third Series: The Holy War.* Public Domain Literature reprinted by Astounding Stories, 2017. Originally, Edinburgh and London: Oliphant Anderson & Ferrier, 1902. Among the four volumes of presentations on John Bunyan's characters, within the years 1893 to 1908, this single volume comprises a Sabbath evening lecture series at St. George's Free Church, Edinburgh, Scotland, on Bunyan's *The Holy War*, by Reverend Dr. Alexander Whyte (1826-1921), notable Scottish divine of the Free Church of Scotland and considered the last of the Puritans.

Wilkinson, David. *The Message of Creation: Encountering the Lord of the Universe.* Bible Themes Series in The Bible Speaks Today. Edited by Derek Tidball. Downers Grove, Illinois: InterVarsity Press, 2002. Carefully focused and articulate background material and insights by a research astrophysicist on the Biblical Creation references to provide helpful thoughts for connection and comparison with Bunyan's handling the nature of God's relationship with humanity.